# I SHOULDN'T HAVE TO PLAY THE VICTIM

*My Experience with Domestic Violence and the Criminal Justice System*

CHELSEY DE GROOT

**LANDON**
**HAIL**
PRESS

Paperback ISBN: 978-1-959955-92-4
Hardback ISBN: 978-1-959955-93-1

Published by Landon Hail Press
Book Cover Design by Rich Johnson, Spectacle Photo
Author cover photos by Bailey Parkinson

*This book is dedicated to the women and children who are no longer here to share their stories because their lives were taken too soon. It is written to inspire hope in others who have experienced something similar and to create meaningful systems change in front-line police officers who respond to domestic violence and the court system that is supposed to protect victims of violence.*

*"I am ever hopeful that, if the court has a blind spot today, its eyes will be open tomorrow.*

—Ruth Bader Ginsburg

# CONTENTS

# Author's Note

## Content Disclosure

This memoir was not easy to write. No matter how many times I've told my story, writing, editing, and rewriting hit different. I felt guilt, shame, and embarrassment, but I also felt hopeful, proud, and resilient. I wrote to inspire hope and systems change, and little did I know I was healing deeper parts of me.

This book is a deeply personal account, drawn from my lived experiences. It contains sensitive subject matter, including references to domestic violence and suicide, that may be distressing or triggering for some readers. These experiences are shared with care and intention, but reader discretion is strongly advised. Names have been changed throughout, to protect privacy.

# Preface

I want to acknowledge that not every police officer is a terrible person, and many wish they could do more to help. I've met some along my journey. I also want to recognize that it is not necessarily the individual who has been the problem, but rather it is failed systems. Systems that have not been updated or revisited for many, many years, and an outdated criminal code that fails to recognize other types of abuse outside of physical. It is a system with old-school mentalities, in which older, powerful individuals make decisions about people's lives with little regard for or understanding of the impact domestic violence has on victims, especially children.

Abuse can come in various forms, including psychological, emotional, spiritual, and physical. Unfortunately, it is the physical type that is readily recognized and easiest to identify. My hopes are, by sharing my story and bringing more awareness to this issue, we can do better in identifying and recognizing the different types of abuse and then begin to change these very systems, along with the criminal code that has failed many women and children. Without creating this change, they will continue to fail victims for years to come.

I want to preface what I have to tell you by saying, although I use the term "victim" throughout this book for simplicity's sake, I do not like the word *victim*. To me personally, victim means giving someone your power and then you remain stuck there. It means you are powerless, hopeless, with no way out.

This is true for many people; I was in that place once, too. When the person you love strips you of your power and makes you feel small and that neither you nor your voice matter, this can make you feel worthless.

I want you to know it's possible to move past the place of victim and to thrive again. It's also possible to take your power back, returning to define what life can look like on *your* terms. It takes a hell of a lot of intentional work to get there, but it's possible. I'm living proof of that. I share my story with you in hopes you feel inspired by the fact that, no matter how stuck you feel and no matter how many systems are stacked against you, with the right amount of work and support, you can create the life you deserve. A life that is safe, secure, full of joy, and, most importantly, peaceful.

We can and should do better. As a justice system, as professionals, as non-profits, and as community members. Domestic violence is everyone's business and does not discriminate.

Join me on this journey as I walk you through my experience. From early on in my relationship, including the early warning signs, through my experiences with police, schools, court, lawyers, and the criminal justice system as a whole.

If you are a victim or experiencing domestic violence, know that you are not alone. It is my hope, as you follow my journey throughout this book, you find a way to take your power back and to gain hope and support, while learning to love yourself again.

We all have a choice. There are a wide variety of resources available, online, at the library or bookstore, or in person, if you or someone you know is struggling. It's important to note that different communities will have different resources available to them.

# A Letter to my Younger Self

*Dear Younger Self,*

*You didn't have to go through the things that you did, and I wish you didn't know what it felt like to never feel good enough for your dad. Little did you know the impact that would have in the future, on relationships, with male bosses, etc. I am proud of you for leaning in and doing the work so you could break through the cycle, along with the pain that came with it. To learn that you are loved and worthy and that real love shouldn't feel like abandonment.*

*I am really proud of you and your willingness to repair the relationship with your dad, even when it's hard, because it has also healed you. I am proud of you for speaking your truth and for understanding and creating boundaries that will serve you later in your life.*

*I am proud of you for deciding to stay. That life was worth living. As I write this, I recognize how proud I am and how many times I have written that in this letter, but it's an indication and acknowledgment that that's all I wanted as my younger self. To feel validated, proud, and to have a sense of belonging. Perhaps you were searching for that all along, until you found it in yourself, as an adult. You have always been a fighter, and even when it has sucked and all you wanted to do was give up, the resilience you gained through experiences will teach you how to navigate all of the crazy life challenges that will be thrown your way, as you grow. I want you to know that you will always be okay.*

*You will learn to love and show up for yourself, because you choose to. I want you to know you will always come home to yourself and find a safe place there. You may feel lost and walk a different path for a bit until you find your place, but you will find it. As you evolve, so will those places. Remain curious. Don't let the experiences keep you jaded. Always be willing to learn about yourself and others.*

*Happiness isn't found in material things. It's found in how you live your life, the people you surround yourself with, and the joy you find in what you do.*

*Life will have twists and turns, but you will be okay, because you always have yourself.*

*You turned broken into beautiful, and the journey is just getting started.*

*This is what freedom and self-love look like. You found it. Everything led you to here. In this moment, with these people, and these opportunities.*

*Your voice is being heard, and it's going to shine. It's going to inspire others and change systems. Your voice is going to be heard in a good way, because it's coming from a good place. You have all the reassurance you need.*

*Thank you for choosing to live so that others could, too.*

*With love,*

*Your older self, Chelsey*

# Chapter 1

## But I Can Change Him...

We all know that famous line, right? "I can be the one to change him" or "This time will be different" or "It's different with me."

It's funny, the messages we give ourselves when we just want to be loved and think that we've finally found someone who is paying attention to us. Especially when that is what we have longed for throughout our childhood and, subconsciously, into adulthood. This is how many of these unhealthy relationships begin and why it takes many of us so long to leave. In reality, it's not about changing anyone. Because we can't. It's about learning to love ourselves, so we can create a different life, one where we love ourselves first, so others can love us the same.

When I first met Johnny, I had been working in the field of human services for a few years, and my mission was to help people. I wanted to help others because of my own personal experiences of being bulled throughout most of junior high and high school, plus struggles with my dad while never feeling good enough for him (cue the desire for validation and seeking approval from men), and my own suicide ideation.

During high school, I was connected to our school counselor, who was instrumental in helping me work through some of the toughest times of my life. There, I found a passion and desire, wanting to be that person for others. Naturally, the "I can fix him" motto was very much engrained in me. Knowing what I know now, "fixing people" is not the mission of human services or the end goal, but early in my career and due to my own story, it was the motto I carried with me and believed to be true.

During Christmas season, 2008, my friend and I were at a local horse racing track/bar, having a drink and some food. This was the first time I'd ever tried eggnog. I'm not sure why that memory has stuck with me for so long, but it has.

We were catching up about Christmas and the latest gossip when we heard a loud group of people in the back of the building making their way through toward the front exit. We learned they were getting kicked out for being intoxicated and disruptive.

As the group was exiting, one of the men stopped to talk to my friend. I sat and listened, observing deeply. I was briefly introduced to him, and then he carried on his way with the rest of his group. I was intrigued, so, once they left, I asked my friend who he was and how she knew him. He was a tall, dark skinned Indigenous man. If I am being totally honest, I thought he was good-looking.

She told me his name and very quickly followed with, "Stay away from him. He's a womanizer."

I received the message but shrugged it off. *When do we ever listen to our friends*? I never thought I'd see him again, so it didn't hurt to inquire for curiosity's sake, and I thought maybe, just maybe, if I did run into him again, I'd find out for myself and prove her wrong.

A few weeks later, he messaged her, telling her he would pay for her and me to visit him in Texas, where he was working on the drilling rigs. Long story short, we never went down to Texas. But this was not the last time I saw him.

Fast forward to several months later. It was nearing summertime. The weather is nice, and it was BBQ season. One day, I was working with a co-worker, doing a supervised visit with a family. During a break, she informed me she had gotten back together with this guy. I was curious and wanted to hear more, but that space was not the most appropriate to have this conversation. We pressed paused until the visit was over.

When the visit came to the end, we resumed our conversation, and she told me about this new guy. He was someone she had dated before, and she shared the story of how they'd reconnected. I learned he was quite a bit older than I was, but so was my co-worker. Nonetheless, I thought it wouldn't hurt to ask my next question.

I was somewhat joking when I asked, "Does he have any relatives?"

She chuckled and said, "Yeah but he works in Texas."

I thought to myself, *There is no way this guy is the same guy I met around Christmas.* I probed further and asked, "Is his name (who I'll call) Johnny?"

Turns out, it was! And he was the same person I had met months prior. I would be lying if I wasn't even more intrigued than I'd been months prior. Time had passed, which maybe had given him time to change, if he really was a womanizer.

Later that day, my co-worker invited me to a family BBQ, which included some of her boyfriend's family. I thought, sure! Why not? I'll go. What are the chances our worlds would connect again? *It's meant to be. What a story to tell. What did I have to lose anyway?* I approached it like I had nothing to lose and everything to gain.

I ended up meeting his family before I really had an opportunity to get to know him. Nothing happened there, nor was Johnny present at the BBQ. I enjoyed my time with my co-worker and Johnny's family and dreamed of the potential of it all working out.

Timelines become blurred when you endure trauma. Sometimes, it's hard to recall how events are associated with which timelines, so I'll do my best to recall the next part. In the fall of 2008 or 2009, I entered into a relationship with an individual I had been friends with for some time. This relationship did not last long. He wasn't as consistent as I had hoped, but again, the messaging of "I can change him" ran through my head.

This individual was still into partying. He was in the process of becoming a police officer, and I'm sure we can all guess how much the ladies love a man in uniform. This drew attention to him for sure, and I think he took deep pride in it all. I remember one night, when I called him, it sounded like there were lots of females in the background.

I will admit, I was also quite insecure back in my early twenties. I became super-uncomfortable and maybe a bit jealous, as the suspicions crept in that he was likely cheating on me. During the conversation, he was quiet and reserved and appeared not care to engage in a conversation with me. I was pretty hurt by this and ended the phone conversation moments later. I'm not sure what happened after that, but the relationship ended shortly after.

Still hurt by this interaction, I was looking for a distraction and someone to validate my feelings. *Deep down, I just wanted someone to choose me and love me.* This was such a common theme and pattern of behavior for me back then, and it followed me around for longer than I'd like to admit.

The following day, I went to my co-worker's house for a visit, as I knew it would distract me from the hurt I was feeling. Surprisingly, her new man was there. They told me Johnny was on his way back down from Edmonton and heading over to the house, that he should be there within the next few hours. I thought to myself, *Perfect! Maybe this is my chance to meet him again and see where things go.*

Hours later, he showed up. When he arrived, he looked quite tired but also excited to see me there. Did he know about me? I wasn't sure.

I later learned he had driven back to town (about five hours from where he was coming from) quite intoxicated, which was why he appeared so exhausted. This was a red flag after the fact, much like the many others. But of course, when we are in the thick of it and so badly wanting to be loved, we ignore the very flags that warn us to stay away. We can be so quick to put our blinders on when our feelings take precedence. I was more naïve than I'd thought.

The four of us hung out as a group for the rest of the day. Johnny and I seemed to hit it off well and spent the entire time engaging in good conversation. The comment my friend had made almost a year prior, "He's a womanizer. Stay away," still echoed in my mind. However, based on the present moment, what she'd said couldn't have been further from the truth. *Ha! I'll prove her wrong,* I thought.

During that time, I really felt maybe I had found someone who would love me and want to spend time with me. I knew I didn't deserve to be cheated on or have my partners out at parties without me, but I didn't know how to achieve that. I thought, this time, it would be different.

Johnny and my relationship basically kicked off from that point on, and we officially started dating in September 2009. He continued to work down south in Texas, and I stayed in our community, a relatively small city in Alberta, to continue my post-secondary education. I was living with my parents at the time, and when Johnny was back home, he would come stay with me or at his mom's house.

Things started off great. I was so happy. I felt loved and appreciated and that he *truly* wanted to be with me. This was so important to me. We travelled around Alberta, doing fun things together, and we went to Manitoba to see my grandparents while they were living there plus visited other family members.

I felt like I was getting a taste of a life I had always wanted. I had no inclination that things would get as bad as they did; that I would be left alone many nights while he was out partying, and that I would be cheated on and eventually become a victim of domestic violence.

# Chapter 2

# Childhood Trauma

Having been a young child who'd had anxious abandonment issues, I found this new relationship feeling good to me. I felt maybe my core wounds were being healed. Looking back now, I'm not even sure I knew what that meant.

As I mentioned briefly, I never felt like I was good enough for my dad. These core wounds followed me into my adulthood. Not only did it show up in the relationship between my dad and me, but it showed up in most every other relationship I had with men. Relationships with male bosses, in particular. I wanted the validation and approval that I was doing a good job, and when I didn't get that, I often felt like I wasn't good enough.

But not until I attended one of Dr. Gabor Maté's presentations on intergenerational trauma did it hit home for me. The feelings of never being worthy or smart enough or good enough for my dad had followed me around into these relationships, too. I had to learn that I didn't need this external validation, that I had it within myself. But until I recognized this deep-rooted issue, I could not begin to make changes.

I didn't know that I had anxiety until I was thirty years old. Thirty! I'd struggled so much growing up but never knew why. I worried a ridiculous amount that my mom would die, and I didn't know how I would live without her. I wanted to be with her every second, because that made me feel like I could control the outcome. (Now I recognize how irrational that thought process was.) I wouldn't have sleepovers at friends' houses because I hated being away from her.

Sometimes, when my parents went out on a date, my siblings and I went to sleep at my grandparents' house, and my anxiety would go through the roof. My attachment issues obviously started there. Whenever I was at school, I worried obsessively about being away from my mom, so much that I would feel nauseous. I complained about stomach aches all the time. I would leave school to go home, complaining of feeling sick, or I would wait in the infirmary until I could be picked up. It got so bad that, in grade four, my dad had to sit in class with me just so I would remain in school.

I knew my mom struggled with this, and it probably wasn't easy for my dad, either, although he never told me how he felt. During that time, my mom was a stay-at-home mom, raising me and my siblings, while my dad was the sole provider. Every moment he was sitting with me at school was a loss of income for our family.

I was the oldest of four children. My mom took me to the doctor because of my ongoing complaints, and they tested me for my appendix and various other medical conditions. The appendix appeared to be the most rational and apparent diagnosis during that era. I remember being told to drink this nasty flax drink (powder added to water), as they figured it was something with my bowels.

In the early nineties, mental health was not talked about the way it is today, nor did people have awareness about it. Our Western medical system is not great when it comes to mental health, and doctors receive very little training on mental health. Worse back then than it is today. From my experience, the way our parents navigated and spoke about mental health was minimal. If it was brought up, it was in a dismissive way.

My dad would say, "We didn't go to counseling and all that shit when people passed away or when we went through hard times. We just got over it."

My mom echoed this sentiment, adding, "That never happened when we were growing up" or "We didn't have these issues growing up."

Now, we recognize all the damage of this disregard, in addition to the work we have to do internally to undo that damage, but this was just part of the time when I grew up and my parents' narrative around mental health, whether right, wrong, or indifferent.

Being bullied in junior high and high school didn't help with my anxiety, either. I carried on, still without knowing what was truly wrong with me. I knew what I was experiencing wasn't normal, but I had no answers. (I'll share all of this journey in far more depth in my second book, but it was definitely hard.)

I didn't date at all in junior high, although I had crushes. I did find myself in online relationships, but that was so silly and, as I reflect back now, could have been quite dangerous. I just wanted to be loved, and I looked for love in all the wrong places. I had a few boyfriends in high school, but my choices were not great. I was going through a self-exploration phase while feeling quite lost. Some might say I was trying to find out where I belonged. Knowing what I know now, I may have the gift of not belonging.

I found myself hanging out with punks, the "skids" as they were often called, and other misfits. This group would skip class and get high all the time, and they would drink on weekends. I never engaged in that behavior, although I would sit with them and wonder, *What is so great about this?* I never got high or drunk (until I was an adult), because I was worried I would become addicted.

The only thing that changed for me was my appearance: I started to wear all black and spikes (bracelets, belts, etc.), and I was often referred to "Avril Lavigne." I went to school on the northside in grade nine, after being bullied at my previous, prominent "westside" school for grades seven and eight.

The northside where I transferred was considered more rebellious and "hood." At this high school, we had the "wall," where all the rebels, smokers, and misfits hung out. I found myself drawn to that crowd. I dated a guy who had dyed his hair exactly like a clown's. That was an interesting time, to say the least. He was a nice guy, but *what was I doing or thinking?* That relationship only lasted a few months.

He used to hang out with some older guys who were also students at the school. I became very intrigued by one boy in this crowd named Tony. He looked like such a badass. He had a mohawk and dressed like a punk, and he had the cutest smile. I don't recall how we were introduced, but it wasn't too long before he and I started dating. There was one problem, though, which seemed to come with the "punk rock" lifestyle: copious amounts of drinking and smoking weed.

I was never comfortable with all that, and because it did not align with my lifestyle, it became a point of contention in our relationship. He had to be high or drunk whenever we hung out; this was a non-negotiable for him. It really bothered me. I remember lying on my friend's living room floor, talking to him on the phone one afternoon, and feeling as though I would never be good enough to hang out with him, if he wasn't high or drunk. My abandonment wounds showed up, subtly, but they were not at the forefront in my decision making. I thought maybe Tony would smarten up, if I threatened to leave, but that wasn't the case.

We dated for a little while longer, but I finally came to terms with this not being what I wanted in a relationship. About six months into the relationship, I ended it. Days later, I found him crying in the hallways, and he attempted to talk me into staying with him, but I couldn't handle the substance use. It wasn't for me.

So many girls at school wanted to beat me up after we broke up because of how hurt he was. That never made sense to me, and I couldn't understand why.

As I reflect back, this was my first lesson in the importance of the alignment between personal values and any relationships we have—intimate, work, friendships, etc.

# Chapter 3

## Front-Row Seat to the Fire

When I was enrolled in my college Child and Youth Care Program at the beginning of my relationship with Johnny, I learned so much in our family violence class about family dynamics and systems and the impact those wounds have on children, youth, and families. It's easier to recognize the situations outside of yourself, though. Much harder to turn the lens inward, especially when you're in the middle of it all.

Johnny worked a rotation in the drilling industry. Most times, he was gone for two to four weeks at a time. There were times when we did not see each other for a couple of months. When he was home, we went out together and took small trips to Montana and northern Alberta. This felt good. I was still a bit into my party phase at the time, so it didn't seem to bother me much that he was drinking quite a bit, too.

I'm not going to lie: college was a bit of a rough time, especially my first year. I drank and partied a lot. I missed a lot of class due to being hung over or choosing to skip out on night classes to go drinking, instead. One time, I skipped to go see Alexisonfire. I thought it was totally worth it, especially since we got to hang out with the band afterwards. But it spoke to a larger issue: I was going down a dark path with alcohol, and my life could be impacted, if I didn't make some better choices.

I was put on academic probation after my first semester of college, as my GPA was 0.34. I chose to make some changes for the following semester, which included cutting out all alcohol consumption. I attended all my classes and promised myself I would try harder and do better. I did, but it still wasn't good enough. My GPA that term was 1.4, which was a substantial increase from what it had been the previous semester; but it needed to be at 1.5 for me to remain in school. I got kicked out.

I thought to myself, *Now what?* I felt like such a failure. I didn't know what to do, but I didn't want to give up or feel like I had let myself down. I knew I was capable of so much more. So, I applied to another program and talked to the dean. I owned my mistakes, shared the lessons I'd learned, and laid out what I would do differently, if I were to be readmitted. Thankfully, I was accepted back for the fall term, this time to the Child and Youth Care Program.

The unhealthy relationships I had with men followed me into my first year of college, as well as the year I took off between high school and starting college. I slept with more men than I care to admit. I so desperately wanted to find someone who would love me and treat me the way I deserved. I went about in all the wrong ways.

Sometimes, it's hard to admit that, but I believe in transparency and vulnerability. While those experiences are a part of my story and helped shape me into the person I am today, they do not define me. If my daughter decides to read this book, I am sorry you had to learn this part, but I'm sure we will have conversations about this as you get older. I hope you love yourself more than I ever loved myself then. (It's evident you already do.)

About a year into the relationship with Johnny, the drinking became more of an issue. It would get to the point where he picked fights with me in order to go out drinking with his friends. Many times, I did not know where he was, and I wouldn't see him for days. There were countless nights when I could not sleep, wondering where he was, worried sick if he was okay, and not knowing what he was doing.

I would call his friends to see if they knew where he was, and sometimes, if they were willing, I would bring them with me to try to track him down and bring him home. If I wasn't home but knew he wanted to go drink, I would try to stall him from leaving the house, so I could buy enough time for me to get home and prevent him from leaving or even hoping I could go with him.

Again, my core abandonment wounds were surfacing, yelling silently in my head that I was being abandoned and the only way to fix it was to find him and bring him back home, where I could feel safe again. As I reflect back now, this was such a distorted way of thinking and did not provide any sense of safety.

One night, I drove all over the reserve, looking for him. His mom lived in a neighboring community, so I would often check in with her to ask whether she had seen him or could help. I don't know how we found Johnny that night, but we did. We were near his dad's house when we located him. His mom got out of the vehicle to talk to him. Emotions were high. I stayed in the vehicle and watched from the driver's seat.

Johnny was never rational when he was drinking and often became rude and dismissive. I had no idea how this was going to go. My headlights shined on the two of them as they engaged in conversation. Moments later, things escalated, and voices were raised. The way he spoke to her, yelling and screaming in her face, scared me.

I remember thinking, *Oh my God, what happens if this escalates further?* I felt conflicted. I wanted so badly to help him but didn't know how. I continued to watch from my driver's seat as they continued to yell and scream at each other.

Johnny would get really mad at me when I would look for him. When I was able to find him, he would look at me with disgust. I will never forget that facial expression. But as someone who just wanted to love and be loved, I ignored those expressions and my reactions, despite feeling so heart-wrenchingly sad on the inside. I just thought, *At least I found him. When he sobers up, he won't be mad anymore and we will be together.* It was still the line, *I can fix him… I just have to hold on.*

As tensions brewed or whenever he experienced grief or loss, his first coping mechanism was to drink and grieve amongst his friends. This was yet another red flag for me, but I continued to ignore it, thinking, *I can help him. He just has to see it and want it, too. I'll show him.*

What bothered me was it felt like, even if he was trying to choose a different way of living and coping, his friends would pull him back in. He always had money, and the friends would often follow, even if it was short-lived. With his lack of coping skills and the money he had available to drink, it was almost the expectation that Johnny would fund every grievance party. If anything, he and his friends would all go down together. It didn't matter how this impacted me or our relationship. It became a selfish endeavour.

We had been dating for a few years by this point and were living together at the time. One day, I got a crazy idea: having a baby with him would help change the narrative. *Maybe that will be what finally sobers him up.* When he was sober, he often told me that having a child is what would make him quit drinking for good. And I believed everything he said, even when his actions and words did not align. I held on to every word. This is something I still do to this day, regardless of who is telling me something, especially in relationships. Maybe I am a little too literal, at times.

During this period, I had given up drinking myself, in the hopes he would follow. I was grasping at straws. Giving up alcohol wasn't a difficult task for me, despite my massive alcohol consumption phase during college. The outcome was going to be worth it, or so I thought. I did not have a drop of alcohol for nearly two years, and it was no longer a part of my life.

I don't remember much of this time, but I do recall we lived together for quite some time, and his drinking remained steady. I figured, if he was drinking at home, that was better than him being out and my having no idea where he was or who he was with. There were times when he prioritized purchasing alcohol over paying portions of our bills. This should have been another red flag. In the back of my mind, I think it was, but I continued to push forward. The way I justified his behavior and minimized it all is insane to me now, but it seemed to make sense to the lost, desperate girl I was at that time.

My memories of previous occasions when he'd take off haunted me. One time, he was brought home in a car full of females. It was late. I was at home and couldn't sleep, so I was on the couch, in and out of sleep, anxiously waiting for him to come home.

When I saw the vehicle pull up outside of our house, I didn't recognize it or the people who got out. Moments later, he came inside, and I noticed his behavior was off. He started acting irrational, and I told him, if he continued to act like that, I would call the police.

He said, "Go ahead," and handed me the phone.

As I looked at the phone, I noticed the timer was going, but I assumed he had just hit the "talk" button to dial out. I failed to realize he had dialed 911. Because of my assumption, I hung up the phone. I didn't actually want to get the police involved, but I desperately wanted him to stop doing what he was doing, and I knew how much he hated police. As I look back, I see how I was grasping at any mechanism I could, to control the situation and change the outcome.

The phone rang moments later, and it was dispatch. "Hello. Is everything okay? We received a 911 hang up call from this location."

My heart was racing. *Fuck, now what?* I needed to be honest, so I replied, "I did not mean to call, and I am okay."

The dispatcher proceeded to tell me that any time they receive a 911 hang-up call, police have to attend. *This is not going to end well,* I thought.

The police arrived a short time later and had a conversation with both of us, separately. After the conversation, they agreed they would be taking Johnny away for the night. Just when I'd gotten him back, he was being taken away, and I had no idea where to. *Here we go again.*

My heart ached more than I care to admit. I would have to go through the process of trying to track him down again tomorrow. I was also really embarrassed by this, but I was also hopeful that maybe this would wake him up and he'd realize the damage the drinking was causing to our relationship.

The next day, I woke up feeling sick to my stomach. I'd barely slept the night before. I had no idea where the police had taken Johnny, and I had no way of getting a hold of him. He was notorious for letting his phone die and not bothering to charge it. I went on a wild goose chase to try to find him again, because I wanted to apologize for what *I* had done. I'd been blamed for many of the issues and fights we had, and I was always the first to apologize, even if, deep down, I knew I hadn't done anything wrong.

I should have been able to express how I feel and feel safe enough to do so, but I just wanted to keep the peace and make things right. I did this because I was often consumed by the fear he would leave me for good. I feared I would never find someone who loved and cared about me. I would rather stay in this relationship and hope things changed rather than navigate life alone. I also recognize now the number of boundaries I failed to establish in my own life, in allowing this to keep happening.

This was the first of several police interactions.

After a few days on a bender, while I had no idea where he was, Johnny showed up and appeared to have hickies on his neck. I was immediately flushed with emotions. I had a huge pit in my stomach, and I wanted to interrogate him, but I knew it would send him back out the door, so I had to tread lightly and remain calm.

There I was again, desperately trying to hold onto a man who continuously hurt me and disregarded my feelings. As I approached him, I asked, "What is on your neck?"

He scoffed. "I got into a fight with someone, and they put their hands around my neck." He shied away and disengaged.

I didn't believe him, despite my badly wanting to. But I let it go because I loved him and wanted so badly to be loved. I was still holding out hope that things would change and get better. I kept envisioning a better life for us, although it's clear we were not envisioning the same future.

Johnny gaslit me many times during our time together, I even started to gaslight myself. I thought I was the crazy one and making things out to be way bigger than they were. This led me to being the peace keeper and constantly apologetic, even when I didn't think I had anything to apologize for. I just wanted things to get back to normal.

And I couldn't bear him being mad at me. I hated that feeling. I felt like a child who was scolded constantly by their parent. Like a kid who was so scared of getting into trouble or shamed, they would hide under the table. This continued even after our relationship ended.

Those are hard habits to break when you are stuck in the weeds for so many years.

# Chapter 4

# What Happens When the Dream Dies

I don't remember exactly when I went off of birth control, probably around the same time I stopped drinking alcohol, in 2010. I was off it for two years before I got pregnant, which was actually quite shocking to me. Also, a bit silly to choose, looking back now, given the turmoil I was experiencing in the relationship. *The things we do when we so desperately want to be loved.*

Around Christmas time, Johnny and I went to a rodeo. This was something he was very passionate about, and he competed throughout the entirety of our relationship. I wanted to support him, so I travelled around to different locations in Alberta to watch him ride and compete. I was so proud of him, and I always thought to myself, *I could get used to this life. I can't wait until we have an acreage of our own. Maybe we can even use some of his land and live this beautiful life on the reserve.*

(For those who may be unfamiliar, a reserve in Canada is similar to a reservation in the United States where many First Nations or Native Americans live.)

My day dreaming quickly ended, because I had a bad experience during the rodeo. It's funny now, but not when it happened. I got hit in the face with a patty of dirt and manure, which ended up busting open my lip. The entire arena made this, "*Oooo*" sound as soon as it happened. I was incredibly embarrassed.

I stayed for a while longer, because I couldn't fathom standing up in front of everyone and walking out after they'd just seen what happened. I wanted to assess my lip situation, so I relied on the camera on my phone to take a look. I was sitting with Johnny's aunt, and I turned the camera on and saw my upper lip was cracked open and bleeding, and I had dirt and manure in my teeth. After I mustered up the courage to do the walk of shame out of the area, I ended up leaving.

I went to a local convenience store near the rodeo arena. As I drove in and parked, I pulled up next to one of Johnny's cousins. We chatted briefly, and he asked me where Johnny was.

I responded, "Still riding," then I shared what had happened, resulting in my busted lip. I told him I was going home.

He asked, "Can Johnny come drinking with us after?"

I didn't want to feel like the controlling spouse, but I knew that situation would lead to nothing good. I replied, "I don't really want that to happen, because then he never comes home."

His cousin begged for at least a couple of drinks and promised me he would make sure Johnny got home.

As I drove away, I realized I had no control over the situation and could only hope for the best, but I was sure tired of living this way. This led to yet another drinking rampage and a night he did not come home.

The following year, Johnny was at another rodeo. This time it was New Year's Eve. I'm not sure why I hadn't gone with him, but I didn't. I stayed home and chose to go to bed somewhat early, worrying about when he would come home. I thought, if I just went to bed early, I would wake up and he would be home, so I could put all of the anxiety to rest. All would be well. Unfortunately, this was not the case.

My friend, Mike, texted me later that night, asking what I was doing.

"Lying in bed, doing nothing," I replied. "Johnny went out drinking, and I'm worried about him."

Mike indicated he was not doing anything either and asked if I wanted to go for a drive. When I agreed, he picked me up, and we went to get a milkshake and then drove around. We talked about our college days and everything in between. Eventually, our conversation led to my relationship with Johnny.

Mike inquired why I stayed, when I was feeling this way and clearly upset about how things were. He then said, "Chelsey, I can't believe you haven't gotten pregnant yet."

I kind of chuckled and said, "I know," thinking *it probably won't happen to me*. Little did I know, I was actually pregnant during that conversation and had only been playing with fire. I just hadn't taken a test to confirm… *yet*.

A few weeks passed, and my breasts were quite sore, more than typical period stuff. My period was late, and I felt exhausted. *So exhausted.* I was attending college at the time. Although I had graduated from Child and Youth Care, I decided to go back to obtain a degree. But I was finding it so hard to find the energy to wake up, let alone get to class on time. Something wasn't right. I had never felt this way in my entire life.

I called a friend of mine, who came over so I could take a pregnancy test. I didn't want to be alone during the process. Johnny must have been away at work during this time, because he was not home. I peed on the stick, and it immediately came back as positive, indicating 4-6 weeks. I was hit with emotions. Shocked, happy, sad, confused, and scared. *Fuck. Now what?*

For the days following, I lay on my bed, thinking, *What kind of life am I going to give this child? Maybe it's best if I consider my options.* Abortion being one of them. My thoughts continued to race a million miles a minute. Johnny hadn't changed. He was drinking often, took off on me, and I was truly not happy. I would be stuck raising this child on my own. These thoughts were among many overwhelming emotions at the time.

I contemplated abortion more and more, and this option became a strong contender. I am very close with my mom, and I thought about calling her. However, she was in Hawaii with some family members. I had a pretty rocky relationship with my dad growing up, as I mentioned, and it still wasn't super-strong at this point in my life, but he was the person I decided to call.

When he answered the phone, I began to tell him the news and how I was feeling about it all. To my surprise, he was quite supportive of my decision about an abortion. It was most surprising to me because, during my first year of college, I supported one of my best friends in getting an abortion, and he was very opposed to that decision. Maybe because things were different now, because it was his own child in this situation. I don't know, but I was grateful for the conversation and the support.

He told me he would support me in whatever I decided to do. I actually believed him, whereas, in previous situations when I had struggled with suicide ideation and depression, he said things like, "Forget about it" and "Don't let those people bother you." But when the suicide ideation got worse and I was put on suicide watch for a period of time, he told he was always there for me and that I could talk to him about anything. I didn't necessarily believe him at the time, because I felt no connection or safety with him, but thinking back now, I do believe this was a turning point in our relationship, where maybe I could learn to lean on my dad more than I ever had before. It was an opportunity for me to trust the process.

A few days passed, and after being consumed by my thoughts, I decided that abortion was no longer an option. I weighed the pros and cons and told myself, since I had some post-secondary education under my belt and already had a decent job, "I can do this. Even if I am raising this child on my own." I could always make changes in the future.

I went to the doctor to confirm the pregnancy and followed all of the proper protocols. This was one of the biggest decisions I had made in my life; little did I know, it would not be the last. It was also a decision that contains a consistent message, one that remains most true for me: I would be raising this girl on my own, but I will always be okay and will figure it out. It may even turn out better than I imagined, but it would not come easy.

I don't remember how or when I told Johnny that I was pregnant. This part of my life is a blur to me, like some others. As time went on, though, I remember having conversations in my head about whether this was the right choice and whether staying with him and trying to make this work would, in fact, work.

I was making the choice to stay, which meant it was time to get serious about where Johnny and I were at and what we were doing. At the time, we were renting a house, but I felt we needed to own property, if we were going to bring a child into this world. That felt like stability to me, and would maybe be a commitment on his end, too. But when I brought this up to him, he was hesitant to do so. I really pushed for this, maybe more than I should have. I was still dreaming of a happy little family life. Isn't that what we all want?

After Johnny found out I was pregnant, he quit drinking. Within a few months, though, he turned into someone many refer to as a "dry drunk," meaning he was no longer drinking, but the behaviors he displayed were very similar to those of someone under the influence of substances. I am not sure which is worse or if there is even a difference or justification for it. In the end, that didn't really matter.

I vividly remember driving around with Johnny one day, looking for houses. I was in the passenger seat of his truck, gazing out the window, deep in thought about whether or not this was going to work. I don't know why he was so reluctant to purchase a home with me. It was something I had wanted for quite some time, and now, with a baby on the way, it seemed like the next logical step. If we were really doing this, then having a stable home was important to me.

I was confused as to why this was not as important to him. *Maybe we have different understandings of home and what a future looks like,* I thought. *And more importantly, about what type of environment we want to raise our daughter in.*

We eventually bought a house together that following April; our daughter was due to be born in September. I was excited for this next chapter and had convinced myself things would be different. Everything was going to work out. This was an opportunity to try, giving it my all, and no longer ruminating on thoughts from my past. I thought to myself, *Maybe things will be different. He told me they would be.*

We even had a conversation about letting go of the past, no longer using past experiences in arguments, and focusing on the future. I was so hopeful.

# Chapter 5

# A Womb Full of Hope, A Mind Full of Dreams

I made the choice to go back to school, thinking it was time to explore my options and pursue a degree in social work. I thought this degree was my next logical step, as it was a related field to my current job and would open more doors for me when I was able to return to the workforce. I was always planning ahead so that, no matter what happened, I would be able to take care of myself.

Turns out, the social work program was quite competitive, and I did not get in. I pivoted and looked at other options. I wasn't able to relocate due to obvious reasons (just having a baby, being in a relationship, and having all of my supports locally), so I started looking into other programs offered by the college. I had always had an interest in policing and other areas of the justice system, so when I saw the Justice Studies Applied Degree was offered and that it was an automatic acceptance, if you had completed any diploma from the human services or justice programs, it was a no-brainer. This was my opportunity to apply and open more doors.

It was not an easy in, however, as they used my grades against me and wanted me to write an entrance exam. This made no sense to me, as I had graduated from two of their programs already, which was evidence I could participate and had the academic standing to take on any other course the college had to offer. I was getting pretty good at navigating challenges and advocating for myself, so I sent an email to the president of the college, asking for clarification as to why I had to follow this process. They agreed and waived the entry exam for me.

I share this because it's an example of another opportunity where I had a choice. It was also about exercising personal advocacy, which you will see has served me well throughout my journey, especially in my court battles.

After Johnny and I purchased our home, we settled in nicely. I had always wanted a dog, and this was my opportunity to get the one I wanted. We'd had dogs while I was growing up, but it was always the choice of my parents, and we never had the money to buy expensive dogs. We usually rescued them or paid a smaller price for a mixed breed. This was my opportunity to get the dog of my dreams. *I got to choose.*

A few months after moving into our home, we got a German Shepherd named Nalah. I thought to myself, *Finally! Life is coming together, and things are going to be so good.* I felt so proud. *Finally.*

I bit off a lot during that time—more than I could chew. Perhaps this was the ambitious part of me that would serve me in years to come. I don't have many other memories until our daughter was born, mostly because things were going well.

My birthday rolled around on August 26, 2012, and we celebrated with family. My parents came over to my house for cake.

Later that evening, I said to Johnny and my mom, "I'm having cramps. What if I'm going into labor?"

Johnny dismissed it and went to play hockey or something. I remember him leaving the house, while my mom stayed behind. We spent some time visiting on the patio. As it got a bit cool, we went inside.

I was still feeling cramps and said to my mom, "What do I do? I think she's going to come today."

My mom sat with me for a bit, unsure of what to do, but she was there to support me, which is all she could do.

I thought I might get the greatest gift of all, which was the birth of our daughter. But I was wrong. I was having Braxton Hicks contractions and would have to wait a few more days for her arrival.

# Chapter 6

## She Changed Everything

I remember so vividly the day before I went into true labor and our daughter was born. We were going to build a fence at Johnny's dad's property along with his brothers, who were quite a bit younger than we were because they were from his dad's second marriage.

Shortly after we arrived there, I went inside to use the bathroom. Then, I walked back to the truck, hopped into the passenger seat, and waited for Johnny to finish his conversation with his brother, so we could get to work. We didn't even make it off the driveway when I felt this sudden urge, like I had peed my pants.

I was so confused. *I literally just went to the bathroom. How could this happen?* I took a moment, and then reality hit me. My water had just broken. I looked at Johnny, who was sitting in the driver's seat, and told him what had just happened. We were no longer building a fence; we were now on our way to the hospital, as our daughter was soon to arrive.

We were about fifty minutes away from town, so we had a bit of a drive before we reached the hospital. On our drive, it felt so easy at first. I thought, *Why do women complain? The pain isn't even that bad.* Little did I know what was about to come… It was only getting started.

I was in labour for fifteen hours, and during that time, I made a few trips to the hospital before they admitted me. The last time, they sent me home before being admitted, so I went to lie down for a bit to try to rest. I was so tired, but my body was working overtime, making it difficult to rest.

When I woke up, I felt this incredible urge, as though I was going to defecate in my pants. I came out of our bedroom and saw Johnny not too far from the hallway. I proceeded to the bathroom, saying, "I feel like I really need the bathroom."

He didn't say much. I requested that we go back to the hospital. I was starting to feel a bit scared, mostly because of the unknown and because things were getting real. I requested again that we go to the hospital.

He responded with something along the lines of, "You're fine. It's probably nothing."

I felt so dismissed but filled with internal panic. I could not describe this feeling. I tried to use the bathroom and felt like I needed to sit on the toilet but nothing was there. I later learned this is what it feels like to be dilated. I felt like I was navigating this all by myself, and that the man who was supposed to be there to support me felt very distant. It made me sad, but I had bigger fish to fry. I had to figure this out. I basically had to beg him to take me back to the hospital.

Finally, he agreed.

When we headed back to the hospital, I was finally admitted. The pain was excruciating by this point. I had to be wheeled in via wheelchair. I tried not to cry, but I let some of the tears flow, because it was unbearable.

Because of the delay, I almost missed the opportunity to get an epidural, which by this point I desperately wanted. I didn't know how much more pain I could take. Initially, I thought I could do it drug-free, mostly because my mom had. There is no shame in those who take drugs for labor; I just thought it would be quick and easy like my mom's experience. The joke was on me. The pain was so unbearable, I was willing to take anything just to get through the next while.

Prior to the epidural and being admitted, I'd been given morphine and some other drug. One of them did not sit well with me, and I'd ended up throwing it up before I even left the hospital.

My mom was allowed in the delivery room, which I was so grateful for. It was one of her only wishes, to watch her granddaughter being born, and there was no way I was going through labor alone. Johnny was there, too, but he spent the entire labor process sleeping.

My delivery nurse was someone I had worked with previously, and I was so excited to have her. She brought me a peace of mind that I desperately needed at that time. I remember her asking me, "Are you okay if I am your nurse?"

I responded, "Of course! I'm so glad it's you."

Labor was intense, and as I was trying to push, I was told I had to wait. My doctor was in the other room, delivering another baby, but it shouldn't be too much longer. I thought to myself, *Are you kidding me? This is painful, and there is no stopping. I have to keep pushing.* And so, I did. As I continued to push, the doctor was able to make it into my room on time.

Our daughter, Grace was born on September 8, 2012, at approximately 6:30 a.m. She shares a birthday with her father.

I watched the doctors and nurses clean Grace, suction the fluid from her nose, and wrap her in a blanket. Not long after, I was asked if I could stand up and feel my legs. I stood up from the hospital bed and told the nurse, "Yes, I can feel my legs." I had no idea what was happening, but I was so tired after labor that I was just going with the flow.

"Great," they said. Within minutes, I was directed by the nurse to sit in a wheelchair. The nurse carried Grace over to me and put her on my lap, then I was wheeled from delivery to the maternity ward.

I'm not sure where I got the idea that I would get some time to rest up before going into full-time parent mode. It may have been from the movies or a story I made up in my mind, where I envisioned Grace being taken to a nursery and cared for by nurses, at least for a few hours while I got to rest. Wherever that narrative came from, it was not true.

I was wheeled to my room. I'd wanted a private room, and our benefits covered it. However, there were too many people having babies that day, so they had to double-bunk us. This was the last thing I'd wanted.

My bed was closest to the door, which meant that my roommate's guests had to walk past my bed and space to get to her. I had no idea how long I would be in the hospital, but I couldn't wait to get out of there and into my own space at home.

Johnny went home after the birth of Grace, indicating he was tired. I don't recall what happened for the rest of the day, but I do remember, later in the night, Grace started crying. I thought the nurses would come and help me, but they didn't. I had all of these assumptions as to what childbirth would be like, and I was far off course. Nobody came. I knew I had to do something, but I felt like a fish out of water.

I am the oldest of four siblings, and I helped care for them growing up, so I was no stranger to babies. But it was a totally different feeling, knowing you are solely responsible for this newborn baby and have to figure it out. It was a whole new level of intimidating, something I had never experienced before.

I thought to myself, *What do I do? I wonder what's wrong with her.* I began to change her diaper, and thought she may be hungry. I had trouble breastfeeding and just wanted to use formula, because the process of breastfeeding and trying to pump was stressing us both out. It took quite a fight with the nurses to allow me to use formula, but I persevered and finally got a nurse the following morning who was supportive of formula and the thought process, "Fed is best." It was such a relief.

I spent the first night at the hospital alone. Johnny did not come back until later the next morning, indicating he was tired and needed to sleep. Our dog was also at home, but there were others who could have helped take care of her, so he could have been with me. It's not like I wasn't totally exhausted myself, after fifteen hours of labor and pushing a baby out…

The following day, I was cleared to go home. Johnny came to the hospital to pick me up. It was such a relief to go back into my own space, where I felt most comfortable and could adjust to being a parent.

Over the course of the next few days, I received an influx of requests from family members who wanted to come visit. To be honest, I was so overwhelmed and exhausted, I didn't want to visit with anyone. I didn't want to hurt anyone's feelings, but deep down I knew I needed to be honest about the way I was feeling.

For a period of time, my feelings were respected, but there was turmoil to follow. A few months later, Johnny's family members started asking me if they could take Grace for the day. I felt uncomfortable with these requests. Not because I didn't trust them, but because she was still so young, and I felt this need and desire to be with her all of the time, as most mothers do.

One day, Johnny said to me, "My dad wants to take the baby for the day." The request became more specific. "They want to take her away from the house."

I inquired as to why they could not come visit us at our house, since I was still not comfortable with letting people take Grace for the day, family members or not.

Johnny's response was, "You are White, and my family doesn't know how to act around White people." That hurt. I felt this kick to my stomach, provoking anxiety. I wondered what my race had to do with anything. I wasn't sure how to fully receive that message. I was most confused because I thought his family and I got along great. While I respected their approach to culture and the different way males and females interacted, I had never gotten the sense from his family that they thought differently of me because of the color of my skin. This led me to wonder what it would mean for Grace, being mixed-race.

As time went on, this narrative sharpened. Johnny began to share with me how his friends didn't feel comfortable coming to our house either, because I was White. I could never figure out where these comments were coming from or what the real message was behind them.

I started to question myself, feeling as though I may not ever be good enough for them. Again, the thought crossed my mind, *What does this mean for my mixed-race daughter? Is there going to be conflict with her being mixed? What messaging is she going to receive? Will she have a hard time identifying with either race?* I fell into old, unhealthy patterns and resorted to justifying and trying to prove I was good enough for Johnny's family and friends.

I received my Blackfoot name in 2011, *Naammiitapii Aakoiyiiniimaki,* which translates in English to "all people pipe woman." I received this name from an elder due to the way I worked with all people, no matter where they come from or their background or how vulnerable they were. I carried that name with immense pride. The story that went along with my name was beautiful, and I knew I had an obligation to live up to this name.

Old patterns of behavior snuck into my consciousness again. I felt the need to justify my relationships to the Indigenous community and the understanding I had of their culture. I said to Johnny, "I was given a Blackfoot name for the way I work with people, no matter what their experiences were or who they are. I had a connection not only to the culture, but to the people, too. I am accepted. Many elders told me that."

It was hurtful, what he said, because I'd been told by so many in the Indigenous community that I was accepted, but here, I felt least accepted from someone I loved the most.

I was met with a snarky response from Johnny. "Do you want a gold star for having an Indian name?"

My heart sank into my stomach. *Why couldn't he just be as proud of me as I was to carry this name and have this connection? Something I take such pride in, he is so quick to dismiss.* I sat deep into the couch, feeling so ashamed and pitiful.

This was the first of many comments and behaviors like this. During arguments, I would sometimes be brave enough to point out that Johnny was behaving in an abusive way. I was met with comments like, "You don't know what abuse is," because, from his perspective, if I wasn't getting hit, it wasn't abuse. He would outright say that to me, and he would justify his own behaviors, saying how bad others in his life have had it.

There were other times when, while holding Grace in his arms, he would get so mad, he would smash furniture with his fist, while he proceeded to yell and swear at me.

One night during an argument, we were standing in the kitchen, and there was enough distance between us. But I moved in closer, because I just wanted him to hug me and make things better. I was tired of fighting and feeling small. I always hoped that a switch would go off, and he would change the way he dealt with conflict.

He did not reciprocate the closeness. Rather, he half turned to me and said something I will never forget. This was probably the most hurtful comment he has ever said. "I hope Grace is nothing like you when she grows up."

I was flooded with emotions. I felt so unworthy. Deep down, I had a sense of pride. As parents, we want our children to grow up to be like us, because we strive to be role models for them. It felt then like any opportunity Johnny had to strip away any positivity and make me feel small, he would take. And he did.

On another occasion, during an argument, I was sitting on the stairs down to the basement. Johnny spent a lot of time down there, as he considered it his "man cave." The couch faced the stairs, and the television was against the wall, next to the stairs. I don't know what we were fighting about this time, but the fighting was becoming a consistent theme throughout our relationship.

Oftentimes, it was around parenting, but it felt like he would pick a fight with me over anything, even just being who I was. I always felt the need to play small and shrink myself in his presence, especially when he was upset. We were in this same place when Johnny smashed the table in the basement. Grace was in his arms again, and he was angry. All I wanted to do was shrivel up and cry.

How could this man speak to me in this way, while holding our daughter? She may have been an infant, but I couldn't help but wonder what type of damage and trauma she was enduring, even at this age.

We know children can inherit trauma from the womb, so there was no doubt in my mind she was inheriting trauma then, being on Earth and in his arms. The pain was so real. I felt so raw and exposed. I wanted it all to end.

A gut-wrenching feeling came across my body, one I will never forget. *You will never change him.*

# Chapter 7

# High Horses, Low Blows

Our relationship was not improving, and we had not even gotten through Grace's first year around the sun. I stayed home with Grace while Johnny worked away. He was still working in Texas for most of Grace's first year of life.

One week, he returned home on a Friday and already had plans to rodeo for the remainder of the weekend. I was excited for him to come home so I could have a bit of time to myself and take the dog for a walk, with us sharing the parenting responsibilities. It was a lot to do on my own, and I had a partner, which meant I shouldn't have to do it on my own once he was home. I was looking forward to having time to decompress my mind, recalibrate, and continue completing some of my outstanding tasks.

I decided to ask Johnny if I could take some time for myself to do the things I needed to do. I was immediately met with resistance.

"You can go gallivant around without Grace and me?"

I felt a sudden surge of panic and anxiety through my body. *Here we go again. I need to justify myself again. Why can't I get thirty minutes to myself?*

As always, I began overexplaining. I came up with a list of reasons why I wanted to go for a walk alone and do the things I needed to do, one of which was to complete my application to go back to school to obtain a degree. I didn't feel heard at all. I was met with more negativity and resistance.

Suddenly, Johnny wanted to go to the grocery store and asked, "Why should I have to bring Grace to the grocery store?" He followed that comment with a demand. "You better have that application completed by the time I get back."

This wasn't the first time he delivered demands and orders. I thought to myself, *What happens if I don't complete my application? What are the consequences going to be?* Fear began to creep in, and I started to fear for my life and my safety. I felt many vague, underlying threats, and I knew he had access to firearms, which made me feel the most uneasy.

I relied on my friends and family a lot during Grace's first year and in the years to come, as Johnny worked out of town, often for a month on and then two weeks off. When he was home, he had other commitments that appeared to be more important than being at home as a partner or a dad. There were times when I fell ill and my friends had to come put Grace to sleep for me, just so I could catch up on some sleep. Other times, when Johnny was home and Grace was unwell, I asked if he could wake up with her, since I was exhausted and was always the one to do it, especially when I was on my own and he was away at work.

Lying in bed, exhausted, I could hear Grace fuss and wake up. She wasn't feeling well and hadn't been since the night before. Johnny had to get up early to leave for Calgary in the morning anyway, so I hoped he would go check on her before he left, letting me maybe get just a little more sleep before having to tackle the rest of the day with an ill child.

I nudged Johnny and said, "Hey, Grace is awake. Do you mind going to check on her?"

No answer.

I tried again a few more times, but he either ignored me or slept through it all. After becoming a mom, I became such a light sleeper. Even with Grace being in the next room, I heard everything—every movement, every sound.

Finally, Johnny heard my request and immediately addressed me with hostility. "What do you need sleep for? The gym? A thirty-minute appointment?"

Pain and sadness seeped through my skin. There I was again, feeling so worthless. The things that had brought me joy and allowed me to be a better mom were slowly being stripped away from me. Plus, I was being verbally punished for even wanting those things for myself and, worst of all, for trying to taking care of myself, so I could show up as a better mom, partner, friend, sister, daughter, and every other role I play in life. It was like I'd made the most absurd ask on the planet: a little support from my partner. I started to gaslight myself, wondering whether I really did have unrealistic expectations of a partner. *Maybe I am the problem.*

This was one of the many instances when I began this self-doubt and self-questioning, plus the unhealthy behavior of comparing my relationship to everyone else's.

When I had the courage to call out the verbal abuse, I was met with more. Johnny would say, "Why don't you get off your high horse and cry about it some more?"

I sank further and further into despair, which soon became depression. I wanted so badly to run away to a place where I felt safe, or at the very least to crawl out into a hole where I wouldn't have to feel. I desperately wanted to be in Johnny's arms, to feel loved and cared about. In fact, the more he pushed me away, the closer I wanted to be to him. In the same breath, though, I was realizing more and more what a pipe dream that close relationship really was, that it would likely never become my reality, no matter how much I hoped, wished, or dreamed. It was such a bizarre feeling, and quite polarizing. I learned over time that both things can be true at the same time.

During another incident, we were driving home from somewhere when Grace was only a few months old. She was feeling under the weather and was not eating her typical meals. As a new mom, this caused me to worry. Maybe more than I should have, but that doesn't matter.

I shared how I was feeling with Johnny, and he responded coldly, "You just can't handle stress," minimizing every concern I had shared.

That sinking feeling reappeared in the pit of my stomach, and I thought, *What? I care about our baby and the fact that she is not eating well. And I am unsure of what to do. How does this equate to me not being able to handle stress?*

Then, I reviewed in my mind the number of stressful incidents I had encountered, whether in my personal or professional life. I was too exhausted to recount them out loud, and I knew it would fall on deaf ears, anyway.

When we pulled into our garage and parked, Johnny turned off the vehicle and let himself out. I remained in the passenger seat momentarily before making my way to the backseat to get Grace out of her car seat. She was fussy and crying, so I jumped to worst-case conclusion and started to worry about what I could do to help Grace. She was only a few months old, so she could not communicate with me other than through crying and fussing.

I wanted to be safe rather than regret my decisions not to act, so I made the decision to call 811 (health link), which is a number we can call to speak to a nurse, explain what is going on, and seek medical advice. Sometimes, they tell you to see your doctor or seek immediate medical attention at the hospital. Sometimes, they provide you with advice you can try at home and how to monitor symptoms. It's a great resource.

I put Grace on my lap in the passenger seat of my vehicle, still inside of the garage, and I attempted to feed her while I spoke to one of the nurses over the phone.

Johnny had remained in the house since we'd arrived home. A few minutes into my phone call with the nurse, he opened the door and stared at me with an intense glare. He had a clenched jaw and fist and was thrusting his hand downward, demanding, "Get in the house now."

I attempted to remain present with the nurse on the phone and deescalate the conflict that was unfolding in front of my eyes. And I was scared. *What will happen if I don't go into the house right now? What are the consequences when I get off the phone and enter the home?* My time felt limited, and I was also tired of living in the unknown with this threat looming over my head.

The nurse must have clued in that something was happening, because she suddenly changed direction in the conversation. She asked, "Are you okay?"

To minimize the situation and lessen the conflict, I said that I was. But this wasn't the last time I'd lie and say I was okay, when, inside, I was scared for my safety and wasn't okay.

As I continued to speak with the nurse, I looked up toward the door, where Johnny continued to stand, giving me the middle finger. When I hung up the phone minutes later, I attempted to enter our home and realized Johnny had locked me out of the house.

I waited in the garage momentarily and then banged on the door until I was let in. I don't remember what happened next.

# Chapter 8

# From Scarcity to Self-Trust

Johnny made far more money working on the drilling rigs than I ever did supervising visits between parents and children who were involved in the child welfare system. I began my career under the child welfare umbrella at the ripe age of twenty. I thought I was making bank when I received my first paycheck of $500. I'd never received that kind of money before. I was on cloud nine.

But now, my reality had changed. It was a great starting point, but I would have to pay for everything on my own if I got out of this terrible situation. Grace was only nine months old when I first contemplated leaving Johnny. In Canada, we were allotted twelve months of maternity leave at that time. (It is now eighteen months.) However, I was so unhappy, I needed to make some changes, so I cut my maternity leave short. I needed to come up with a game plan.

As my career developed and expanded, so did my pay cheques, but the reality of paying all of the bills and expenses on my own had me deep in planning mode, with a bit of fear as to how I would make it on my own. But I knew, no matter what, I would figure it out.

So, three months before I was supposed to return from maternity leave, I was back at work. Little did I know the government would come looking for me years later, saying I owed them money because I returned to work while still collecting government benefits for maternity leave. I tried to explain my situation; however, they did not seem to care that our lives were in danger. They prioritized the debts owed and how quickly I could pay them back.

The drastic difference in our earned income caused me a lot of despair. Johnny will say and continues to make claims that it's always been about money for me. On numerous occasions, Johnny has claimed that I only stayed with him because of money, but that couldn't be further from the truth. I was being strategic about money so that I could figure out how to survive on my own.

The money issue became more significant and leverage to hang over my head. Not only was I worried about paying for rent and everything else on my own, as a single mom and dog mom, but also, Johnny often threatened me with his money. One time, when we were arguing, again in the basement of our home, as I sat on the couch, he stood on the stairs, his full height above me, and told me, "I make more money than you do. I will make sure I hire a lawyer, and you will never see Grace again."

Another gut punch. The last thing I wanted was for my daughter to be taken away from me. I also knew from working under the child welfare umbrella that Indigenous bands have band delegates who get involved when Indigenous children are in the care of non-Indigenous foster homes, and they assist in determining where Indigenous kids in care go or whether they can be adopted by non-Indigenous families, etc.

While our case was a bit different due to the fact that Grace was not being apprehended and we were not involved with child welfare, I had the deep, looming question in the back of my mind: "Could they get involved in our situation through the courts and determine where Grace goes?"

As a White person, I wouldn't stand a chance, I thought. I would fight to the death for my daughter, but the intimidation and fear of the unknown weighed heavily on me. *What if he does take her away from me, and I never see her again? How could I go on?*

I felt like I had to walk on eggshells from that point on, because at any moment everything could change. That was the message I kept telling myself. I believe my skin color could put me at a disadvantage, and the thought of losing my daughter devastated me more than I can put into words. This fear followed me for many years to come, and the issue of me being White would come up in court years later. Culture can be weaponized; I've lived that firsthand.

In Canada, families receive a child tax benefit, which is non-taxable income the federal government provides to parents to assist with some of the costs of having children. It is based on family income, so monthly payments vary, but it is still helpful. They are direct deposits now; however, when I first started receiving them, they came as a check in the mail. I was always the person who picked up the mail, and the checks arrived around the same time every month. When they came in, I stashed each check away in one of my drawers. This was going to be a large part of my exit plan.

For almost a year, I saved the checks and didn't even think about cashing them. Then, one day, I realized that checks were only valid for so long, before they expired and could no longer be cashed, so I had to make some moves. I went to the bank a few days later and cashed them all. I put the money into my account, while I continued to make a plan, one small step at a time. *Every time I put a check away, I dreamed of a better future for Grace and me.*

Over time, I got braver with Johnny and began to stand my ground. I tried to end the relationship on a few occasions, the first time in 2013, when Grace was one. I can't remember what led up to that moment.

Despite my bravery, the conversation did not go well. Johnny threatened to take his own life if I ended the relationship. While I did not believe this to be true, given all of my training in suicide intervention, I knew that, regardless my own thoughts about the situation, comments like that must be taken seriously.

This weighed heavily on me, too, because the thought lingered: *What if he actually does something like that? Could I live with that? Would I blame myself?*

Sometimes, it felt like, no matter how hard I tried or how courageous I felt, something always drew me back in. *So close, yet so far.* This very well could have been the first of Johnny's many manipulation tactics, but coming from the professional mental health world as I did, I didn't take suicide threats lightly.

# Chapter 9

# The Exit I Couldn't Ignore

Beginning in 2012, leading up to our daughter's birth and for many years after, I documented the details of our relationship. I started this process because something deep inside me told me I needed to do it. My professional background supported this practice, as did the advice of others in the field who kept recommending this process to me. I thought, if anything, I would have all of this proof, should I ever need it. Trauma can impact our ability to remember things, especially as they happened. As more time passes, it becomes harder to remember the details. This way, I would have a recollection of everything that had happened, because I'd documented in real time.

They say, "Hope for the best, plan for the worst," and I was at the point where I was planning for the worst. I had been hopeful that things would change after the birth of our daughter, but I was proven wrong as time went on. Things didn't get any better after Grace entered the world. In fact, it only gave Johnny more leverage and control. I didn't think I would come out of my relationship with Johnny unscathed, whatever way it looked.

There's a large gap in my documentation. Maybe it's because this was the most daunting time of my life, and I was merely surviving each and every day, walking on eggshells and trying to keep my own sanity. *I don't know.*

In 2014, I ended the relationship and was making plans to move out. I tried to lessen the blow by attempting to make it not seem definitive. Instead, I told him he needed to work on himself, because we could no longer live like this. I think part of me was still hopeful that maybe it would all work out, but I knew I needed to remove myself from the situation, the home, and everything else, in order to be able to see things clearer and from another perspective, outside of survival.

Nobody dreams of this life, with a broken home, a broken family, and a lot of dysfunction. I knew I needed to protect my inner peace. Not only mine, but Grace's, too. That was my priority. Whatever happened after that would just happen. I thought, by leaving, it would send a stronger message to him that there was a lot on the line, and that our relationship required a lot more work than he was currently putting in. Johnny did make counseling appointments and attended them occasionally, but doing so was short-lived. I still resided in the home during this process, though I was fervently looking for another place to rent. Staying there was not the best option overall, but it was my best choice in that moment. *I don't recommend....*

A few weeks later, I found a rental on the westside via an ad on social media. This was a nice house in a prime location and within my budget. But the rental price involved a key oversight on my part; I should have realized the price was too good to be true. Not only that, there were other warning signs, as well. I look back now and laugh at how stupid I was to get sucked into this, but in the midst of my panic and survival, I chose to ignore the red flags. Unfortunately, this mistake put me out almost $1,000.

The rental wasn't far from where I was living with Johnny, so I decided to take a drive past the house one night. I noticed lights on inside and people in the windows. *Interesting,* I thought. *First red flag.* Also, the house was fully decorated, including pictures on the wall—it appeared as though a family lived there. *Second red flag.*

But I ignored the things I saw and convinced myself that this house would be mine. There could be a million reasons why the house was fully furnished with people inside, when I drove past. However, I did do what I do best: sought clarification.

I sent a message to the "landlord" and inquired further, indicating what I'd observed. They responded to me almost immediately, writing, "We don't live in the house and are currently out of the country. The people there are taking care of the property and should not be there long." The desperate side of me believed what they'd told me, despite my suspicion that things were not adding up.

They proceeded to tell me the best way to get them their money for my damage deposit was through Western Union. Later that night, I got into my vehicle with the information I needed and headed to Safeway, our nearest Western Union.

When I arrived at Safeway and parked, I had a pit in my stomach, questioning whether this was legitimate or not, but I convinced myself to carry through. I walked up to the customer service counter, which was closed. *Shoot, I guess I'm not sending the money today.*

I sent a text message to the "landlord" and informed them, adding I would go back first thing the next morning and transfer the money to them. They seemed so patient and understanding… *Third red flag.*

The following morning, I woke up and headed back to Safeway to send off this money. When I approached the counter and told the clerk, "Hello, I'm here to send a money transfer," the staff member asked me, "Are you sure you want to do this and this is not a scam?" *Fourth red flag.*

I almost hesitated but convinced myself in the moment that I did not want to look stupid. That I was sure I wanted to do this. "No, this is not a scam," I said and proceeded with the transaction.

I learned within hours that this was, in fact, a scam and I was out $900. *Great. Now what?* I had no other money put away. I had no other options. I would have to continue to live with Johnny and expose Grace to the ongoing chaos.

Let me tell you this. If you think the universe is sending you messages or when you have a gut feeling about something, *TRUST IT*! The universe will always have your back, if you're open to receiving. At this point in my life, though, I was not yet ready to receive, not in the way I should have. I was more naïve than anything else, even though I was able to briefly acknowledge the not-so-subtle hints. And I was very good at suppressing my gut feelings when I shouldn't have.

For some reason unbeknownst to me, I kept Johnny informed about what I was doing and the houses I was looking at. I remember approaching him after this experience full of shame. I mustered up the courage to explain what had happened. I assumed he would be grateful and excited that things didn't work out for me. I also expected him to be quite spiteful. Johnny didn't want me to leave, so there was a relief in his eyes and voice when I told him.

Meanwhile, I was feeling trapped, wondering, *What the fuck do I do now?* I continued my search for housing in my price range, but it proved to be quite difficult, especially because I had a large dog in tow. Many rental properties were out of my range, and if you had a large dog, landlords often required an additional monthly payment or some restrictive clause in their agreements, which made things more difficult for me. In the meantime, I continued to save even more money.

A month or so later, I found a place on the northside of the city. I'd never felt comfortable on that side of town, even though I went to school there. Johnny and I had briefly lived on the northside, when we first moved in together. I'd felt a bit more comfortable, since he was there with me. But to live there alone didn't feel the safest. I grew up on the westside of town; that was where I felt most comfortable. But at this point in my life, I couldn't be too picky. I wasn't as much of a risk taker as I am now.

The rental was an entire house at a decent price, under $1,000 a month, and included a large yard for my dog. It even had a garage. It reminded me somewhat of my great-grandma's house and her garage; for whatever reason, I did not feel comfortable utilizing it. Regardless of those small details, I thought it would be a great opportunity for Grace and me to start again. Johnny came with Grace and me to look at the place. Part of the reason I included him was to lessen the blow and make this a safer exit for us.

After the tour, I decided to take the house. Johnny did not appear thrilled. The landlord did not require I sign a full year's lease; instead, it was month to month, which was nice. I figured, if the house didn't work out for me, I only had to give one month's notice. Given the uncertainty of my life then, that was the perfect scenario.

Very soon after moving in, I realized the house was too much space. It did not feel like home *at all*. It was too big and empty. I tried to give it some time, to make it feel like home, where we could add more furniture, pictures, and whatever else complimented the home, but I couldn't see it through. I felt lost, disconnected, and maybe even a little afraid.

I lived there for a few months until I found a different, smaller place on the westside. It was such a relief to be back on the westside. It was in an area quite a distance from where I grew up, but in this familiar side of town, I could finally let my shoulders down and breathe. It was closer to my parents, as well, which gave me a sense of security in its own right. Grace and I resided there with our dog for a year. I sacrificed a yard for my dog, which was a huge inconvenience, but overall, it was the right choice for all of us at the time.

During that period, I was a full-time student plus working full-time as well during most evenings, to facilitate programming. I was also training my dog to be a search dog, and I volunteered with Search and Rescue. Looking back now, I had far too much on my plate, but I was building my future, *our future,* and escaping the reality of home life. It was a massive distraction and perhaps what I needed at the time, although not sustainable long term.

Johnny and I were not in the best place, but certainly this was not the worst it had been. I was still walking on eggshells, trying to keep him happy, because I was so tired of the fighting. Having my own place gave me the space I needed, so I was not entrenched in his chaos and uncertainty all the time.

Johnny was not very consistent about his parenting, but that was okay with me. The less I had to deal with him, the better. As time went on, the old messages from Johnny continued to haunt me. I often thought, *Maybe nobody will love me the way Johnny claims to.... and I won't find anyone else. Maybe I should go back, so Grace has a family and is not living in what society tells us is a broken home.*

Money was also tight. While I was working in the field and doing a job that I loved, which was great, the work didn't pay very well yet, and we weren't offered benefits. I was often living pay check to pay check. Buying groceries was often tough. Grace and I spent a lot of time at my parents' house, especially for dinner.

Grace often reminds me about the time we lived at "that house in Sunridge," where we had no food. It's interesting what kids remember and mention to us. It's a lesson about how our children observe and remember far more things than we give them credit for. In hindsight, I don't think I ever used that oven to cook. In fact, I didn't do much cooking there at all.

I'm incredibly grateful for my parents and the place of refuge they offered, always ensuring we had something to eat. Johnny did send me money sometimes, and I think he even helped cover the cost of some of Grace's daycare on occasion. But it never amounted to what he should have been paying for our daughter's care.

# Chapter 10

## Back to Familiarity

I took that year of living in Sunridge to build my self-love and to heal after all the chaos I'd endured over the past several years. I signed a full year's lease at the place on the westside, and when it was up, I let old narratives fill my head.

*He's right, nobody will love me the way he did,* I thought to myself. Also, *I've been single for a year and nobody has taken interest in me, so I guess I am just meant to be with him.* It was such a distorted way of viewing relationships and love. I chose not to sign another lease. Instead, I moved back in with Johnny, back into the house we'd bought together.

This probably sounds like a crazy idea, because I had found my way out and built the love for myself that I'd so desperately wanted and needed. But old habits die hard.

It took only a few months for our old relationship patterns to resurface and things to go back to the way they'd been before I left. The fighting ramped up, my self-worth plummeted, and the love for self that I had worked so hard to build up was stripped away. Again, I feel deep into despair. And most sad, I knew: *I let myself down.*

Johnny was still working on the oil rigs during that time, but eventually, those jobs dried up and work became limited. Not long after that, Johnny decided he no longer wanted to work on the rigs, that he wanted to change careers so he could be home more often. As much as many partners would want their partner home more often, I felt the exact opposite. I thought, *Great, now he will be around more, which will only make things worse. More fighting and hostility.*

While searching for alternative work, he found things to fill his time. I supported him through this process, despite wanting more for myself. When he chose to pursue a career as a paramedic, I was really proud of him. I celebrated his wins and cheered him on along the way. Soon, he was in school to become an EMT (emergency medical technician) and was hired on by his reserve as an EMT.

I was doing the brunt of the parenting, even though I was also in school. I never received the same level of support from him as he did from me. This was upsetting, but I was beginning to expect nothing more.

In June 2016, I cocreated a program for the agency where I worked. They were short staffed, so I decided to help out, on top of my leadership position. This was in a frontline gig that I loved. It put me out in the community, engaging with our vulnerable community and connecting with stakeholders. It was a lot of fun. However, I had no idea what fresh hell it would bring for me…

The position required us to be mobile, in a van, for most of the shift. We were ensuring our vulnerable population was safe, while assisting EMS and police with non-medical and non-criminal calls and transporting individuals to safe places. Due to the nature of the work that I did, we were required to be in a male-female partnership. I was fortunate to be paired with a good partner. We got along well and had a lot of fun, which made working together on those long days so much easier. What didn't become easier was my home life.

I was putting in approximately fifty-to-sixty-hour work weeks during this time. It was a lot, but it was a distraction from my home life. It also allowed me to save up more money, as I was still planning for my final exit. It was also an opportunity for Johnny to step up his parenting. I worked these insane hours for a few months until our organization lost the contract to another one.

Johnny always complained about my work hours and was more concerned about his own priorities. There was no coparenting or support in the relationship. He did not like how much I was working, but what bothered him most was the fact that my partner was male. It wasn't long before he started accusing me of cheating on him and sleeping with my work partner. Despite my attempts to explain the job dynamics and why we were always partnered with an opposite-sex colleague, it fell on deaf ears and was a waste of breath. Yet there I was again, trying to justify and explain myself, just to keep the peace and calm the storm at home.

I am not sure how Johnny found my partner's contact information, but he did. Soon, he started sending messages to my partner, accusing him of being with me. I wasn't aware of the messages at first, but our work dynamic started to shift, and I was left feeling confused. I wondered, *Why did things dramatically change between us all of a sudden? Why does it feel like he barely talks to me during our shifts?*

I wasn't great with addressing conflict back then, and I had enough turmoil going on in my life at that moment, so I didn't need more. But I did feel obligated to figure out what was going on between us and why there was such a shift in my work partner's energy. He did have some understanding of my situation. How could he not? We drove around for twelve hours a day. It is hard *not* to talk about our personal lives when you spend that amount of time together.

This awkwardness and tension went on for a couple of weeks before he finally came clean about what was going on. He texted me one day, explaining that Johnny had somehow gotten his contact information and had been sending him accusatory text messages, making him feel super-uncomfortable.

"It's tough to show up to work sometimes," he said. In turn, this had made it quite difficult for me, as well. So, what had felt like my "safe space," an escape from my home life, was now being impacted by Johnny.

I knew something had to give, and I just wanted to get off the roller coaster. Feelings of anxiety, sadness, anger, and a million other emotions rushed over me, as I wondered how the hell I was going to get out of this. But I knew I needed to do something soon.

Not only was Johnny harassing my work partner and me, both, he also started to share inappropriate messages with Grace. One evening when Grace was about four years old, she and I went for a walk.

She turned her little body, looked up at me, and asked, "Why did you tell my dad we are not a family anymore? You made him cry."

I was immediately flooded with all sorts of emotions. *Now Grace is getting dragged into the manipulation?* I thought. *Why would he tell her something like this!?*

I calmed my angry, internal voice before I replied, "Those are messages that should not be shared with you. And it is not true."

Johnny was doing shift work, so he was away some nights. Grace's behavior started to be impacted by this schedule, and I became concerned about her wetting the bed for the first few nights after Johnny returned home after being away for a few days. This wasn't normal; she was already fully potty trained. It was a clear indication that something more was going on with her, that she was being impacted by his schedule more than she could verbalize. This wasn't the last time this would happen.

One morning, out the blue, I woke to Johnny saying how much of a pathetic loser he was. That is not how anyone wants to wake up. Dazed and half asleep, I was very confused. He had to go to work that morning, and I was hoping he would just leave.

Rather than engaging in the conversation, I told him, "You need to go to work, and I don't want Grace to wake up to this commotion." Like usual, though, anything I said fell on deaf years and tended only to escalate the situation. Still, I continued to ask him to leave.

Johnny remained in the room, standing near the doorway, and said, "The damage is done. I cannot go on like this anymore." Johnny's behavior escalated. He lay down on the floor beside the bed and pounded his fist on the ground. This scared my dog, who got up and left the room.

Then, Grace woke up, making me furious. That was the last thing I wanted. So, now, I had to deal with two upset humans, including one who should be able to manage on his own.

I asked Johnny to leave again, saying Grace was worth more than this. Then, I closed the bedroom door and told him to go to work.

Instead, he walked into the living room and started yelling at me, *"Get out here right now!"*

I refused. I lay in bed, hoping he would get tired of ordering me into the other room. I wasn't so lucky. I didn't want to engage in this type of conversation. I was so done.

Johnny always liked to control the conversation and its outcomes. Moments later, he shifted, accusing me, "You're kicking me out."

I replied, "I am not leaving this time. I left last time, and it's too hard for me to find a place with a dog and a baby. You have another house you own and somewhere to go to."

He continued to repeat himself. Despite his being late for work, he continued to yell and argue with me, refusing to leave.

I was at my wit's end and didn't know what else to say or do. I suggested we both retain lawyers, as it was clear we could not navigate this on our own.

He responded, "I will be homeless," and then engaged in more manipulation tactics.

I well knew that homelessness was not going to happen to him: he had another property, and he also had land. I remember thinking, *My sanity is worth more than this. He can figure it out. It's not my job to worry about that. It's my job to worry about Grace and me.*

Then, the conversation's energy shifted again. Johnny started to cry, apologizing to Grace. When I again asked him to leave again, he changed it up, saying it was his house. Now, it was his and Grace's. So, he wasn't going anywhere.

I felt suddenly terrified. I didn't know what to expect next, as he changed behavior and answers so rapidly. I didn't want to leave, but his comments were always threatening and left me wondering what was next for me.

I decided to take a different approach, an old tactic I had tried once before. I said to Johnny, "If you don't leave, I will call the police."

Johnny was supposed to be at work at 8:00 a.m. He finally left the house at 7:55 that morning. As soon as he'd left the driveway, he called me over and over. When I picked up eventually, he went right back to accusing me of texting other guys all of the time, and he demanded to see my phone.

Rather than disengaging or ignoring him, I found myself defensive, saying I had no reason to show him my phone, that I was not talking to other men. The only men I had communicated with were coworkers or friends who were in my life prior to meeting him.

Then, he shifted the narrative and blame yet again. "You left your ex so quick to be with me. I'm sure you would do it again." He continued to accuse me of being with other men until I ended the conversation. It had already gone on far longer than it should have.

A week or so later, after Johnny had left for work, Grace and I were in the kitchen, getting ready to eat breakfast and tackle the day. She glanced up at me and said, "Mom, are you being nice to my dad?"

A fury came over me again, and I thought to myself, *What the hell did he tell her now?* I was so tired of being made out to be the bad guy. But I knew it was not my daughter's problem to own. I reminded myself, *She's a child who is observing her environment, a sponge who is receiving messages and soaking it all up.*

I took a moment to gather my thoughts so I didn't come across as angry and then replied, "I am nice to your dad. You don't have to worry about those things." It was the best response I could think of at the time. She was only four years old; she couldn't comprehend much more than that, nor should she have to.

Grace stood there for a moment then agreed in the way any four-year-old would and ran off to play.

A few days later, though, Johnny started another argument with me, this time about staying together. I repeated my answer, the same one I'd provided time and again. "The damage is done."

In response, he ramped up the manipulation and began accusing me of not being as supportive of him as he was to me, then he brought up money issues from five years ago. Yes, there was a significant gap in our incomes when I was still in school. It was true, I had never made $140,000, but I'd been helpful in other ways.

Shortly after that fight, Grace began to hit me. Although I was not being hit at that time, children are sponges and soak up their environment. It's like she felt the anger and hostility in our relationship, and this was her way of acting out and moving through what she was feeling.

Although Grace was an infant and too young at the time to remember this, once Johnny and I were arguing while I was changing Grace's diaper. I had walked into Grace's room and placed her on the change table, and Johnny had followed us.

He was talking to me while I was busy changing Grace, and already I was tired of being yelled at and all of our arguing. He demanded I look at him, and when I didn't, he grabbed my shoulder and pushed me, to make me look at him. He said, "Look at me when I am talking to you!"

This was an abrupt push, and I was scared I was going to fall, so I grabbed onto the changing table. In my panic, I almost pulled Grace down with me. The table did rock a bit, but thankfully, there were no injuries. I didn't fall, and Grace wasn't pulled off the table in the chaos. Still, she was startled and began to cry.

I'm sure our verbal fighting made her the most upset. We learn a lot about nature versus nurture in school, which applies to children of all ages. The nature of their environment sets the tone for their development.

As Grace grew older and continued to witness our fighting, she attempted to referee between the two of us. Sometimes she would say, "Be nice to my mom."

Anytime she said that, Johnny's response was, "I am, but I want answers."

I was never sure what type of answers he was looking for. But I was becoming increasingly scared for my life.

# Chapter 11

# My Exit Plan

As we entered the month of July 2016, things between Johnny and I were as rocky as ever. I was sitting on the couch in our living room, cross-legged and facing the window, feeling so sad and defeated. I thought to myself, *I know this feeling. I've been here before. This is what depression feels like. The only way out of this situation is suicide.* Or so I thought.

I felt numb and lost, like my brain had shut off but I still had a million thoughts running through it at the same time. I contemplated the freedom I would feel, if I just took my own life. Soon, that voice became the loudest one in my head. I could get away from this monster for good…

B*ut wait!* said another voice that became even louder. *What about Grace?* I couldn't leave her behind. There was no way I could leave her in this mess. I realized I needed a better game plan, one that involved me staying alive. But if I was contemplating suicide and feeling like it was the only way out, that was a sure sign that things were not good. I needed a plan, and I needed it quick.

A few days later, I knew Johnny had plans to meet someone at 7:00 p.m. My typical work schedule was from 8:30 a.m.-4:30 p.m., Monday to Friday, so that gave me plenty of time to get my workout in at the gym and then get home, so he could make it to his meeting on time. I received a text message from Johnny at 4:00 p.m., asking if I could be back by 5:15, so he could go golfing.

Immediately, there I went again, justifying my decisions for why I could not make it back by 5:15, while still feeling mom guilt, like *Why am I not just going home to be there for Grace?* I did know I was a better mom for practicing self-care, which I needed more than ever those days.

He continued to text me until he finally wrote, "I will just take Grace golfing, if you can't be here on time." Then, he texted me again at 5:45, asking me to be home by 6:10, instead.

What a weird time, I thought.

"Grace wants you."

I replied, "Okay." When I finished my workout at 6:11, I sent Johnny a quick text to let him know I would be a bit late but was on my way.

Part of me was proud for pushing the boundaries just a little bit and standing up for myself and my time. Like part of me was taking back a small piece of my power. But I did not yet know what hell awaited me, when I got home.

Johnny wasn't done. He blasted me, "I can't ask for anything anymore."

I replied, "Grace has not seen you in a while. You should be grateful to spend some time with her."

He responded, "My requests and Grace's are just too much to ask for."

He made me feel so small. Nothing I said or did mattered. Even though I felt small glimmers of pride when I stood up for myself, these types of remarks still sent me spiraling. Deep down, I knew it wasn't my fault, but it was hard not to blame myself.

When you experience psychological manipulation, gaslighting, and emotional abuse, you begin to doubt yourself, and your perception of reality. I was made to believe that I was the bad person and always in the wrong. These are just a few of the tactics Johnny used to make me feel there was no way out.

On my drive home from the gym, I mustered up the courage to call Johnny and ask where he was. He answered, "I already left."

I felt sick, thinking now I had to go on a wild goose chase to find my daughter. Just like in the old days, when I used to have to go looking for him.

Johnny eventually told me they were at his friend's house, which was not too far from our place. I said, "I'll meet you there, so I can take Grace, and you can go golf."

He replied, "It was too much to ask for in the beginning, so don't bother."

I had understood I had until 7:00 p.m. to return home, but the plans kept changing and the manipulation was stronger than ever. I couldn't keep up.

Summer 2016, which is a happy time for many people, was not so much for me. Johnny renewed his accusations of my being with other men in the community. My friend, Mike was mentioned, someone I hadn't seen or talked to in quite some time. In fact, the last time he'd come over to our house was to meet Grace when she was a few months old, and Johnny had been home during the visit.

"You are devious. You used me. If it wasn't for me, you wouldn't have half the things you have."

*Here we go again,* I thought. More accusations and comments started to come, and now he made them in front of Grace. Some of his complaints referred to the property we owned and who would get it in the separation. I had already sought legal advice from a lawyer previously, so I knew what my rights were. *Knowledge is power.*

I told him, if we could figure it out on our own, we wouldn't need a lawyer.

He laughed at me and said, "You're a joke." Then, he turned toward Grace, who was still only four years old at the time. "I will be your only dad, and I mean it."

A few nights later, I was stepping out of the house for a bit, and Johnny had asked me to be home by 9:00 p.m., so he could go play pool. Moments later, the deadline changed, and he asked for me to come home earlier. He seemed to have no desire to take on any parental duties. That night, I learned, after I left, he did not even feed Grace dinner and did not return home that night. Yet I was the one constantly accused of being with other men.

When some work became available on the rigs again, Johnny made the decision to leave home for a bit to earn more money. He was gone for a couple weeks at a time, and Grace started to tell me she missed him. Despite me feeling frustrated and wanting to limit my conversations with Johnny, I decided to share the message with him about how Grace was feeling via text message.

His response, "I miss her, too. I miss texting you, too."

Johnny and I were not together at this time. However, we were still residing under the same roof. I had set some strong boundaries around what he could and could not say to me, and when I would disengage in conversation. I responded, "It's not like you cannot text me, but there are conversations I will and will not engage in, like I've told you before."

Johnny didn't appear to like that answer, because the tone of the conversation immediately changed. He began name-calling, saying I was heartless. Then, he continued, "I don't want anyone else stepping in as Grace's dad."

I reassured him, as long as he was in her life, that was not going to happen, and she wouldn't need another dad.

Then, the conversation went darker. Johnny said, "I want to die."

I briefly wondered whether his statement was genuine or not, but it was not up for me to decide. My past training kicked in, and I did what I needed to do.

"If this is true and you are truly thinking about hurting yourself and want to die, I need to call the police."

On a dime, he again flipped the script and went back to accusing me of being with other men.

Grace had another episode of wetting the bed that night, and I couldn't help but to wonder how much vicarious trauma she was experiencing due to all of the turmoil inside of the home.

A few days later, Johnny still wasn't home and daycare was closed. Children are not allowed at our workplace, but I had no other option, since we didn't get sick time or paid time off, and I needed all of the money I could get. When I reached out to Johnny to see if he could help me out, he said he could not take Grace, because he was on the reserve, helping his dad, and would not come back to town to pick Grace up.

I asked around to family members and friends, to see if anyone could watch Grace, even if it was for a bit. But everyone else was working, too.

A few days later, Johnny returned home. I was walking on egg shells, trying to navigate the situation as best I could. I didn't want to rely on him or ask him for much, so I continued with my hyper-independence and did what I needed to do. I woke up and started preparing Grace's lunch. She needed a bath, as well, as she had an exciting day planned at day care that day. I attempted to wake her up but was not successful.

When Johnny woke up, he told me to leave her alone, because she wasn't going to daycare today. He wanted to spend time with her. There were plenty of opportunities to spend time with her, if he'd only plan his time and take advantage of all of the other times he had, but he chose not to. Yesterday had been another example, and I told him so.

He lashed back at me. "So, what, I can't spend time with my culture?"

Confused, I thought, *That's not what I said.* I replied, "That is not the point I am trying to make. But you could have picked a better time, so she, too, could spend time engaging in the culture."

He said, "You could have brought her out there."

Yet I was at work with back-to-back meetings yesterday… *Here we go again.*

Johnny told me to leave, because I make Grace cry. Then he said, "If you bring Grace to school this morning, I am going to show up there and take her."

I told him, if he did that, I would put things into place so it cannot happen. Children need routine and consistency. I got Grace ready so she could be dropped off at daycare and I could continue on to work.

As I was walking out the door, he said in a threatening tone, "I am coming to your work, and we are finishing this conversation."

I felt so scared and embarrassed that this was my life. I went to my go-to response. "I will call the police and have you removed, if you show up at my workplace."

In the back of my mind, though, a million questions swirled. *What if he shows up at my work? Will I risk losing my job because he is going to cause a scene? What are people going to think of me? Are the police going to have to come? Fuck. I don't know what to do. Do I tell my boss there is a potential, and ask they make sure he doesn't have access to me? Am I blowing this out of proportion? Am I putting others at risk by going to work and risking him coming to the property, so they have to deal with him? I just want out.*

He replied snidely, "Go ahead, call the police."

In my job, I worked closely with the police in the downtown core. The last thing I wanted was for them to respond and see this side of me, even when it was out of my control.

Every summer, we took our annual family trip to Manitoba. I brought Grace as I always had, and our first stop was always at my grandparents' house. My grandpa and Grace had a special bond. She was the highlight of the trip for him. As much as he loved catching up with my siblings and me, Grace always stole the show.

Those memories will forever be engrained in my memory and I am deeply grateful. This particular trip was a nice break for Grace, too, to get out of the house and be in a less stressful environment. Although, when she was young, she may not have been fully aware of the chaos she, too, was living, the holiday was a reprieve from all that.

On the drive from Manitoba back to Alberta, my uncle decided to ride with Grace and me, since I was leaving a few days earlier than my mom and the rest of my siblings. This way, I could break up the trip and sleep at the halfway point, in Regina, where my uncle's husband's family lived, so we could stay for free. We were also going to be celebrating some event at his husband's sister's house.

I was so excited for BBQ food. We made the choice to break the trip into two days and spend an extra night in Saskatchewan, at his husband's sister's place. My uncle would finish the trip back to Alberta with his husband, while Grace and I drove back alone.

We had a huge BBQ, filling our stomachs to the point where we could not possibly take another bite, and then decided to chill for the rest of the night. Grace was jumping on the trampoline with some of the other children when she suddenly hurt her foot. It wasn't anything major, but enough to upset her and get her off the trampoline.

We were both quite exhausted from the six-hour drive to Regina, so I thought it best we go down to our sleeping corridors and spend the rest of the night watching TV before bed. It was still too early for bed time, but I thought this would be the perfect way to wind down. But our night was about to end differently.

Grace was still a bit upset from the incident on the trampoline, so I had her in my arms as I carried her down the stairs to the basement. The stairs were quite narrow and steep, so I tried to take it slow and steady. I misstepped near the bottom, which I thought *was* the bottom, but it was not. I fell down the remaining stairs with Grace in my arms.

I remember two things: one was the sound of the crack, so I was certain I'd find bones sticking out of my leg once I fell to the bottom; and two, I remember protecting Grace's head as we went down and hit the ground. The sound of the snap in my bones was so disgusting, I was terrified to look at my leg.

A sudden rush of sickness came over my body, like I was going to throw up. Moments later, I couldn't feel my arms. *This feels super-weird,* I thought, then remembered all the food I'd eaten and how badly I did not want to get sick.

Grace was still in my arms, and when she looked at me, she said, "Mom, how come you're green?"

I had no idea what she was talking about, but I knew something had to be wrong based on how I felt. An adult in the basement sounded the alarm for others to come help us, while someone else went to get a nurse who lived down the street.

Things happened quickly, and my only concern was that I please not puke! I needed to remain calm. Someone asked me if I wanted an ambulance, and I said no—I did not have benefits at the time. When the nurse came, she got me situated and explained why my skin had turned green: I had gone into shock. *No wonder my face is green in color.*

A few adults fireman-carried me out of the basement and put me into my uncle's husband's vehicle. He took me to the hospital and waited for me to get assessed before we returned to the house. Grace had a chill night, watching movies with the other children and my uncle, while I spent the evening in the hospital.

Hours later, when we finally returned, I had a fancy new accessory—an air cast. The doctor informed me that I had torn the ligaments in my right leg and needed to wear the air cast for six weeks. This may seem like a vacation or a reason to slow down for a period of time, but I had other plans, and slowing down was not on the agenda.

I had taken up the sport of running a few years prior to this injury. The freeing feeling that running gave to me allowed me to escape my problems even momentarily. Running provided me with the opportunity to connect to myself and the land. A sense of peace and safety that I could not find at home. Unfortunately, this new accessory and the condition I was in were not aligning with my summer plans.

*Great. I've signed up for two upcoming races and paid for them. What am I going to do?*

The logical thing would be to not run them, but I had another idea and solution. The Dutch in me said, "You paid, you can't miss out." The stubborn and ambitious part of me said, "You'll find a way to run it." And that I did. I also drove home wearing the air cast, which was super-uncomfortable. My determination (and maybe a little bit of stupidity) led the way.

Two weeks later, I was on my way to Red Deer, Alberta. A large group of my friends and I had planned months in advance to do the mud run, long before my injury and new foot accessory. I didn't want to leave Grace, and the mom guilt came over me like a tidal wave. But I also knew I needed space and time away, and that it was okay to give myself permission to do so. This trip may have been just what I needed.

The night before we left for Red Deer, I figured I would need some type of ankle support to complete the run; I couldn't run it in an air cast. I found a tensor bandage ankle support brace at Shoppers. The next day, we were off to our destination. In hindsight, this was a stupid choice, and I shouldn't have done any type of intense exercise with torn ligaments. Unfortunately, I would pay for it later. In the moment, though, it was a lot of fun, very freeing, and the laughter was just what my soul needed. It was an escape and worth the memories.

As I was getting ready to leave for Red Deer, Johnny started again with his accusations about my work partner, with whom he had made contact with. "I know Timmy is going," he said.

I ignored the accusations and instead asked Johnny about his work schedule. We were supposed to share parenting responsibilities and create some type of schedule, because our routine for Grace had started to become inconsistent and chaotic. He still would not provide me a schedule and hadn't for weeks. So,

I made the decision to pick Grace up from daycare before heading to Red Deer.

When I made the comment about our schedule, he replied, "I'm the bad guy, yet you get to go gallivant around in Red Deer."

During this conversation, Johnny mentioned the suggestion of his fire chief, to have a drink, since he was going through a tough time. I thought this comment was strange and alarm bells started to ring for me, because Johnny had had issues with alcohol. As I headed out of town for the weekend, I was concerned and wondered what his comment meant for Grace.

*Will he go out drinking? What about Grace? Will he drink in front of her? Or where will she go?* This made me feel really uneasy, yet I felt I had no control over the situation. I should be able to go away for the weekend and trust that my daughter is in good hands with her dad. But at this point, I wasn't so sure.

I had to ask the question, "Does your chief know you struggled with alcohol misuse? And does he understand the impact it's had on your family?"

Johnny shrugged his shoulders and carried on, again flipping the script and hurling more accusations, this time about *me* not keeping Grace on a schedule.

As I drove Grace to school that day, she asked, "Why are you mean to my dad?"

I replied, "I am not being mean to him" and changed the subject. I was a bit hesitant to leave Grace with Johnny in this state, but I was hopeful his anger was only toward me, and that he would be fine with Grace.

*Living under the same roof with a manipulative, abusive person, while being separated and trying to coparent is not easy. In fact, it was one of the most challenging things I've ever done.*

I returned from Red Deer a few days later. Much of what came next is a blur.

Chaos ensued almost right away. Johnny left to go hang out with friends. When Grace asked him where he was going, Johnny replied, "To my friend's house. I'm going to sleep there."

Grace began to cry. "I'm going to miss you," she whimpered.

Johnny ignored her comment and turned to me to say, "I can't stand being around you. I'll be back in the morning."

While I understood the turmoil he must have felt inside, I shared his sentiment. However, I wanted desperately to put our feelings aside so we could coparent Grace. Then, Johnny left the house for the night with no further conversation. I wished it was that easy for me to say I couldn't stand being around him and then just disappear for the night. But my priority was Grace, and I knew there would be more hell to pay if I didn't come home some night.

As time went on, I continued to make my exit plan, which took much longer than maybe it should have. Meanwhile, Grace's behaviors started to escalate. She would become physically violent with me, head-butting me, hitting, and kicking me, plus screaming at me. One day, Grace took a water gun and pointed it straight at my face then made shooting noises. That was not something that was modelled by me or in the way I grew up. Firearms were not a part of my life.

While this may be something three- or four-year-olds go through, I couldn't help but to reflect on what she was being exposed to and the vicarious trauma she was enduring. Johnny was a hunter and enjoyed shooting guns, so sometimes, he took Grace along for the ride when they went out to shoot gophers.

One time, when Johnny returned home with Grace, they shared their experience shooting gophers. Johnny laughed as he told the story about how, when the gopher was shot, Grace went over and kicked them. I thought to myself, *Where would she learn to do this? Why would she do it?*

A pivotal moment and the biggest red flag of all occurred one day in the living room. Johnny was watching a show, and he, Grace, and I were sitting together, with me passively watching whatever he had on the TV.

A show came describing how a man had killed his wife and children. Johnny said with a cold stare toward the TV, "I could see how he could do that. If he can't have her, nobody should."

I immediately felt so sick in the pit of my stomach and thought, *Fuck. He's going to end up killing us.*

I met with a lawyer shortly after that, to discuss my options. Unfortunately, I needed a new lawyer, since my original attorney went on sabbatical. I was disappointed about that, because I felt my first lawyer would have really fought for me.

I went through the same law office but decided to use a student lawyer, as money was tight. I was well prepared by this point, so I presented him with my documentation, including all of the incidents that had occurred to date. I shared with him how I am scared for my life, given the homicidal comment, added to the fact that he had firearms in the house.

Unfazed and appearing unconcerned, the student lawyer looked across the table and said, "If he hasn't done it yet, he won't."

This was another gut punch. I thought, *Are you fucking kidding me? What kind of response is that?* So many women and children were dying because of domestic violence, and this was the kind of response I got? Either this man was poorly trained or he simply doesn't care. Either way, I couldn't have him representing me….

But I didn't have a lot of money and I didn't want to keep paying consulting fees, so I decided to choose the lesser of two evils and stick with this lawyer. Sometimes, he consulted on my case with a senior lawyer, to ensure he was "doing the right thing" according to the law, but I didn't feel he gave me much support at all. And they both seemed to share the same mindset, which was the most concerning thing about this experience. *Why wasn't anyone seeing this for what it was?*

When you are in survival mode, you do not think clearly. You're merely trying to make it through, and you take what you can get. Desperation is the best way to describe it.

Little did I know how much power this would give to my voice later on, as I grew, evolved, and became a fierce advocate for myself and Grace.

A few days later, I was driving to pick Grace up from daycare when, out of the blue, I received a text from Johnny saying, "You stabbed me in the back. You are not the person I thought you were."

Suddenly, I was flooded in fear. I wondered, is this the time he is going to hurt me? Or worse, kill me? What was going to happen when I got home?"

I could feel his hate and resentment toward me building rapidly.

I didn't respond to his text message, but Johnny continued to berate me, writing, "You always pawn Grace off on your mom."

As Grace and I pulled into our driveway, she saw Johnny's vehicle there already and asked, "Why is he here? He makes me cry."

Curious, as I took her out of her car seat, I asked her why. But before the conversation could go any further, she ran off, saying she was kidding.

A few days later, Johnny asked me, "When are you moving out? I found a roommate."

I replied, "I'm not sure, likely September." This was the middle of August, and I still hadn't figured out where I would go. But I knew I needed out. I was trying to find someplace that was available and I could afford.

He replied, "Take all of your stuff."

Johnny and I had previously had a conversation about the house and his keeping it, because I had made up my mind I wanted nothing to do with it anymore. I wanted a fresh start, and our house was tied to too many bad memories, but I did not tell him that part. I just wanted to create something new with positive energy.

During this process, I came to the conclusion that material possessions were simply things, and I could acquire them all again. They did not provide the happiness and safety we so desperately needed.

Part of the conversation had been around keeping my name on the mortgage, so Johnny could for sure keep the house. I am not sure now why I had agreed to that or even considered agreeing to it, but I did.

I said to him, "You want me to keep my name on the mortgage, but I can't keep anything here for any period of time?"

He had no answer to that, but I believe it was all part of his desire to control the narrative.

As I reflect on why it took me so long to leave, there were many factors, but some weighed heavier on me than I initially realized. I cared about Johnny's family deeply and, for the most part, had a great relationship with them. I was worried, if I left the relationship, I would lose them, too, especially on his maternal side, and that was a hard pill for me to swallow.

When I was deep in my head about all of this, one night I thought I'd reach out to some of the family members I was closest with, to see if they would still talk to me if I left. I shared pieces of my unhappiness. One aunt expressed she would always talk to me, and she has. But the conversation I had with Johnny's mom was quite different. She told me she would stay connected with me would have been a hypocrite, if she told me to stay, given she also was a survivor of domestic violence.

Another hard piece to moving out was having to leave the neighborhood. I loved our neighbors and was sad I would no longer be able to sit on my deck and visit with them, while they sat on theirs. There was also stigma attached to that. I didn't want them to think less of me or question what was going on, and I didn't want to share with them why I was leaving. I was a bit ashamed I'd even "allowed" this to happen to me. So many mixed emotions, but I knew it was my time to go. The neighbors and the family were not what was going to keep us safe. It was me.

I felt more confident about my exit strategy this time. A few weeks before I left, while I was making breakfast, I asked Grace, as I often did, who she wanted to take her to daycare today. She said, "My dad."

Grace went to make efforts to wake Johnny up, but she was not successful. I wasn't going to try and wake a grown adult up or risk getting into an argument over this. So, I ended up taking Grace, because he refused to wake up. This was becoming a common theme: his commitment to parenting was inconsistent.

He picked Grace up from school that same day, in the midafternoon. I had plans to take some time to prepare for a test, because I had applied to the local police service. Math was never an easy subject for me, and I needed assistance in that area to prepare for the APCAT, which is one of the tests many police services use to assess candidates.

As it grew close to dinner time, while I was studying away, I received a call from Johnny's number. He knew that I was studying, so I was surprised to see him calling.

When I picked up, it was Grace on the line, asking, "Will you be home soon?"

This was not a question she typically asked, and I couldn't help but think Johnny had put her up to it. I replied, "I will be home soon, but I am studying right now." The phone call ended shortly after.

About an hour or so later, I received a text message from Johnny. "Grace says don't bother."

*Don't bother with what?* I wondered. I knew Grace didn't talk like that, so those were his words. Johnny continued, "She won't care whether you come back or not."

These manipulation tactics made it difficult for me to focus on anything else, and it seemed he was being quite strategic in how he implemented them. All I wanted to do was better our lives, but

Johnny always seemed to be in the background, causing chaos. As much as I wanted out, sometimes a little voice in my head would show up and say, "Maybe it would be easier if you just stayed." I'm so glad I didn't. But I had no idea just how difficult this fight would get.

My friends were becoming increasingly worried about my safety, as well. They would ask me to text them when I got home and would check in with me periodically, to make sure I was safe. One night, as I was getting ready for bed, I plugged my phone in on my nightstand. I didn't think anything of it, but I put my phone face down.

Johnny noticed and began accusing me of texting men yet again. The voice that had told me it might be easier if I stayed suddenly went silent, and the overpowering voice saying, "Get the hell out of here" took over.

In the days following, Grace started to complain of stomach aches and not feeling well. The average person could attribute this to simply being unwell or having a stomach bug. I knew this was something more, likely due to the stress and other things going on in our home. To me, this was another slap in the face, as our reality was becoming starker. It was one thing for me to put up with the constant attacks and unhealthy environment, but knowing I was allowing that for Grace, too, was something I was just not willing to accept. I knew then, *I have to find an exit plan, and it has to happen quick.*

I have heard many true stories from other women about how hard it is to leave. You, too, should believe them. The difficulties are very real, especially when there are pets and children involved. Children are allowed in women's shelters, but pets are not. Our current laws and limitations do not make it easy to leave a domestic violence situation, and the systems favor the abuser, who get to stay in the home, living comfortably, while the women and children are left scrambling to make a plan where they can take their entire family—because pets count, too.

This was another part of why it was hard for me to leave. Many rentals were not accepting pets, especially one the size of my German Shepherd.

At the end of summer, on August 26, I celebrated my birthday. My friends planned a night out for me, and it felt really nice to be surrounded by people who loved and cared about me. The celebration allowed me the space I needed to escape the constant chaos we lived in, even if it was for a little while.

That night, we made a game plan together for the following day, when we were going to move me out of that house and into my parents' house. I was a bit skeptical about how this would go, given how hungover some of us might have been, but we woke up the next day and put the plan into action.

# Chapter 12

## Exit Strategy: Executed with a Hangover

Johnny was away that morning, so my friends and I decided to do this early-morning move. My friends and I had had a little too much fun the night before, so I was impressed we all stayed true to our word and got to work.

We packed up what was mine and left the rest behind. I just needed the necessities; anything else, I could buy or replace when I became more situated. Material things did not mean much to me at this time. My happiness and freedom did. I am so incredibly grateful for my friends who showed up and made this possible. I don't think I could have done it without them. With the task at hand and the emotions involved, it was a lot, and something I had to grieve amidst the chaos.

I rented a storage locker to store all the things that did not fit in my parents' house. My parents were not expecting their child, grandchild, and dog to move back in, so it's not like they had a ton of space for us and everything else I had.

I was moving back into my old bedroom. I knew this could be chaotic with my dog, since my parents had two of their own, and the space was limited, but I knew Grace, the dog, and I would be comfortable there, and it was safe. Also, this was for the short term, giving me space and time to get us back on our feet, so I could purchase something of our own someday. I needed to let the dust settle and find peace. The rest would come.

My box spring didn't fit down the stairs, so Grace and I had to sleep on just my mattress on the basement floor, with our dog, Nalah, sleeping on her dog bed next to us. This was our life for the next two years. The space was cramped and less than ideal, but it was a roof over our head. I was not losing sight of our North Star. I am constantly reminded how fortunate I am to have parents I could stay with for a while, as we got through this tough time.

I had my eye on furthering my education and pursuing my master's degree, but I knew this was not yet the right time. I promised myself, once I found my own home, I would pursue this goal more seriously. Thankfully, my parents allowed us to stay at their house rent free. This allowed me to pay off debts and put money away so I could afford a down payment on my own home. I was tired of paying extreme rental prices, and I wanted something of our own that nobody could take from us.

Grace's birthday was coming up. I planned a celebration at the local swimming pool with her friends. She was so excited. Johnny showed up an hour late and did not engage with Grace or her friends at all, nor did he offer to help cover the costs of her birthday. I was determined to give her a good birthday, regardless of whether he contributed or not, but I was surprised he put in no effort to contribute to her birthday.

We did not have a formal parenting order during this time. We'd had many conversations back and forth, and although his parenting was inconsistent at best, I wanted to save money and do my best to stay out of the courts. I was very hopeful we could make small, incremental progress with coparenting. We finally agreed to create a schedule of our own and keep things out of the courts, knowing neither of us wanted to pay those astronomical legal fees. I was also hopeful we could be amicable. I did my best for a period for time, but my hopes were shattered and the dream of coparenting dashed. Ultimately, I knew I needed to get the courts involved again.

Johnny was scheduled to have Grace in the following days. Grace did go over to his house, but soon thereafter I received a text from him indicating he had a headache and didn't think he could keep Grace until 8:00 p.m., the scheduled time for me to pick her up, as we had agreed.

I was chairing a meeting that evening, as I was the president for a local volunteer organization, so I suggested he reach out to my parents, to see if he could bring her back a bit earlier. I don't know why I still played the role of problem solver for him, but because it had to do with our daughter, I wanted to do what was best for her. Johnny sent repeated text messages to me, indicating he had a headache. I ignored them, as I was in my meeting.

Moments later, I received a text from my mom. "Grace got dropped off here." With no communication from Johnny. My mom said she heard her door open and close, and when she went to look, Grace was inside. Johnny didn't even walk Grace to the door.

I got home an hour or so later, and while putting Grace to bed, she asked me, "Do you think my dad is happy?"

I replied, "I think so. Why do you ask?"

She said she didn't think he was.

*I didn't care, but I wasn't going to let Grace know or see that.* Children are so observant of their environments and sensitive to the world around them. We often don't realize how much we inflict onto our children, if we are not in the right mindset. I didn't want to probe the issue further with her, as it was not her responsibility to figure those things out. But it was becoming evident she was taking on a caretaker role, which was the last thing I wanted for her.

As the president of our local search and rescue group, I met with this organization on a monthly basis and chaired most of the meetings. Soon after the above, I was at another meeting while Grace was with Johnny. He was scheduled to have her overnight for a couple of nights. But my phone started to ring over sixteen times in a matter of minutes, followed by numerous text messages, indicating he was outside the building where my meeting was taking place.

I had to pause the meeting and go outside, to see if he was there, but Johnny was nowhere to be found. This started to scare me, but I knew I had to keep my cool, because I was at this meeting. I certainly did not need this distraction of being pulled out of my meeting, believing he was outside with our daughter.

And I started to worry about Grace's safety, due to this behavior, though I didn't yet feel this was enough to get the police involved, no matter the negative impact on my mental health. The stigma attached to all of this was also quite difficult for me to bear. All I could do was hope that she was okay. Although the thought did cross my mind, if I went to the police, I could start building a file about Johnny. In case things escalated, there would be a paper trail.

# Chapter 13

# Fear Was Loud, Courage Became Louder

I didn't know how much longer I could take the mental stress of Johnny's manipulation tactics. The following day, I talked to some friends who strongly encouraged me to go to the police. Despite the stigma, I knew they were right. I would have to put away my pride and shame for our safety and the betterment of our future.

I didn't want Grace to know what was going on, so I made arrangements for her to spend some time with my friend, so I could head down to the police station and file a complaint. I walked into the station. Above the counter was a sign that read "complaints."

The uniformed officer there waved me over, indicating, "I can help you over here."

My heart was pounding and felt like it might beat out of my chest as I greeted the officer. After she asked what they could do to help, I explained what had been going on and provided her with some background information. I showed her the repeated calling and text messages on my phone.

She looked at my phone and said fairly confidently, "Would you like us to contact Johnny to let him know we are aware of the constant calls and to ask him to stop, or we will charge him with harassment?"

I replied, "Yes, that's exactly what I want."

The officer then said, "We can't do that here. You have to leave, call dispatch, and file a complaint that way."

I was so confused. I was literally standing at a desk with the word "complaints" above my head. *Why do they have a complaint desk if that's not what they handle here?* Just when I felt heard, even momentarily, my trust and faith in the service dissipated. Now, I had to muster up the courage to retell my story again and navigate this process another way. I walked out of the police station with my emotions quite high, feeling confused and frustrated.

I walked to the parking lot, got in my car, and after a few moments of deep breaths, I made the call to dispatch. After a few rings, when someone from dispatch answered, I retold my story for a second time, hardly a trauma-informed approach. It's hard to tell and retell your story over and over again. I felt frustrated, overwhelmed, embarrassed, and retraumatized.

I explained again what had happened at the complaint desk and informed her I'd been directed to call this line and file a complaint.

The dispatcher took some information from me and then said, "This is nothing. Nor is it domestic violence."

My mind was blown. I thought to myself, *Excuse me, your job is to take the information and let the officers decide how to proceed. How is this not domestic violence?*

My emotions get the best of me and I began to cry. The dispatcher said, "I can tell you're upset."

*No kidding I'm upset. Do you know how much strength and courage this takes, to come forward and explain all that is happening? Especially when I've been made to feel the years like I am making this up and that my experience is not that big of a deal.* I don't recall how the rest of the conversation went, but I do remember an officer being dispatched to talk to me the following day. Cue the first of numerous delayed responses by our local police service.

The next day, when I was at an interagency meeting with various stakeholders across our community, my phone rang. Caller I.D. said it was from someone in my community. I had a feeling it might be the police, so I stepped outside the room to take the call.

I was right. I spoke with the officer, who asked me where I was, as he would like to come and speak with me. I informed him of my location, and he came to meet me. I felt sudden panic and a sense of embarrassment. Like, "What did I just do? He's going to come here and meet with me, and people are going to wonder what was happening." But the urgency of the situation and my sense of safety overrode all the other feelings I had. I didn't want to miss this opportunity to share with him, because who knew whether I would be able to speak to someone the next time.

The officer took a statement from me. He informed me that he would tell Johnny not to contact me, and if he did, I needed to let the police know right away. The police also informed me, if I was to pursue a court order, including a police clause would be helpful.

This experience was not what I had been expecting, given how I'd been treated the previous day at the complaints desk and with dispatch. I felt heard and supported by this officer, which prompted me to provide feedback to the service. It's not often that the good police officers receive positive feedback on a job well done. Usually, they hear only complaints or silence.

Also, I wanted the officer at the desk and on dispatch to be held accountable for their poor service and communication, as I didn't want others to experience what I had. After those conversations, I felt so hopeless and defeated, even though I am someone with system navigation and advocacy skills, unlike so many victims of violence and others who require police services.

I received a relatively quick response from the department that received my "shout out." She inquired about my treatment the day prior and thanked me for the praise of the officer I had dealt with that day. I shared my experience, which led to me filing a complaint to the manager of dispatch, as well, about my experience. This gave me a glimmer of hope and felt like a small step toward taking my power back.

Shortly after I spoke with the police, they spoke to Johnny. Within hours, I received a text from Johnny. "You ran to the fucking cops!" As per the officer's direction, I sent him an email because contact had been made. I never once received a response from that officer or from any others that were assigned to my case.

A week or two later, I was at work when I received a call from the manager of dispatch. He informed me that he'd received my complaint about my interaction with one of his staff a couple of weeks prior. He continued, "We received your complaint, and I want to thank you for bringing your concerns forward. We reviewed the call you had with that particular staff member, as all calls are recorded." He assured me he'd also had a conversation with the dispatcher I spoke with that night, and it should not happen again. He apologized for my experience.

I felt relieved and proud of myself for taking that step, even though I had no idea what the outcome would be. The manager made small talk with me after we discussed the important parts of my complaint and then said to me, "Your name sounds familiar. I'm pretty sure I taught you in the justice degree."

I was immediately flooded with embarrassment.

He asked, "Do you remember me?"

I did not, but I couldn't escape the punch of shame for being connected to the justice world through my work and education, then now being in this position, as a victim of domestic violence. *People with this experience and level of education should not be in my shoes. We should know better.* This voice repeats in my head regularly, even though I knew deep down this was not my fault.

As victims of domestic violence, we may have left the home and the relationship, but that is only the beginning. So many other things follow, including thoughts, feelings, and emotions. Leaving almost seems like the easy part. I began to wonder whether I would ever truly be exempt from these experiences. I would later learn, as things progressed, that I would not be exempt and they would only hit closer to home.

Grace was in a Blackfoot-based program called HeadStart, which was great, because it allowed for her to learn about her culture and provided her a wonderful educational foundation. Once she had graduated from that program, she was moving into kindergarten. This was an exciting time, and I couldn't believe how fast she was growing.

A few weeks later, it was Meet the Teacher Night at Grace's new school. Grace had been with me during the pre-K interview, per our scheduled parental rotation, but I always made sure Johnny was kept informed and knew what was going on. I let him know it was Meet the Teacher Night.

Grace and I arrived at the school before Johnny did. When he arrived, Grace greeted him with a hug. I approached Johnny and suggested we go meet the teacher together, rather than stand in the entryway, awkwardly. Johnny ignored me. Moments later, we made steps toward the classroom to finally meet the teacher.

As we are standing outside of the classroom, one of the staff approached to give me an envelope for Grace. I noticed her last name was written incorrectly on the front of the envelope. It wasn't a big deal, but I was going to tell the staff member when she came back that it required a small edit. Before I could say anything, Johnny noticed the same error and immediately got mad. They had used his mom's last name, so it wasn't a totally random error, but Johnny immediately started yelling at the staff member. She apologized profusely, saying, "I'll fix it right away."

The teacher came over moments later to introduce herself. Johnny began to yell at her, too. I was so embarrassed. Shortly after, he left the room. I felt the need to apologize to the teacher and inform her that Johnny and I had recently separated. I also asked, if she noticed any behavioral concerns from Grace, to please let me know.

The teacher thanked me for the information and said, "I will definitely let you know if any concerns come up."

Johnny spent the rest of the night walking around the building with his jaw tight and fists clenched. I hated the way his intimidating behaviors made me feel. We had to sign some paperwork for Grace to attend their programming. After Johnny completed his portion, he threw the papers at me across the table. There were others sitting around the table, and when they saw that, I felt so embarrassed and ashamed that I'd allowed someone to treat me that way.

I had an appointment scheduled after the parent meeting, so we had agreed that Johnny would take Grace afterward, so I could attend my meeting. Johnny said to me, "Don't you have to be somewhere?" almost as though he wanted me out of his presence.

I responded, "My meeting isn't until seven. I have some time." It felt like he watched my every move.

When it came time for me to leave, Grace was quite hysterical and did not want me to go. I asked Johnny how he wanted to go about the exchange, returning her back to me, and whether it was easier if I went to his house to pick her up. He did not respond to me, so I asked again.

All he said was, "I don't want to talk to you."

I attempted to make contact with the police again, because Johnny continued to call and text me repeatedly. They never responded to me. I continued to send emails to the officer who had initially responded, and I did my due diligence, keeping my file up to date with them, as I'd been directed to do. But I started to feel like the police didn't care. This feeling would only exacerbate over time, and many more officers would send a similar message after our interactions.

A few days later, Grace and I had gone to the store, and she began to hit me. I asked her why she was hitting me, but as a five-year-old, she could not really articulate why.

She said, "I don't want to spend more than one night at my dad's house." When I asked her why, she replied, "I don't like it there."

I'd finally had enough of the unknown and made a doctor's appointment to get a referral for Grace to attend counseling. But I very quickly learned that it didn't matter whether a doctor ordered counseling for a child. The way our counseling system is set up requires both parents sign up for counseling, unless a court order states otherwise. I understand why this is standard practice for general scenarios, but it makes it quite difficult for people who are dealing with power and control, and who refuse to get their child the help they need. The only person who gets harmed in that process is the child.

Although I was living at my parents' house and didn't have a ton of bills to pay per se, I was working hard to save money and pay off debt, so I could buy a house. I began looking for ways to earn additional money. One day, my mom asked if I wanted to help set up for a wedding with her friend, who had a small wedding planning business. It was an opportunity to earn more cash, so I jumped on the opportunity. Grace was with Johnny that day, so I wouldn't have to worry about childcare. I just had to pick her up late that evening.

That afternoon, I received a text message from Johnny. "Grace wants to come back to you."

I responded, "I am busy and have things to do. I'm helping set up for a wedding and will grab Grace when I am done, likely around 7:00 p.m."

He replied, "So, 6:00 p.m."

I texted, "I said, likely between 7:00-8:00 p.m."

"You said 7:00-8:00 p.m., but I was hoping it was closer to 7:00." When I didn't respond, he continued to berate me. "It's okay for you to be abrasive to me. Maybe I'll just keep her, since you'll be so late. I figure she can miss you for one more night and stay here."

I finally replied, "I'll be there by 8:00 p.m."

At 8:01 p.m., I received another text message from Johnny. "She's sleeping here. You're not here."

I replied I was one second away. As I pulled into the driveway and approached the door, Johnny opened it, with Grace behind him. She was acting strange toward me, almost shy.

Johnny picked Grace up and handed her to me, saying, "I'm surprised you didn't bring the police with you." I left without saying anything back.

As I put Grace into the vehicle and buckled her in her seat, she asked, "Are you mad at me?"

I replied, "I am not," then asked, "Why did you want to come home tonight?"

She responded, "I didn't ask to come home."

I thought that was weird. I didn't want to probe further, but I was also desperate to get some clarity on what was going on. So, I said, "Your dad said that you wanted to come home tonight, which is why I came to pick you up."

Grace said, "I told my dad that I missed you, and he told me to stop saying that or I wouldn't be able to spend two nights with him, so I stopped."

I reassured Grace it was okay to say that she missed me, that it was okay to miss anyone. Then, I followed up with that officer yet again to provide an update, and I asked for a No Contact Order. I never received a response from him regarding this incident, either.

I became fed up with the nonsense and instability of what was going on with our parenting and scheduling, so I sought legal advice again.

I met with a lawyer, and over the next few weeks, they got to work, drafting up some agreements.

Not long after, I received a call from Johnny. He was crying. "I got served. Do I need a lawyer?"

I replied, "If you agree to what's in the letter, you don't need a lawyer."

Johnny said he couldn't pay the requested amount of child support.

I replied, "I didn't ask for that amount. It's based on your income. There are federal guidelines that determine child support." I encouraged him to call and speak to my lawyer, an invitation in the letter Johnny had been provided. I told him I was willing to allow him some time to get on his feet before I went forward requiring child support.

He said, "I gave my mom a few months to get out of the house. I may need to sell it."

I replied, "That needs to be in writing. And if you can get it in writing, then I am willing to wait." I didn't want to get screwed over, and I had been patient and understanding for far longer than most. I continue, "I have been more than fair in this process. I didn't fight for the house, and the only thing I asked for was that you pay off the line of credit that you maxed out. This was to be completed through the sale of our house."

Johnny said, "I'm scared you will keep Grace from me."

I assured him I would never do that to him or withhold our child over money. The only reason I would ever withhold her was if he put her at risk.

Johnny never agreed to what was written in the documents. I did my best to continue on as best I could, mitigating the inconsistent parenting time as I planned my next move. But I was so exhausted by the court system and forking out what little money I had to continue to pay for a lawyer to chase him around. Again, I thought, by giving him the benefit of the doubt, maybe he would change his ways and we could coparent, even if it was minimal.

A few nights later, it was time for Grace to go to Johnny's. As Grace was getting ready to go, she said to me, "I don't want to go." I wished it was that easy, to always follow what the child wanted, but it's intimidating when threats loom over you, despite your knowing what's best for the child. I knew I didn't have enough "reason" for why she did not want to go on that night, so it would never hold up in court. This process killed me. Little did I know, it was only going to get exponentially worse as time went on.

The following year, when we were at another Meet the Teacher Night, Grace refused to go home with Johnny afterward, so he passed her to me, saying, "She doesn't want to go with me, so I am going to work." This despite it being his scheduled parenting time.

As Grace and I were driving home, she told me she never wanted to go to her dad's ever again. I really began to wonder what was going on at his house during their time together, because this reluctance was becoming common, often part of our weekly conversation.

I didn't want to pry, since I felt Grace was still too young to articulate herself or understand what I was asking, but I knew I wouldn't get answers from her dad, so I had to be resourceful with the resources I had. I had to get to the bottom of this.

When Grace told me, "I don't want to go anymore because I will miss you," I responded, "I miss you, too, but it's important for you to spend time with your dad."

Grace then said, "I don't want to see him."

It was getting to be increasingly difficult to force my daughter to go somewhere she didn't want to be, but I had little concrete information or evidence to base my judgment on. I had no support from police and was feeling very lost and alone. But I wouldn't give up.

As I was about to drive away from Meet the Teacher Night, I was stopped by Johnny in the parking lot. He approached my vehicle and proceeded to tell me, "I met someone."

I paused momentarily then asked general questions, like, "Who is she? What does she do? Where did you meet her?" I thought it was a bit early, but his wasn't my life to live. There was a glimmer of hope that perhaps he would leave me alone and make my life easier, now that he was with someone else.

He told me they met about a month ago, at Hudson's, and that she was a teacher.

"I'm happy for you," I said. After our conversation, I drove home. As I reflected on this news, I felt a bit uneasy as to what it meant for his relationship with Grace.

I sent Johnny a text message saying, "If you can afford to date and do those things, you should be able to help cover some of the costs of Grace's expenses and pay child support." I didn't have a problem with him dating, but he should be able to share parenting costs with me.

He replied, "I have no money. My girlfriend, Rosie, offers to buy me groceries. I feel like a bum, because I cannot afford to live on my own." Then, Johnny changed the subject. "I want Grace to meet Rosie on Friday, and I want to include you, as well."

This was a surprise. Just a few text messages prior, he had indicated he was not sure how serious this relationship was. But now, he wanted us all to meet.

I felt this was too soon to be introducing Grace to his new partner. If I were to meet her, it wouldn't be that big of a deal. But Johnny was failing to see that his relationship with Grace was a bit rocky and unstable. I don't think he had thought out how introducing her to his new partner would make Grace feel or the impact it might have on their relationship.

I asked Johnny to give it some time, to see how the relationship played out, prior to him introducing everyone. Deep down, I knew I had very little control over the situation or anything that happened when I was not around. Likely, I would never know, but I felt it necessary to express my concern, for whatever it was worth.

I encouraged Johnny to spend more time with Grace, so they could strengthen their relationship before introducing her to a new girlfriend.

A few days later, Grace inquired how many nights she had to spend at her dad's next time, adding "Not too many." This conversation was becoming more and more frequent, almost as though she was preparing for stress and anticipating what was next.

I worry she was being consumed by the stressors around where she was to be and when. I said, "You are only staying with your dad for one night."

Again, she told me she did not want to go. I expressed my concern to Johnny about Grace not wanting to go to his house and how this was becoming a frequent topic of conversation between her and me. Rather than reflecting on this information, Johnny disregarded my comment and asked for more time with Grace. I told him I was not willing to allow more time at the moment, that we needed to stick to the schedule we had created.

A few days later, after more conversation between Grace and me about how she did not want to go to her dad's, I tried to bring up the conversation with Johnny again. I tried to encourage Grace, but her response remained the same: she didn't want to be there. When I brought it up with Johnny, it almost fell on deaf ears.

His response was still, "I need more time with her."

I asked if he would be open to letting Grace decide when and how much time she spent with him, even just for a little bit, to see if it made a difference. I was hopeful she would continue to want to spend time with him. Grace was still a bit young at this time, around five, but I was trying to figure out different ways to make this a good situation for everyone involved.

Johnny did not agree. He said he needed more time with her because that was the only time he was happy. I suggested we try my approach and see if it made a difference. I tried so hard to be encouraging during this conversation, even though he was so difficult to deal with.

Johnny replied, "I am keeping her. If she refuses to be here, I'll bring her to you." It felt very self-serving rather than what was best for Grace.

I took another approach and encouraged him to spend more time with Grace after school, so they could build up their time together. Johnny was not interested in that option, either.

He then said, "Everyone I love leaves me and doesn't care about me anymore."

As the caregiver I appeared to be back then, while trying to keep the peace as best as I could, I tried to navigate this new territory. I encouraged Johnny to change the way he thought about things and suggested what he could do to make the situation better and the experiences better for Grace. I also suggested that Grace may be picking up on his energy and maybe that was a contributing factor to why she did not want to be there at his house. I also let him know that, when they were not together, Grace said she missed him. *God, is it ever hard to be the adult for everyone in the room,* I thought.

Unfortunately, this conversation went nowhere. Johnny ended it by saying, "Tell her I love her and I miss her."

Fast forward a few days. Grace was scheduled to go with Johnny. Prior to her leaving, I gave her a bath and got her ready. As we were doing this, Grace began to get upset and started to cry.

I asked what was wrong, and she said, "I don't want to go with my dad." When I asked her why not, she said she would miss me.

I replied, "I will miss you, too, but you should try to spend some time with him." I encouraged her to tell her dad how she was feeling, and if she didn't want to sleep there, she should tell him.

She continued to cry, saying, "I don't want to go there." In a matter of minutes, she was hyperventilating, repeatedly saying she didn't want to go. I attempted to calm her down, but I was not successful.

I felt terrible and immense guilt for forcing her to go somewhere she did not want to go. I held out some hope that, if I shared this with Johnny, perhaps he would have some understanding and either come up with a different solution or let Grace stay with me.

I sent Johnny a text message to inform him about what was going on. He didn't appear to care. His response was, "Bring her. I want to see her. Calm her down, and get her to go."

As if I hadn't been trying that for the last thirty minutes or so. I described my efforts already and said I would try to make her some lunch, to see if that changed anything. Then, we could try again. After she ate, she did end up going, but I didn't feel good about the entire situation.

I began to notice how, when Grace came back from spending time at her dad's house, she would talk back, spit at me, throw things, and hit and kick me. This appeared to be more than typical behavior for children her age, and this would go for hours on end. It was exhausting to deal with.

On one wintery evening, Grace and I decided to go for a walk to get some fresh air. On the way home, she said to me, "My dad still loves you."

I tried to navigate this situation by telling her I knew that, but we were not together anymore because we were not getting along. Trying to explain separations to children is not easy in the best of times. It became much more difficult when I was navigating these types of comments, including my own feelings about the entire situation.

As we continued our walk, Grace said, "I wish we still lived with my dad."

I validated her feelings and provided comfort and reassurance that it was better for us to live apart, to give her a better life. "Moms and dads need to show love and respect for one another. If there is too much fighting, it isn't good for anyone." As the conversation carried on, I explained, "There was too much fighting between your dad and me. I didn't want you to see that all of the time."

Grace responded, "It's okay. You're allowed to fight."

While this was true, relationships do have ups and downs, the level of fighting between Johnny and me was unacceptable, something I was no longer willing to entertain. I didn't provide much more to that conversation, just changed the topic to something lighter and more enjoyable.

Soon, Grace also changed the topic, saying, "My dad is selling the house. I am worried, because it's my house."

I replied, "It's okay, Grace. I'm not sure what's happening, but you don't have to worry about that stuff right now." In my mind, though, I wondered, *Why on Earth does this poor child have to deal with all of her own feelings, plus take on such adult responsibilities and concerns?*

A few days had passed and I was still concerned about what Grace had shared with me during our walk. I sent Johnny a text message, asking about it. He replied, "I'm not going to lie to her. Stop micromanaging the way I parent."

I asked him to keep things age appropriate with her.

He responded, "I tried to keep the family together. Stop micromanaging me and my parenting."

The inconsistencies in Johnny's parenting time continued to be an issue. I dreaded going back to court, because it was a drawn-out process. Even though you can do it without legal support, I was avoiding it. I attempted to go back the lawyer I had used previously, when I had first inquired about leaving, but I was told she was still on sabbatical. *Great*, I thought. *Now what?*

It's so hard to find a good lawyer, especially one you trust and believe will represent you well. But I knew I had to do something. The last person I'd hired did not do anything for me, and that court battle was short-lived. I'd had a few new requests regarding our parenting plan, one of which was for me to be able to take Grace to counseling, so she could work through some of these issues. It was denied, because Johnny told the court, "My daughter doesn't need counseling." Rather than any further inquiry, my lawyer did nothing to stand up for me or advocate. It was ruled I could not take Grace to counseling, and nothing else was granted from my application, either.

The next time Grace came back from her dad's house, she started calling me ugly, on repeat. The name-calling was so hurtful, even if she didn't mean it. Also, Johnny continued to ask for Grace to spend two nights at his house, but was never consistent and often didn't keep her during his time. This was starting to feel like a broken record, but I felt like I had no more resources available.

Johnny would say, "I miss her. You get to spend more time with her than I do."

I didn't bother engaging in that conversation. He was never interested in what I had to say. It wasn't worth the battle for me, but I was left with the question, "Why can't you just be consistent with the time you do get with her?"

The next time I picked Grace up from school after her time with Johnny, she shared a story about her dad's friend, Rosie, and told me how she'd spent time at Rosie's house while her dad was at work. I was confused by this, since Johnny and I had had a specific conversation about his waiting to introduce the two of them. I reflected on this new information for the rest of the day and then decided to inquire about it further with Johnny. I never wanted to take everything as fact from Grace, as children don't always interpret or explain things in the way an adult can.. And I always wanted to provide Johnny the opportunity to explain himself, despite my feelings toward him.

I sent him a text message, asking whether he had introduced Rosie to Grace, because she had mentioned their spending time together. Johnny denied it.

The following day, when Grace was at Johnny's, he asked me to pick her up early. I thought, *Here we go again with him parenting only when it's convenient for him.*

Next, the accusations reared their head again. The following weekend, Johnny asked for Grace to spend three nights with him. I suggested two, as I was doing my best to keep her on somewhat of a consistent schedule, and she was still struggling around spending nights there.

Johnny said, "You gave me no reason not to let her stay for three nights, and if it's about the money, we will figure something out, so I can see my daughter."

It had nothing to do with money; that had never even come up. It was always about consistency and routine. Johnny then accused me of denying him access to Grace, even though I have documented all the time she spent with him, plus the outcomes and how many times he had ended his parenting time early. I shared with Johnny all the times I could account for their spending time together.

Johnny wasn't willing to hear me. He responded, "There are numerous times when you have denied me access."

This simply wasn't true, and I had all of the documentation to prove it. The only time I would say no to him was if there were plans in place and he asked last minute. Next, the conversation shifted to him saying he would like to coparent with me and keep things outside of the courts, but if he had to, he would ask for "dual custody," since Grace meant just as much to him as she did to me.

I ignored those text messages because I could anticipate the spiral, and I did not have the energy to deal with his ongoing accusations and inability to engage in a meaningful conversation.

Later that day, I received a text message from a friend. She told me that Johnny had reached out to her to help get a third-party, educated opinion on whether Grace should spend more time with him. My friend had been around for all of the chaos, and she knew better than to get involved in this manipulation tactic. My friend had respectfully told Johnny that she was my friend and so would not weigh in on this matter, that he should seek his own supporters. Instead of respecting her wishes, he continued to tell her how upset, frustrated, and heartbroken he was.

About a week or so later, Grace came to me and said she wanted to see her dad more, but that I wouldn't let her. Immediately my mind went to, *I wonder where she got this information from.* But I knew exactly where it was coming from.

*How unhealthy is this? How do I stop it? Why does he continue to get her involved in this stuff, when it's not appropriate?*

I asked Grace why she felt that way. She said, "You won't let me." So, I asked the follow-up question, where had she heard that? She said, "A horse told me." It felt like she was trying to place blame outside of people, as though she was protecting someone.

A few days later, Grace was at Johnny's house again. He sent me a text message indicating Grace wanted to come home, because she was lonely. That was an interesting notion, as feeling lonely wasn't something I'd heard in Grace's vocabulary. Johnny continued, "I don't want Grace to have a bad experience here, so I want her to go back with you."

This parenting inconsistency was starting to drive me insane.

Another day, Johnny brought up the document my lawyer had asked him to review many months ago and wanted to talk about it. I asked what, in particular, he wanted to talk about.

He told me he had received his lands check and would transfer $150 to me for childcare. He then asked if he could put off paying any type of child support until he was done with school. While initially I didn't care about money or material things, the fact that he had ignored the agreement for so long, and gotten the house, the fifth wheel, and everything we'd owned together was getting old. Although all I wanted was my belongings, I felt like I was being taken advantage of, and I was tired of playing nice and being patient all the time, when I couldn't get the same understanding in return. I was always expected to be the flexible one.

The conversation did not go anywhere. I began to push back and tell him I was done granting all of these excuses. It wasn't easy, paying for everything on my own.

A couple of days later, I get flooded with text messages from Johnny. "I feel like giving up. I've tried my best. I am letting Grace down. I am such a failure." He continued via numerous text messages. "I am alone, yet I keep trying so hard."

As someone who had been through so much with him and on my own, and who had had him make me feel so small and worthless, it was hard for me to show any compassion toward Johnny at this point. Eventually, I responded, "I don't know what to say. Life throws us curve balls, and we need to learn how to deal with it.

He replied, "It's hard because I've never been given a fair shot."

By this point, I really didn't care. I wanted to keep the conversation respectful, because I was so tired of the back and forth and unpredictability. But I wasn't about to show him any support. I'd tried for so long. Now, it was time he found support elsewhere.

But no matter what I said or how cold my text messages were, he continued to blow up my phone. "I tried everything to keep this family together. It was all in vain. The universe thinks I am a loser."

*It is the most draining, ridiculous position to be in when you're a victim and have to deal with the victim mentality. And it is one that is difficult to navigate.*

A few days later, we were back in the blame game. Johnny blamed me for tearing our family apart and for the potential costs we might be charged a penalty fee for selling our house before our term was up.

Then, he said, "You took everything away from me. It's not like I cheated on you, and you're making me out to be the worst person." He continued, "You act like I didn't financially support you or help you with your post-secondary classes. What you have done to me is ten times worse than I ever did to you."

Then there were more phone calls and ongoing text messages, but I ignored them, because I was at work and had other things to focus on. He continued to send messages, worried about signing his daughter away, saying he did not want to do that, as she was his child. One of his last texts that day read, "Since you got a lawyer, you have now affected Grace."

The following summer, Johnny brought his girlfriend to the powwow. I asked if he was going to introduce us, since they had now been together for quite some time. His response to my question was, "You had your chance."

Even a decade later, I've never been formally introduced to Rosie.

# Chapter 14

# From Self-Protection to (Broken) Connection

After a year or so of staying single, while rebuilding myself and learning to love myself again, I decided to start dating. It was a bit weird to be dating while living with my parents, but I thought it was time to put myself out there and see what happened. I deserved love and happiness just like everyone else, despite my current living situation.

I resorted to online dating. I met someone on one of the dating apps, and we began seeing each other, agreeing to take it slow. His name was Sam. He worked on the rigs in Texas—sound familiar? He lived in Calgary but was originally from Vancouver Island. I had a fascination and love for this island in British Columbia, although I hadn't spent much time there. The way the mountains met the ocean set my soul on fire.

I had my eye on attending Royal Roads University, which was on the island; when the time was right, I wanted to apply there to complete my master's degree. Once I got out of the chaos, I was a big dreamer. I hoped, one day, I could live out there, and maybe this guy would be the person beside me, living the life we dreamed of.

Somehow, Johnny found out I was dating this guy. This was weird because I had not introduced him to anyone yet, not even my friends. When I went to pick Grace up from Johnny's house one day, he confronted me about this relationship. He said, "Sam is a piece of shit."

I asked him how he knew that.

"I'm not telling you."

So, I asked Johnny how he knew about the relationship, which he also refused to share with me. I will never forget the look on his face during this conversation, full of hate, yet like he had some advantage or power over me. He acted like he had some information I was not privy to, which excited him. He chuckled snidely as he gave short little responses I did receive from him.

When he behaved this way, it was hard for me not to fall back into my old patterns of beating myself up and questioning my own sanity. I couldn't help but wonder, though, if there was some truth to whatever he was saying… Or was this just another of his scare tactics. There was only one way to find out.

A tool I found helpful as I was building myself up was the practice of positive affirmations. Whenever I left Johnny's presence, I engaged in this practice to ground and regulate myself again. I also wrote affirmations on sticky notes and stuck them to my bathroom mirror as constant reminders. This practice served me for many, many years, and became something I incorporate into my daily routine. Those sticky notes? They're still on my bathroom mirror.

One day, I went to pick Grace up from Johnny's and was met with a million questions as soon as I entered the doorway.

"What's this? You let your boyfriend take our dog to the dog park? Nalah isn't his dog—why are you letting him take care of her?"

I just stood in the doorway, giving no response, which appeared to upset him.

He continued to berate me. "You are replacing me with everything. I can't believe you would do this, but I should expect that from you. *And* him. You allow him to sleep in the same bed as you! That's inappropriate, don't you think? I would never do that to you."

We had been broken up for over a year by this point, and he was still in a relationship with Rosie, so this was odd, coming from him. I finally said, "I will not be engaging in this conversation. I have done nothing wrong."

Johnny argued, "You have done plenty to me. You are allowing another man to replace me. You've gone behind my back. The only reason you don't want to have this conversation is because you know what you are doing and you know that you are heartless. I've never done these things to you."

I couldn't take much more of this. I said, "You've been in a relationship almost the entire time we have been broken up. Focus on that relationship."

Johnny totally flipped the script when it came to the rules and regulations that I established for him and his parenting.

He made comments, "I try, but you continue to have free rein. You spit in my face and disrespect me. I don't care what you and he do, but don't bring my daughter into this shit."

Grace had not even met the guy I was dating, so I had no idea what Johnny was talking about, but I was beginning to learn that the best tactic I had was to not engage in these conversations at all, although it was still mentally and emotionally exhausting to have to cycle through this chaos all of the time, with no accountability on his part.

Johnny and I were still battling out the separation agreement that he continued to put off and not sign. I asked him, "If we write everything down that we talked about and then add it to the agreement, will you sign it?"

It felt like we were nearing the finish line with this document. I really looked forward to our having something concrete to follow, bound by the courts, even if we amended the original document that had been drafted by my lawyer. I was also sure the courts would be grateful that we'd come to an agreement on our own and could close this out for good.

Johnny knew that one of my goals was to get out of my parents' place and purchase my own home for Grace and me. In order to do that, I needed some things to be finalized, like that we needed to sell our house, etc. But Johnny threw up more resistance, saying, "You've disrespected me too much. I've changed my mind since we last talked about things."

By this point, the relationship was going well between me and Sam, and I had introduced him to Grace. Dating as a single parent when you have your child most of the time can be difficult, but it felt right at the time and I knew that I could figure things out.

Grace and I had spent the weekend in Calgary at Sam's house. Johnny was made aware after the fact, but I did not tell him prior to going. This was not the approach I would typically take with partners and introductions; however, I did not want to introduce him to Sam, given the hostility I'd experienced and the comments made previously, and I sure did not want anything bad to happen in front of Grace.

Johnny said to me, "You are a female, and I'm a male. I can do those things without being at risk." The comments continued. "Sam's a piece of shit. My rigger friends told me that he's a piece of shit." When I asked for clarification, he laughed and said in a snide manner, "I'm not telling you."

I felt so small, like I wanted to run away and cry. A million thoughts went through my head. *Why can't he just be supportive and leave me alone? He's in a relationship, and I'm not doing this stuff to him. Why can't he just let me be happy and accept the relationship is over?*

These little comments had such an impact on my mental health and made me feel unsafe. *Where is he getting his information from? Are people watching me? Who's talking about me and why do they care so much about my life and what I am doing?*

Later that evening, I received a text from Johnny that read, "If you want to draw up that paper, there are a few things that need to be addressed. I'm not asking for a lot, I'm asking to be respected, plain and simple."

I didn't have the emotional bandwidth to engage in that conversation, so I did not respond and carried on with whatever I was doing.

As I was putting Grace to bed later that night, she said to me, "My dad told me he was going to die."

While I did not think that was true, I did wonder why he had said something like that. *When will this stop?*

It didn't stop. Instead, I got more text messages the following day that said he deserved more respect than what I and my partner had given him, and that I was using our daughter against him, if he didn't sign the order that had been drafted. Johnny never met my partner, and I have no idea where this disrespect piece came from, but it was something thrown in my face on a regular basis.

During exchange times, I was expected to make it happen at a precise time. If I was even one minute late, he would threaten to keep her. Oftentimes, Johnny would be waiting in the window for me, watching.

During one exchange, I asked him what time he would be bringing Grace home. He explained his plans for the day, and on this day in particular, he told me he was taking Grace to a Remembrance Day ceremony and then going to look at a dog.

Seeking clarification as I always did, I asked for a time. "4:00 p.m.," he said.

Time passed. 4:00 p.m. came and went. I waited about fifteen minutes then asked how much longer he would be and where were they.

Johnny replied, "We are at home. I'll get her ready and bring her to you." These seemingly small disruptions started to add up. I felt like, no matter what I did, this man would do anything to control every aspect he could, while trying to make my life as difficult as possible.

The following day, I picked Grace up from school and asked her how her day was. We talked about powwows and the things she'd learned about that day. She was quick to change the subject, though.

"My dad tried really hard to live with you," she announced, "but you left, so he gave up."

*What?* These were not conversations Grace and I would have during our time together, so this messaging was becoming concerning. It did come from somewhere, with the most logical explanation being from her dad.

I felt so frustrated and angry, but I couldn't let Grace see that. I reminded her that when parents no longer get along and there is too much fighting, they sometimes don't stay together. And that's okay.

She changed the subject again and said she wanted to talk to me because she missed me. We carried on our conversation and went about our evening, taking the dog out, eating dinner, and spending time together.

A few days later, Grace went back to Johnny's. As we made the exchange, Grace started giving me more attitude, which was also becoming common whenever she came back from her dad's. This time, she hit and pushed me. This was unlike her normal behavior, but not so unusual during our exchanges or when she came back from spending time with her dad.

I started to wonder what was going on inside that home, when she and Johnny were together, but I knew I would not get an answer, let alone an honest one. I might never know.

I told Grace, "If you continue to hit and push me, you are going to get grounded."

Grace replied, "Are you going to give up on me?" and started to cry.

I wondered, *What is this now? Where is this coming from? This narrative is sounding a lot like her dad's*. I wanted to scream, because I was so frustrated by these comments and the way she was behaving every time she returned. But I felt like I had no control or could not do anything to make this better.

I pull myself together before responding then reassured her that I would never give up on her, but that she did need to listen and be kind.

The next day, similar behavior. Grace grabbed my head and started hitting me. I put her in time out. Another common behavior of hers was, whenever she got in trouble for doing or saying something like this, she would say, "You don't love me. I'm stupid. I'm a bad kid."

This negative self-talk was something I had never seen in a child her age, and I had worked with a lot of children and families throughout my career. I so badly wanted to have a level-headed conversation with Johnny, to get to the bottom of this and have him realize this was not helpful for any of us, but especially not for Grace. I wanted us to try to find a way to move forward.

A few days later, Sam and I had plans to take Grace to the *Star Wars* movie. *Star Wars* was not an interest of mine, but it deeply interested Sam, and he thought Grace would enjoy it, as well. I'm not sure how Johnny found out about it, but Grace shared our plan with him, as kids often share things without a filter. It was no big deal to me, nor was it a secret, but I certainly didn't need to provide day-to-day updates to Johnny about Grace's and my activities.

Later that day, my phone started to blow up with text messages from Johnny. "I would really like to be the one to take Grace to the movie."

I suggested, if he wanted to see it with her, he could take her again during his time with her.

He started to interrogate me. "Since when are you into *Star Wars*? You're more concerned about Grace and Sam's relationship. You will never stop breaking my heart. You are trying to replace me and push me out of Grace's life." The texts kept coming. "I would never do this to you.

I chose not to engage in this conversation because it was inflammatory and not going to go anywhere. That didn't matter, though, because whether I engaged or not, the texts continued into the day.

"Your partner is trying to buy Grace's love. It goes both ways."

It was mind-blowing to me, how Johnny could spend so much time and energy interrogating me and trying to analyze what I was doing. I never attacked him for what he and Rosie chose to do with Grace during their time together. I trusted their time and respected it as such, even though I had concerns about the comments that were being made and the behaviors I saw, when Grace came home.

The following day, I continued to receive text messages. "Please don't let Sam take Grace from me. Grace and I watched all of the *Star Wars* movies, and it's a special bond we have. I would never do anything like this to you." Followed by, "I know it's just a movie, but it's a movie she and I have been watching for the past two months and a bond we have built as father and daughter."

I didn't respond.

Grace then went back to Johnny's for a few days. When she came home, she said, "I don't want you and Sam to get married."

Marriage wasn't even a topic of discussion in our relationship, which was only a few months old, so this comment seemed odd. I asked Grace why not, out of curiosity.

She replied, "Because my dad said that Nalah will be Sam's dog."

I thought, *Holy shit, are you kidding me. Now this?* I pulled my thoughts together and said, "Nalah is our dog, and nothing will change that. You have nothing to worry about."

The following day, Grace had a new concern. She said, "I don't want you and Sam to have a baby. Only my dad and Rosie can." She continued, "If you get married, I will have to choose where I want to live, and I don't want to have to do that."

This was vocabulary that most five-year-olds didn't have, so it seemed like a really strange thing for her to be worrying about. I told her, "Grace, you will never have to choose."

I began to notice, as Grace played with her toys, she became quite aggressive in her games, and there was always conflict. *This was telling.* I remained curious and kept documenting the incidents and behaviors I observed, hoping, one day, this data would serve me.

Later that day, Johnny called, and I put him on speaker phone so he and Grace could talk. Johnny had gotten a dog a little while ago, and he shared with Grace, "The dog misses you. When you aren't around, the dog is always sniffing your toys."

This may seem like an innocent comment, but it was the first of many manipulative tactics and use of other measures to draw Grace toward him and away from me. A part of me wondered if these were attempts to make Grace feel guilty for not being there with Johnny. I kept documenting, as it was all I felt I could do.

# Chapter 15

# The First Court Application

Around New Year's, many people set goals for the year ahead, while others make resolutions. I've always pondered New Year's resolutions but believe that behavior change should happen in the moment, without waiting for some specific time to make it happen. Nonetheless, this year I knew was again going to be one of survival and change. As experiences ramped up, so did my documentation and motivation to make a change.

One night, when Grace was to spend the night at her dad's, she began to cry and said, "I don't want to go. I have nightmares when I am there." Her behaviors escalated, and she started hitting me and screaming in my face. This behaviour was unprovoked, as it often was during the lead up to her having to spend time with Johnny.

I made her go anyway, despite how guilty I felt making her go places she didn't want to, but I felt like I had no choice right now. It felt like I was trying to plan my next strategic move, playing a game of chess only in the dark. I had no sense of direction.

The next day, Grace and I were working on Valentine's Day cards for her class. She became frustrated with her writing. With encouragement, I told her, "It's okay, keep trying. You're doing your best, and that's all that matters."

She continued to escalate, getting out of her chair and punching me in the chest. I didn't respond at all, just quietly gathered up the cards, put them on top of the fridge, and walked away. Grace remained in the kitchen, still upset, yet observing my behaviors. I needed a moment. I was so exhausted from riding this rollercoaster.

Grace followed me up the stairs to the living room. Still upset, she grabbed my clothes as she screamed at me that I was the stupidest mom and that she wanted me to go live with someone else. She continues, "I will go live where nobody can find me."

I was very frustrated about her behavior, but my heart was breaking for her, as she was too young to want to live alone where nobody could find her. I wondered what would make her say such a thing.

The yelling continued and her behavior escalated until, moments later, she grabbed a pen and stabbed it into my leg. I tried very hard not to cry and get upset, but my emotions got the best of me.

Later that day, when it was time for her to go to Johnny's, the comments and behaviors escalated again almost immediately. "I'm a fake kid," she cried. "I'm not the kid you wanted." Moments later, she switched gears, saying, "I don't want to go to my dad's, but if I don't go, he will cry."

Grace had been invited to a birthday party the following day. She asked, "Can you bring me to the party instead?"

I explained that, because she would be at her dad's house, he would have to bring her.

She asked, "Can you ask my dad if you could bring me?"

I promised I would ask.

A few days later, when she comes back from her dad's, Grace was speaking negatively about herself. Later on, she shared a story about her dad not protecting her when they were out shooting gophers and there was a bull nearby. I was confused but asked her more questions, because this was the second time she'd brought up this idea of her dad being a protector. I asked if that was something they talked about often, and she said yes. The other time she'd mentioned her dad being a protector, she'd said that only her dad could protect her and that I couldn't. I told her I was fully capable of keeping her safe, too.

The next day, Grace and I went to powwow club. Upon returning home, there wasn't much time before it was time to get ready for bed. She approached me and said, "You are going to take a hammer to my face and smash it."

This stopped me in my tracks. *What the hell is this about*? My heart was breaking, yet I was also becoming furious. *Why is she saying things like this? Where is it coming from?* I calmed myself down and asked, "Where did that come from?"

"Myself," she said.

She began to say things often like, "Nobody wants me. Call the police on me. You don't want me, you never will. You aren't my mom. I'm not your daughter. I will leave and live with my dad forever. You will never see me again."

I didn't have the words to engage, but it was incredibly heartbreaking to hear my child speak these words. I knew these types of conversations and messaging didn't occur inside *my* home. But I had no control over what my child was being exposed to. And as much as I wanted to make it better, I had very little control or ability to do so.

I had a hard time processing this all. She was just a child who was navigating a lot, but those words stung. I knew she likely didn't mean this and was clearly too young to understand the weight of those words, but it still impacted me. I was doing my best to support her, but it was incredibly difficult. I felt so alone in this parenting fight, because I didn't have someone to coparent with. If it wasn't for Johnny and the things he was projecting onto our daughter, maybe I wouldn't have had to deal with this in the first place. It's one thing to heal on your own, it's another to help your child through the process, especially when they are continuously being exposed.

The next day, it was the same old thing. Grace ramped up her negative self-talk. "I'm a spoiled child. I want to die." This came out of nowhere.

All I could do was monitor her behavior and keep documenting, but I was becoming increasingly concerned. I was still in the dark and at a loss for what to do or where to turn. I sought out counseling services for Grace again, however was very quickly informed that we needed two parent signatures. *Great.* I'd had this conversation before, and Johnny was not interested.

I approached Johnny again with the idea of seeking out counseling for Grace, as I was really struggling with her behavior, and he told me, "I don't see those behaviors at my house. She doesn't need counseling." This would later inform part of my court application, because I wanted Grace to get the help she needed.

Months went by. I was still dating Sam and decided to put a picture of him up in our home. When Grace walked by and noticed it, she said, "You better not show my dad that."

I asked her why. "My dad hates him," she replied.

*Interesting,* I thought. I still had not introduced the two of them out of my own safety concerns. Johnny had been violent toward others and could be, again, especially as emotions and tensions were so high.

When Grace returned from her dad's a few days later, she told me that Rosie had picked her up from school yesterday. I thought it was weird, since she was not on the list of adults or caregivers who could pick her up from school. Grace asked, "Who would pick me up from school, if my dad can't?"

I replied, "I would."

Grace continued, "My dad wouldn't like that. He will come to your house and break everything."

I had no idea what that was about. I asked if her dad got mad a lot.

She replied, "Yes."

So, I inquired further. "What does he get mad about?"

"He gets mad at me and Rosie. Sometimes, when they fight, I lock myself in the bathroom and tell them to stop complaining."

A few days later, it was time for Grace to return to her dad's. She said, "My chest hurts when I am at my dad's. It's hard to breathe, and I worry a lot when I am there."

I felt so proud of her self-awareness, but it killed me to hear she felt this way. And I continued to feel helpless, being unable to help her in the ways I wanted to. I asked her why she thought that was.

She said, "I want you when I am there."

A few days later, minutes after I picked Grace up from Johnny's, the verbal diarrhea started flowing. It was almost as though she had bottled up all of her thoughts, feelings, and emotions from the past few days and could not wait to be in a safe place to let it all out. She said, "My dad's girlfriend says bad words."

I asked what was said, because I am no stranger to potty mouth, and Grace replied, "Fuck you."

"Who does she say that to?"

Grace said, "My dad." I start to worry about her experiencing domestic violence inside Johnny's home, as well. It sounded like it, but my only obligation was to control the protection and safety of my daughter.

Grace's kindergarten graduation was fast approaching, an exciting time. As we were talking about who she wanted at her graduation, she said, "Sam cannot come, because my dad doesn't like him."

One of the most common messages I found myself giving to Grace during this time was that her dad should not be telling her things like that. I continued to encourage her not to worry about that and to focus on who she wanted there.

As our day continued, so did her revelations. "I have something to tell you, but I don't want to get in trouble."

As a mother, my first instinct was to ask, "What did you do?" but I knew I needed to respond differently in this situation. I composed myself, took a few breaths, and asked, "What is it?"

Thankfully, what she told me had nothing to do with her. It was about another thing she'd been exposed to. "Rosie calls my dad a fucking asshole right in front of me."

I asked, "How does that make you feel?" There was not much of a response, so I inquired, "Do you ever tell your dad how this stuff makes you feel?"

She said, "My dad talks to Rosie about the things she is saying and how it makes me feel." A few days later, Grace shared that she had told her dad she did not like Rosie. I asked how he'd responded to that. "My dad told me not to talk like that."

Kindergarten graduation came and went with no issues, though I did bring Sam to the graduation ceremony. We kept our distance, as did Johnny. Grace attended the school's day programming over the summer. She thoroughly enjoyed her time there with her friends.

The program was rooted in Indigenous culture, which was amazing. Before Grace was five, she was able to pray in her language, as well as say her colors and numbers. It had always been a goal of mine to have her feel a strong foundation and connection to her identity, and I believed the cultural approach was more holistic and better aligned with our values as a family. Some families provide religion as a foundation; I felt that culture was best. To each their own.

One day, during pickup from camp, the teacher came out and said, "Can I speak with you?" She then informed me that Grace and another student were hitting other classmates that day. "We are seeing an increase in behaviors from Grace when she is with her dad."

I didn't want to jump to conclusions, because I needed more information. "Can you provide me with some examples of what you mean by that?" This would help me talk about it with Grace, once we got home, because this behavior was unacceptable.

The teacher said, "Grace will either act out physically, as she did today, or become violent with her words." That wasn't much to go off of, but I thanked the teacher for this information and assured her I would be speaking to Grace about it later, as well. As always, I added this to my documentation.

There was a powwow coming up. Grace and I had plans to go attend. She said to me, "Sam cannot come. My dad will be there, and he is the boss." Again, we had to have a conversation about what is appropriate messaging and what is not, and how everyone is welcome at powwows.

We attended the powwow together with no issues, but I felt like I had to continuously watch my back, hoping to prevent any issues while we were there. This became a constant for me for years to come. At times, it felt ridiculous, but it was my reality, and still is.

The cycle continued: wash, rinse, repeat. When I picked Grace up from Johnny's, the stories would begin. "My dad is always out golfing. Rosie puts me to bed all the time," Grace said. "I asked my dad if I could come back to your house, but he told me that Rosie wants to spend time with me."

This was getting ridiculous. There was no consistency in his parenting, and even when he "had" her, he didn't appear to be spending much time with her. *Why does he always fight so hard to have her in his life and feel threatened by others stepping in, when he doesn't even utilize the time he does have with her?* I wondered, *Is this just an image thing for him? What is underneath all of the ruckus?*

During this time, Grace and I made a safety plan. The plan was, if she was ever feeling unsafe, she could go to my friend's house who lived in the same condo complex as her dad. This seemed to comfort Grace a bit, as she was part of the planning process and knew she had a safe place to go, should she ever need it. Later that night, though, Grace wet the bed. The stress was taking a toll on her. There was no other explanation for it, as she was fully potty trained and had been for many years. More documentation.

I felt at a loss, like I was grasping at straws. I knew we needed help and that Grace deserved more than this, but what was I to do? It felt like nobody would listen and everyone was passing the buck. I finally mustered up the courage to call Children's Services, where I spoke to a woman named Danielle. She said she would speak to her supervisor and give me a call back.

A few days later, I received a call from Grace's school, reporting that Children's Services had called them. I didn't get much more information than that. And it didn't really matter, because it went nowhere. Another dead end. Another conversation with no outcome.

When I picked Grace up from her dad's a few days later, her behaviors continued. I asked, "Why are you acting this way?"

She said, "I don't want to tell you." I tried my best not to pry when she answered like this, giving her space in the hopes she would come forward and tell me on her own terms. She continued to complain about being at her dad's and how she did not want to go there anymore.

I asked her, "Is this something I can talk to your dad about?"

She said no. She was only five years old. It was hard to balance respecting her wishes and maintaining trust with doing what I thought was best in the situation.

Grace continued to tell me that she felt lonely at night time and that she wanted someone to protect her. "I feel like nobody loves me and I don't have a family."

My heart broke when I heard her speak those words. Looking at her little body, the way her eyes said more than her words ever could, I knew this wasn't about me. But it was so hard not to feel crushed by this.

I wondered, *What more can I do to show her love and create safety? Why does she keep talking about wanting to be protected? This is not a word that we use. Where is it coming from?'*

I made my best attempts to reassure her that she had many family members and we all loved her very much.

I finally made an application to the courts in November 2017, after five years of this ongoing battle. I didn't have money to hire a lawyer, but I learned about Resolution Services that would allow a neutral party to help you fill out the paperwork and would appear in court with you. The basis of my application was for assistance from the courts to address consistent parenting time, fair and equitable child support based off the federal child support guidelines, and the ability to obtain a passport for Grace and to travel with her outside of the country. I also requested a police clause be included, should we ever need that.

I was lucky enough to get paired with a great staff member. I felt very supported by her, and she made the application process feel easy and less intimidating.

# Chapter 16

# The First Court Appearance

I had my first court appearance in docket court. Grace continued to struggle with sleep, bed wetting, and behavioral concerns. I wanted to enrol Grace into counseling to address these concerns and to learn ways that I could best support her as we navigated these challenges. Johnny was making this process difficult.

I had to complete an update statement and ask for an Interim Parenting Order for Grace to attend counseling. In my application in April 2018, I indicated the above information in my application and provided the courts with documentation from 2012-2018 on all of my concerns, including why I was requesting counseling. This was adjourned, and we were scheduled for another court date.

Rather than appearing in docket court, we were scheduled for a Judicial Dispute Resolution (JDR). It's similar to a mediation, but there were no lawyers involved and the judge acted as the mediator. It was not a good experience. Terrible, in fact.

During this JDR, it was agreed that I would have day-to-day care and primary residence of Grace. Johnny would have reasonable and generous parenting time, following his shift work, and those times were outlined in the agreement. Additional conditions stipulated that neither parent would speak negatively about the other parent in the presence of the child and established where the exchange would take place. Grace was also to attend counseling.

There was another interesting condition specified in this agreement, one that didn't initially worry too much about, but I later recognized it was another means of power and control. It stated that, if I were to travel outside of the country with a male, I was required to provide Johnny with the male's criminal record check fifteen days prior to leaving the country.

There was also a police clause in the agreement, which is standard across many parenting orders. It read:

*If a party or another person on their behalf breaches this order, a peace officer will provide assistance to ensure the offending party complies with the order. If the peace officer decides that compliance with the order is not in the best interest of the child, the peace officer is to compile a report. The officer's report must include a statement describing the events and circumstances of the assistance provided, and the reason for any non-enforcement of this order. The parties have a right to request, in writing, a copy of the report.*

This police clause remained in every parenting order that followed.

After the JDR was completed, we were excused. I refused to leave the room at the same time as Johnny did, because I feared for my safety and what would happen, if we walked out together. Years ago, when I was a teenager, a friend's mom was dragged at knifepoint down the stairs outside the courthouse, after a court appearance that went sideways. I had visions of something similar happening to me, so I asked the judge to sit in the room and wait until he was gone.

The judge sat with me, just him and me in the room. He probed further, inquiring why I feared for my safety. I explained, although I was so sick of telling my story, especially since it often fell on deaf ears. Despite my biases, I thought, *Maybe this will be the time someone listens to me. I won't know if I don't share.*

I was hoping, maybe if I told him directly, something would change. Maybe this was how we would finally get the protection we needed. Still, I thought, *I have all of this documentation, things were addressed in my court order, so why am I stuck retelling my story time and time again?*

I later learned that judges are not privy to information about things prior to the current discussions or court appearances, so they really are just taking the information in at the present time. I can understand this approach, since it helps to limit bias, it can also do a disservice when there is so much history, especially when it includes domestic violence. Reviewing a file to understand the bigger picture of each dispute would be a much more trauma-informed approach.

The judge responded to me very clearly after I shared my reasons. "I had no idea this was domestic violence. You hold yourself together so well."

I became emotional and told him, "I have no other choice but to hold myself together." I've had the opportunity to present in court throughout my career, in various roles, so I knew how to compose myself and present well. That didn't mean I was less of a victim.

A parenting order was granted by the judge that day, with us set to appear again in court a few months later for review. I felt a bit relieved that we had something in writing and hoped it would alleviate some of our issue. In the meantime, there could be some consistency and routine moving forward, until we could figure out next steps.

A few months went by. We were set to return to court. I walked into the court room nervous as hell, sat down, and waited for the clerk to call the judge in. When the judge walked in, we stood until she said, "Please be seated."

As I looked at the judge, I formed some very early assumptions. *She looks kind and compassionate.* I had heard about this judge and her experience with domestic violence. She had sat in that court for quite some time. This provided me a small sense of ease and relief, especially seeing that she was female.

There was some back-and-forth conversation. What I remember most is there being tension in the court room. One comment stood out to me. Johnny stood before the judge and said, "Chelsey is a female and cannot protect our daughter in the same way that I can." He proceeded to ask the judge to be informed every time I left the city with our daughter.

The judge immediately denied that request and said it was power and control. She would not be granting that. A powerful sense of relief came over my body like a rush. *Finally,* I thought. My shoulders dropped, and I could feel the tension leave me. This was the first time I'd ever felt heard, even if it was for a small matter. I wanted to cry.

I got most of what I had requested in my application. The one thing Johnny asked to remain in the order was the clause about my travelling outside of the country with Grace along with any male companion, that the male had to provide a criminal record check to Johnny.

I thought this was insane, but at the end of the day, it wasn't that big of a deal, because I wasn't dating people with criminal records. I couldn't help but think this was a breach of confidentiality, though. I would learn later that it was. Not much else changed as regards the division of parenting time or Grace's having access to counseling, so we carried on business as usual.

# Chapter 17

## Turning Pain into Persistence and Perseverance

My relationship with Sam ended. He cheated on me numerous times and had a fear of commitment. We had broken up a few times because of this, before we ended it for good.

I felt like such a failure, and the negative self-talk seeped through my pores. I wondered why I couldn't have a happy, healthy relationship? What did this say to Grace? What did I do to deserve this? Why couldn't I find a good guy? I deserved love just like everyone else.

There I went again, healing from another heartbreak and another let down. But I couldn't wallow in that headspace for long. I had a daughter to raise, healing to do, and an ongoing fight with Johnny that was far from being over. So, I did as I always did: I armored up for battle.

I picked Grace up from her dad's house a few days later. She ran to me and said, "I missed you so much. I cried for you every night."

I comforted her then asked, "How come you didn't call?"

She said, "I am not allowed to call you, because it stresses my dad out." Later that day, Grace exhibited the same familiar attitude and resistance, telling me, "You're a bad mom." Those words stung. There is nothing worse than hearing that from your child, even if they don't mean them.

I often found myself dreaming of the days when the behaviors and the constant fighting would be a thing of the past. Little did I know, I had many more years of this to come.

A few days later, Grace and I went for a walk. She told me, "My dad forces me to call Rosie *Mom*, and I don't like it."

Johnny and I had had this conversation previously. So had Grace and I. I am a strong believer in a child being able to choose what they want to call the adults in their lives. Adults earn those titles; it's not something that is simply given. Grace called her maternal grandma's husband, "Papa Les." This upset Johnny, because he believed Les was not her grandpa, since he was not biologically related. I stood by my conviction that if she wanted to call him "Papa Les," she should be able to.

I asked Grace whether she talked to her dad about the way she felt, calling his partner "Mom." She replied, "If I told my dad that, he would teach me a lesson and give me a whipping."

I asked her if that was true. She said yes. Concerned about her answer, I said, "If that's the case, we would need to go to the police, because that is not okay, and it's my job to keep you safe."

Grace began to cry, asking, "Will my dad go to jail?"

I replied, "He likely won't go to jail, but adults should not teach their children lessons by whipping them." The conversation ended shortly after that, and we carried on with our day.

About a week later, Grace again disclosed that her dad whipped her. I hadn't seen any bruises, but I was becoming increasingly concerned about these reports and where they were coming from. *There has to be some truth to this somewhere.* I didn't want to immediately panic, in case this was not true, but I also didn't want to sit on it and do nothing about it, at the expense of Grace's safety and wellbeing. I was also aware, given my work experience, that how any questions around abuse are asked is super-important. I didn't want to lead her down a path, but I knew in my heart I had to ask additional questions, because if my daughter was being harmed in that home, I had to take action.

Grace said, "I wear lots of clothing when it happens."

I kept documenting her disclosures and our conversations. I didn't want to discredit or disregard her comments, but I also knew that false allegations could hold a ton of weight, so I had to make sure I had enough evidence to move forward.

I said to her, "If that is true, we need to go to the police." I hated the way I made that statement, because it sounded as though I was doubting her, but I was trying to do the best I could with what I had at the time.

Grace began to cry. "I'm scared my dad will go to jail and I won't be able to see my dog again."

I sat with this for a bit, maybe longer than I should have, but eventually, I filed another report with police.

By summer 2020, we had been following our parenting order and scheduled parenting time that had been established earlier that year. While there were concerns regarding behavior, there were no concerns with the parenting time per se, which was the primary focus of our parenting order at the time. The court order was being followed, but Grace was becoming increasingly reluctant to spending time with her dad.

Once, as I was attempting to help Grace get ready to go, she told me, "I don't want to go to my dad's." My response was that she had to. There is nothing worse than feeling the pain of your child while also feeling hopeless, like there is nothing you can do because you have a court order over your head, forcing the child to go somewhere they don't want to go.

Grace and I got into my vehicle and started driving toward her dad's house. Grace became increasingly upset and started kicking the back of my seat, begging me to turn around and take her back home.

When we arrived at her dad's house, I parked in the visitors parking, and Grace refused to get out of the car. I texted Johnny and explained the situation, asking for his assistance. I hated to do that, but I felt I had no other choice. Turning around and taking her back home would have had dire consequences for me in the court process, but in reality, the real consequences were for Grace and having to go somewhere she didn't want to be. This took a toll on her mental health.

Johnny lived on the second floor of his condo building. I vividly remember him coming down the stairs with his familiar facial expression, a clenched jaw and fists. He approached my vehicle and immediately got mad, demanding Grace get out of the car. He yelled at her and said, "Quit crying." This only made her cry more.

I was standing outside of my car, hopelessly watching. Johnny continued to yell and berate Grace. She would not look at him, just kept looking down at the floor of the vehicle. He demanded, "You need to respect me. Look at me when I am talking to you." Rather than comforting Grace, he took a more aggressive approach. "You think your life is so hard?"

Crying hysterically, Grace replied, "Yes."

Johnny listed off his own childhood experiences, telling her, "Your life isn't hard. You want to cry? Get out of the car and cry. Have a fit in the parking lot. Throw a tantrum."

Johnny stepped away from the vehicle and gestured for Grace to get out. She refused. With hostility, Johnny told her, "You're embarrassed, that's why!" He then began to mimic her in the parking lot.

My heart was breaking by the minute. I could no longer stand by and watch this happen, yet I was scared what would happen if I said something. *Could I make the situation worse? What would happen to Grace once I left?* I finally said, "Johnny, you are not listening to what she is saying."

He was rude and condescending in his response to me, as well.

Grace said, "This is why I want to stay with my mom."

I chimed in, "Johnny, if you spoke to me this way, I wouldn't want to spend time with you, either."

He shifted his focus from Grace to me and started to yell at me in the parking lot.

I said, "I do not deserve to be spoken to like this, and it is no longer being tolerated." *It felt so good to stand my ground, but it still made me feel uneasy as to what was next.*

Grace attempted some compromising, asking to stay for two nights instead of three. Johnny immediately shut that down, saying, "If that's what you want, don't come back."

Grace often referred to "little potatoes," though I wasn't clear on what that meant. While we were still in the parking lot, Grace refusing to get out of the vehicle, she again brought up the "little potatoes," saying "I don't want to eat them."

Johnny responded, "I am not going to cook separate meals for you."

Later, Grace told me Johnny had threatened to shove the potatoes down her throat, if she did not eat them. This led to trauma around these potatoes and meal times in general. Even several years later, she refuses to eat them.

I attempted to mediate the food issues conversation with Johnny about and asked, "If she really doesn't like them, why is she being forced to eat them? Imagine being forced to eat things you don't enjoy."

Johnny's response was cold and direct. "You eat what is served." Then, he changed the subject and said to Grace, "You want to be a big girl and make all of these decisions? Go ahead, be a big girl. Cook and clean for yourself."

The situation was only escalating. By now, Grace was so upset, and we weren't getting anywhere. I didn't want to leave her with him and could only imagine what would happen once I left if he was behaving this way right in front of me and neighbors.

As Grace continued to cry, Johnny said to her, "Come on, let's go get your diapers, if you want to act like a baby."

I intervened again, expressing my concern about his saying these belittling, negative things. He disagreed and continued to harass Grace, telling her, if she decided she didn't want to see him but then one day changed her mind, then he would have to decide if he even wanted to see her then. He ended his rant by barking, "You are no longer welcome at my house. I am going to pack up all of your things and throw them on the lawn." Then, he slammed my car door and went inside.

Moments later, Grace and I drove back home. We needed a minute to decompress. That had been a lot. For both of us. Her little heart was hurting, and mine was, too.

The next day, Grace is again supposed to be at Johnny's house, but given what had happened the day before, she stayed with me. He demanded that Grace again be brought to his house, so I asked her if she wanted to go over there. She responded with a ton of emotion and resistance, saying she felt unsafe with him.

I told her, if she felt unsafe, she could go to my friend's house in the condo complex across from her dad's, just like we'd planned. Grace asked if she could call the police if she was scared, and I said, "Of course." She asked if she could walk home if she was scared, which I agreed to, as well.

Children shouldn't have to plan their exit strategy or even have safety concerns during visits with their parents. The courts continued to expose children to hurt and pain, rather than protect them. This gave me flashbacks to when I used to supervise visits between children and parents in the child welfare system. *How has this become my life?*

At summer's end, it was my birthday, August 26, 2020. Another year around the sun. What a wonderful thing to celebrate. I love a little extra-special treatment, bit of extra love, and maybe a gift or two. To me, it's a day to celebrate *you* with the people you love and care about the most.

That day, I was about to receive the greatest gift of all: one of my most traumatic experiences.

My birthday started off as a beautiful day. My family and friends hosted a BBQ down at the river bottom, which is one of my favorite places. We ate, told stories, and shared tons of laughter. Grace was scheduled to go to her dad's later that evening. I was feeling a bit uneasy as to how this would go, because the last few visits had been less than ideal. I tried my best to enjoy my time with my friends and family and to make the most of it for Grace, too. I didn't want her to get the sense that I was feeling on edge.

On the drive to Johnny's, as we neared his house, Grace began to cry. As her emotions became more intense, Grace begged and pleaded with me not to take her to her dad's and to bring her home. My heart hurt for her. I'd never felt so many emotions all at once.

As I continued to drive, I felt ashamed but trapped, bound by this stupid court order. Grace continued to cry, and all I could think of was, if I breached this court order, there would be consequences. That outweighed my daughter's safety and the clear messaging she was giving me. It never should have, but I felt at a loss, that nobody believed me. *How much worse does this have to get before someone sees it for what it is?*

When we pulled up to Johnny's building, I parked my vehicle out front in the visitors parking, as I always did, and Grace was hysterical. You know that ugly crying, when you have snot all over your face and you sound congested? That was her. I reflect back on this moment often, despite how painful it was, because I will forever beat myself up for the way I handled this situation, due to my fear of the courts.

Grace refused to get out of my vehicle. It was dark out. I looked around, paying attention to my surroundings. My momma instinct came over me, and I suddenly thought, *What if she runs away?* I looked around for the route she might take.

She and I sat outside for a good five to ten minutes. I didn't know what to do. I tried to convince her that she had to go inside. It was only for a few sleeps. And the reason she had to, I explained, was because the court order said so. I felt like a terrible mom, riddled with fear. We both were. I didn't want Grace ever to think that I prioritized a court-ordered document over her own safety, but when you are in this situation, it is not easy. Since all of my previous attempts to get police to help me had failed, I had little hope anyone would be able to help me now, plus I would be blamed. It was the hardest position I had ever been in.

A million thoughts went through your mind, starting with *which is going to be more believable?* I hated those thoughts. Eventually, I called Johnny and asked for him to help me, as Grace was refusing to get out of my vehicle. I felt like I was deceiving her, but I had no idea what else to do.

As Johnny came down the stairs and approached my vehicle, Grace noticed him and became more hysterical. I was so tired of documenting and taking notes on these types of incidents and conversations. *For what? They don't get us anywhere and have served no purpose thus far.* Then, I had an idea: our phones have this magical ability for audio recording. As Johnny approached my vehicle, I hit record.

Grace still refused to get out, but when she caught a break, she did exactly what I'd thought she was going to do. She ran. Johnny said, "Let her run. She'll be back."

I watched her run into the night. I thought to myself, *What parent would just let their child run?* I was worried. I watched, hoping she would turn around, but knowing, if I lost sight of her, I was going after her, regardless of what he said or thought about the situation. I wasn't leaving her to wander in the dark alone. How scary, with her already terrified and rejecting being at Johnny's.

Grace did come back a few minutes later and climbed back into my car. Johnny tried to grab her, telling me to hold her until he could get to her. When he came around to the driver's side, Grace jumped from the front seat to the back seat, dodging her dad's attempt to grab her. I told Johnny I was not going to put my hands on her, especially when she was in this state. She was also still sobbing hysterically.

Eventually, Johnny caught Grace in the vehicle and dragged her outside of it. She screamed, "Help me! *Help me*! He's going to kill me. *I can't breathe!*" Her little hands grasped at the car's seat, mirror, anything to help her stay inside or provide some leverage, to maintain her safety. The look on her face was pure fear.

I watched in disbelief, yet still felt sacred to intervene, because what if he hurt me in the process? If something happened to me, I wouldn't be able to help Grace at all.

A neighbor came out of the condo complex and asked, "Is everything okay?"

I did answer, "Yes," but not in a confident tone.

I kept thinking how the things we do or don't do to analyze safety is insane. I didn't think anyone could understand what this experience was like or could even imagine it, unless they lived through it. It felt like something out of a movie. But at least someone had finally seen something, so I now have a witness plus this audio recording. I hoped they would call the cops, so it was not always Johnny vs. Chelsey.

I prayed, *Please let something good come from this. I am so tired and emotionally exhausted, feeling like a bad mom.* I hoped the police would come and take statements, so they, too, could see that I was not making this up. That would be a positive outcome to this shitty experience.

But no. Johnny finally put Grace down. She was still kicking and screaming, while yelling that she couldn't breathe and he was going to kill her. Grace then jumped back in my car, more hysterical than ever.

Johnny said, "Did you hear what that neighbor said to you? Tell her you're okay."

I reply sheepishly, "I did."

Johnny acted like he couldn't believe Grace had said she couldn't breathe. In the audio recording, you can hear him tell Grace to punch me in the face. I had no idea where that came from or why Johnny was expressing that message. Next, he demanded that I get Grace into his house.

I said, "I am not putting my hands on her. She is in a fragile state."

Johnny's ordered, "Step it up and be a parent. It's called discipline."

Moments later, he went into his house alone. I could see his shadow pacing above us through the window in his door. This, too, was something out of a movie. He would peer through the blinds then go to the living room window.

I was stunned. Frozen. Scared. Ashamed. Lost. I didn't feel like I knew what to do. I sat in my vehicle for another forty-five minutes, scanning my environment, with a million thoughts going through my mind. *What are the consequences if I leave? I can't possibly try to make Grace go inside, even if she calms down. There will be hell to pay by this point, if she goes inside, and I am scared as to what will happen.* I was in the middle of trying to regulate my own emotions, as well as Grace's. Getting out of the situation may have made the most sense, but when you're in the middle of it, it's hard to think practically.

I called my friend who'd just seen me at my birthday. She worked for Children's Services, and after explaining what had just happened, I asked her, "What do I do?"

She gave me a very practical answer. "Get the hell out of there!"

It felt like I couldn't even think on my own anymore. When I bought my house in 2018, I'd bought strategically. My friend owned the house across from me, and another friend lived next to me. I knew, if anything ever happened or I needed anything, I had support right there. I was right, because very soon, my safety plan became a necessity.

I followed my friend's direction and left. We drove home in silence. As I parked in my driveway with Grace in the backseat, I saw a car come speeding down my street, ripping around the corner. Sudden terror shot through my body and then Grace's.

Grace said, "It's my dad!" and she was right. He followed us home.

I tried to compose myself, because I didn't want to traumatize Grace any more than she already was. I immediately called my friend across the street and said, "He's followed us home. Please come outside."

She sounded the alarm and called another friend next door to me. Within seconds, my friends were outside. I felt so lucky to have these friends. I don't know what I would do without them.

My friends approached my vehicle. One friend escorted Grace to the front step. As I got out, my other friend said, "Get inside. I'll get the stuff out of your vehicle."

Johnny was parked in front of my house. He got out and leaned against his car, his body language screaming, "Authoritative."

As Grace walked across the front yard toward the door, she said to him, "I couldn't breathe."

Johnny replied, "You were talking. You were fine."

As I approached my door, Johnny demanded I come to his vehicle. I did not acknowledge him, just followed Grace into the house with one of my friends. It felt good to be inside my house, the safe place, full of peace. Nobody could take that from us.

As I walked toward my door, Johnny called the police. I could hear him say to dispatch in a condescending, sarcastic tone, "Apparently, I am aggressive and abusive. I don't know what I am doing wrong here."

I didn't know what was going to happen next. Nobody did. As Grace finally settled in, she grabbed a few of her Barbies and started playing with them. My friends sat with us after we'd made sure all the windows and doors were locked. In play, Grace reenacted various violent scenarios.

My psychologist friend said, "Notice how Grace is role-playing with the Barbies?" And I nodded my head in agreement. "It's her way of processing what happened."

Some child psychologists or therapists use this method to role-play situations rather than talk about them; it is termed *play therapy*. We weren't in a therapy session, but Grace took it upon herself to work through these experiences.

Johnny was still on my front step. Once he was off the phone with dispatch, he started banging on my front door and ringing the doorbell over and over. All of us ignored him and tried to keep Grace calm, distracting her through play.

Awhile later, someone else joined in: Johnny's mom. I'd had a good relationship with his mother up until this point, and she'd assured me she would stay connected with me and Grace.

But as she stood on my doorstep, she was relentless, knocking right alongside Johnny. Then, she started sending nasty text messages to my phone. This included comments accusing me of being the abusive one and saying I should make Grace go with her dad.

Finally, my friend had had enough of this harassment. She opened the door to Johnny and his mom.

His mom said, "I'm here to get my granddaughter."

My friend replied, "She will not be going with you tonight," and closed the door, locking it behind her.

Even though my friends were with me, I feared for our safety. At 10:27 p.m., I mustered up the courage to call the police and inform dispatch of what has transpired up until this point. I repeated all of the things the Domestic Violence Team (DVAT) told me to say.

"He has access to weapons. There is a history of domestic violence. I am scared for my safety."

Dispatch responded, "Please lock all of your doors and windows, and don't respond to any of their text messages." She added, "We do not currently have any officers available right now."

This was not helpful at all. I'd already done all of those things. Dispatch promised they would send officers as soon as someone became available.

All four of us were confined in my house for hours, not knowing what was going to happen or when police would show up. One of my friends was still breastfeeding her month-old baby daughter. She was worried she would not be able to leave my house to feed the baby. So many unknowns. We tried to keep calm for Grace's sake, but this was especially hard for me, because I was so triggered by what was going on.

As it grew later, we were hopeful the police would be there soon, but there was still no sign of them. After a few hours, Johnny and his mom finally left. I didn't want to keep my friends up all night, so I told them they could go, that we should all probably get some sleep, I thanked them for coming, and we parted ways.

They told me to call them if anything else happened, and I agreed. When I woke up the following morning, there was still no sign of the police, not even a phone call. *This can't be happening,* I thought. *How do the police just not show up, or at the very least, call?*

Later that day, on August 27, 2020, at 4:09 p.m., an officer from our local police service walked up to my yard. I was standing on my step. He asked, "Why are we here?"

I thought to myself, *Great question, Officer. I, too, am also wondering what you are doing here. Sixteen hours after the incident, you are kind of late to the game.*

I was so furious about their response time. Nonetheless, I explained what had occurred the night before. My friend from across the street came over. She, too, was upset about their terrible response time. I kept thinking to myself, *We could have been dead inside. For this many hours, nobody would have known. Who would have been accountable to this? It could have been prevented. But so can domestic violence as a whole.*

As I was talking to the officer, I told him about the audio recording of Johnny dragging Grace out of my vehicle the night prior. He refused to listen to it, telling me, "This isn't a police issue."

My friend and I asked, "If it's not your issue, whose is it?"

He replied, "Children's Services," adding, "I would suggest you hire a lawyer and speak to Children's Services." They left shortly after, saying, as they always do, "If anything else happens, call us back."

My friend asked them before he left, "How come it took you so long to respond?"

The officer replied, "I am not sure. It's something we should look into."

My friend, having worked for Children's Services, was so confused, so she called her supervisor to confirm whether this was indeed a child-welfare issue. She didn't think it was. She called her supervisor and explained the situation, seeking further clarification.

Her supervisor replied, "You have done everything you need to do to keep Grace safe." There was nothing more we could do, and this was proving not to be a child-welfare issue.

Looking back on it now, I feel like I had been gaslighting myself, fighting an entire system, while trying to ensure my daughter's safety. I kept wondering, *Am I crazy? Is this even real? How come nobody believes me or is doing anything about this? When is enough, enough? Do I need bruises to show them to make it real, or worse?*

I reminded myself of the presentation I'd attended on domestic violence and reassured myself that this *was* domestic violence. People were just choosing not to see it, likely because of their own perception of what it was, rather than the reality.

I can't help but wonder if this is one of the many reasons people don't report to police. The result has been cases being underreported and death rates continuing to increase.

Even after all of this, I was still expected to coparent with someone like Johnny. A few days later, I reached out to him about a remaining balance on Grace's dental bill that needed to be paid. The dental office told me, if it was not paid that day, they were going to send it to collections. This was the last thing I needed, as I was trying to rebuild my life and did not need any more stressors or headaches.

I came up with the money myself and paid the balance off. Johnny never responded or helped pay for this bill. Grace continued to act out scenes for a few weeks after the incident, as she played with her Barbies.

As I watched her play one day, she invented a scenario that involved the police. She looked at me and said, "My dad hates the police. He calls them pigs."

I felt so lost and unheard. Grasping at anything I could do to make this situation go away, I thought maybe I should follow up with Children's Services, to see if there was anything they could help me with, despite my friend confirming there was nothing they could do.

The lady I spoke to was nice. She explained, if they were to open an investigation, they would have to investigate both parents. I told her I would be okay with that. I'm not sure what happened after that conversation, but I never heard from them again.

Grace began seeing a counselor for a period of time. During one of the appointments, the counselor informed me that she'd attempted to communicate with Children's Services, in order to try to gain access to any information Children's Services had on file about Grace. However, upon her consultation, children's services informed the counselor they had nothing on file, and there was no documentation of interventions or conversations had. This was another cause for concern.

(People have an obligation to document. How were there no files attached to our case, even if a file was never open?)

# Chapter 18

## New School Year, a Pandemic, and Continuous Chaos

At the beginning of the 2020-21 school year, Covid-19 was still lurking, but children had returned to school and life seemed to be functioning in our new normal. A new school year always seemed like a reset, something I looked forward to. There was more structure and routine, especially after coming out of the pandemic, when everyone's routine was thrown off and we all had to pivot to create a new one.

One afternoon, I received a phone call from Grace's teacher. She said, "Grace told me today she was scared that her dad was going to come to the school and take her. I was hoping you could provide more information."

I explained to the teacher what was going on and why Grace might be feeling that way, though the schools were locked to any visitors. I described the incident from August 26, 2020, when Grace had been dragged out of my vehicle, something I believe caused tremendous trauma. I also told the teacher I had an appointment with a lawyer later that day and would keep them informed of anything that transpired.

The teacher told me, "Any legal documentation you have, the school will need a copy of that."

I promised I would share anything I received.

Then she asked, "Would you be comfortable if Grace accessed the school counselor? It may be helpful for her."

I definitely supported this. Getting Grace counseling support had been really difficult with Johnny involved, so the more support she had at school, the better.

The following day, I received a call from the school counselor. She was a lovely woman with a genuine concern for Grace and her wellbeing. The teacher had brought her up to speed on what had occurred the day before and all I'd shared in our conversation. I provided her with some additional information, thinking, *Here I go again, telling the same story for the fiftieth time.*

The counselor promised she'd be more aware of Grace and who was around the school, and that she'd do her best to keep her safe. The counselor remembered how difficult Johnny had been about approving Grace to get into some sort of counseling last year and said she would check in with Grace tomorrow. At the very least, I hoped this would provide Grace the reassurance and safety she needed to continue showing up at school and focusing on her learning, instead of worrying about her safety.

Later that night, during our bedtime routine, Grace and I hunkered down to read a book. Afterward, she began to cry, saying "I don't want to go to school tomorrow. I am scared my dad is going to come and take me,"

I reassured her it would be okay. How the school doors were locked and the staff was there to help keep her safe."

Grace still struggled to sleep. She paced around for hours, going in and out of her bedroom.

I noticed how the skin on her hands, around her fingers had been chewed to the point where they looked raw. She asked me repeatedly to make sure the front door was locked and the blinds were closed. This became a common theme for years afterward.

Grace asked for tape, and when I asked what for, she said, "I want to tape the corner of my blinds to the window frame." She was so fearful, adding, "I don't want my dad to see in my room." Grace worried that her dad would climb to her bedroom window in the middle of the night, since her bedroom window faced the street, and continued this fear for years.

No matter how many times I tried to reassure her that she was safe and that he wouldn't do that, nothing eased her mind. I told her, "If he ever came to our house and tried to climb in the window, I will call the police."

Grace's trust in the police was waning. She often said, "Why would we call them? They don't come anyway." I had the same thought.

Some nights, Grace would pace, coming out of her room every hour after bedtime, because she was scared and couldn't sleep. We would talk about safety. Wash, rinse, repeat. This was exhausting but something I had to do. It got to the point where, for a while, she slept on the couch in the living room, where she felt most secure.

When I asked her what made the living room feel safer, she always replied, "The window doesn't face the street." Our living room window faced the backyard, and the gate was locked, which meant it was much harder to gain access to this window than her bedroom window. Especially from her perspective.

Grace and I also had discussions around drawing, journalling, and what other ideas she thought could be helpful ways for her to cope. Grace kept a journal in her room. She had used it infrequently, but after our conversation, she began the journalling process. I found one of her journal entries that included a picture.

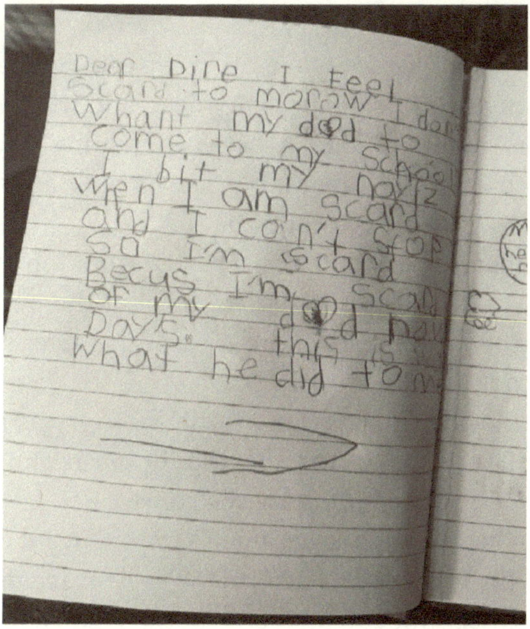
Dear Dire I Feel
Scard to morow I
whant my dad to
come to my
I bit my
when I am scard
and I can't stop
so I'm scard
Becus I'm
of my
Days.
what he did to

DAD
Mom
me
help me

A few days later, Grace woke up in a panic. She said to me, "I had a dream my dad had a gun to my head and tried to hurt me."

There was minimal contact between Johnny and Grace for about a month after her dream, but it was only a matter of time before the crisis cycle would continue.

In November, I received a text message from Johnny saying, "I want to see Grace." He requested we meet at the police station. I agreed to meet with him but informed him that Grace had made it clear she did not want to see him.

I was flooded with an intense guilt. Here I was again, going against what Grace has told me, including her recent nightmares, all because I felt the need to please the courts.

A dark cloud loomed over me. I was worried what would happen if I didn't bring her, because the system seemed to protect the abusers and continue to further victimize the victims.

When Grace and I pulled up to the police station and parked in the safe pick-up zone, Grace refused to get out of the car. Johnny remained in his vehicle, parked next to mine, and sent me a text message. "I am not getting out of my vehicle until Grace gets out."

Grace was adamant she was not getting out of the vehicle. I waited in mine with Grace, feeling conflicted as to why we were there. I watched a police van pull into the parking lot and then release someone from the back. I recognized the officer. As he approached my vehicle, I felt a sense of relief, but also confusion as to why he was coming up to me. Johnny must have called the police.

The officer came to my window and said, "Is everything okay? We received a call, and as soon as I saw your name in the system, I wanted to be the officer to respond."

I was so grateful for him. I had a small glimmer of hope that maybe this officer would actually make something happen. Whatever that "something" was. *Maybe this will be the last of our police interactions*. When he asked for additional information, I retold my story for what seemed like the hundredth time.

The officer asked, "Do you have a police clause in your parenting order?"

I replied, "Yes, we do." He asked to see it, so I pulled it up on my phone and handed it to him. The officer then opened the back door on my driver's side and spoke to Grace, asking her what she wanted.

Grace said, "I don't want to go to my dad's." When the officer asked her why, she said, "He abuses me." The officer indicated that was all he needed and went over to Johnny's vehicle to inform him of this.

Johnny stepped out of the vehicle and spoke to the officer, while I stood outside of mine. Johnny demanded the officer physically remove Grace from my vehicle and put her into his. The officer refused, stating, "I am not going to physically take her and put her into yours. I can't do that."

Next came a conversation between the officer, myself, and Johnny. Johnny's partner, Rosie, was in the passenger seat of his vehicle. When the topic of abuse was mentioned, it appeared to trigger Johnny. In front of the officer, he said, "You don't know what abuse is. You make this all about you."

I replied, "I am afraid of you."

Johnny continued, "Have I ever hit you? No, I've never abused you."

I said, "There are different types of abuse, and you pushed me once. If abuse wasn't present, why did I have the Domestic Violence Action Team staff present with me at court?"

He replied, "I put my hand on your shoulder and turned you around so you would look at me."

No matter what I said, it fell on deaf ears. The police didn't seem to be too alarmed by these statements, either, similar to my interactions with our local police service.

Johnny stood outside of his vehicle and looked at Rosie, then demanded she step out of the vehicle. It almost felt like he needed back up. I wondered what was going on in their relationship. Acting and speaking that way to his partner in front of an officer was concerning.

After two hours talking in the parking lot, the officer informed Johnny it was not in the child's best interest to have Grace go with him. But he added, "This is a family court matter, not a police matter." As we'd heard before.

I advised the officer that we had court coming up the following week, to which he replied, "I hope you figure it out then."

Johnny got back into his vehicle. As the officer and I walked to the other side of my car, he said, "That guy is difficult to deal with." *Tell me about it*, I thought.

A few days later, Grace said, "I don't want to be alive anymore. This is all too hard on me." Another gut punch to the stomach.

This is not the first time she had made comments like this, but they were becoming more regular, which caused me more concern. I felt like I couldn't do anything to make her feel better or eliminate this ongoing circus around her. Grace also became more vocal about the abuse that had occurred with her father, and she shared about it with others, no matter to whom. It was like she had verbal diarrhea and would talk to anyone who would listen. Sometimes, she would even open a conversation with statements about it before even knowing the person.

I was made aware of this when one of her friend's moms told me about it. The mom approached me during Grace's birthday party. As the kids were playing, she said, "Chelsey, I wanted to ask you something Grace disclosed to us the other day. Is it true that her dad abuses her?"

I confirmed what I knew. I was actually grateful Grace was talking about what had happened, that she now felt safe enough to do so, but it was important to recognize who she was disclosing things to. Some people did not have the capacity to understand or deal with it, especially one of her peers.

Grace and I soon had a conversation about the importance of talking about what had happened only to safe, trusted adults. That there were times when it wasn't so appropriate to share, like in a room full of children her age, since they often wouldn't know what to do or say. It would be a lot of information for someone their age.

Grace also started to say things like, "I have secrets, but if I tell you, I am scared my dad will go to jail." I didn't want to force that conversation or make her tell me, but in the back of my mind I was so worried. *What could this possibly mean? What are these secrets? Is something more happening that I do need to be aware of for safety concerns?*

Grace and Johnny had had no in-person contact for a number of weeks when he decided to have a call via FaceTime. I made sure to stay within earshot, just in case. While they were having a conversation about hot takeout lunches, she said to her dad, "We didn't order yet."

Johnny said, "I will pay for it, but you have to come home first."

I thought, *What a way to manipulate this poor child,* especially because she had not been to her dad's in quite some time. Grace told him she was still thinking about when she might be ready to go back there.

Johnny said, "Your friends are waiting for you. They keep asking where you are." He then asked if he could get her tomorrow, to spend some time with her, adding, "I'll bring you back in the evening."

At the time, she appeared excited, saying, "I can't wait to see my dog." They made plans for her to be picked up from school the following day.

The next day, I dropped Grace off at school and wished her the best day. "Have fun with your dad. I'll see you later tonight!"

Grace asked, "When will I be brought home?"

I replied, "I'm not sure. You will have to ask your dad." Grace went on her way into the school.

It was a Friday, which meant the kids had a half day for the kids and the bell rang to go home at 11:25 a.m.

At 11:31 a.m., I received a call from Grace's teacher. She said, "Grace told me that her dad was coming to get her from school today. She is in the office having a panic attack. She is hyperventilating and says she does not want to go anymore." She added, "Grace asked me to call you."

I asked whether she gave the teacher a reason as to why she did not want to go.

"She said her dad abuses her."

I thought to myself, *Perfect. She just disclosed to someone else who has a duty to report.*

I asked, "Has anyone from the school reported that or do they plan to, knowing what they know now?"

The teacher said she would speak to the school counselor.

At the same time, I received a call from Johnny. I told the teacher, "Johnny is calling me. Can I call you back?" Then, I took the call.

"Where is Grace?" he demanded. As though he'd assumed I picked her up and took her.

I told him, "She's in the office. She does not want to go with you."

The school called back to say that Johnny was now at the front door of the school, ringing the buzzer. The teacher stayed on the phone with me while the assistant principal went out to speak with Johnny. She said, "Grace does not feel safe to go with her dad today. Are you able to come pick her up? I am not sure what to do."

I said, "Yes, once Johnny leaves the property. I do not feel comfortable going to the school while he is still there. I also fear for my safety."

The teacher should have known this, but I directed her to report this incident, since she had an obligation to report the disclosed abuse. I thought, *It should not be my job to remind professionals who and what they should be reporting.*

I received another call from the school shortly afterward, informing me that the school counselor had called their police liaison to seek guidance. She'd said, "The police told me this is not a police issue and they don't want to get involved. They said it's a family court issue."

After Johnny left school property, I went to pick Grace up. The school counselor greeted me at the front door and explained that, based on how Grace's body was responding, she was traumatized and triggered. She also informed me that she'd placed a call to Children's Services. "Children's Services told me there has been no file opened or any reports on file. The only thing they could see is one conversation you had with them in 2018."

This was interesting, because I knew that Grace's previous counselor had placed a call to Children's Services, as well.

The school counselor expressed her concern, adding, "There does not seem to be a documentation trail anywhere. Trust has to be rebuilt between Grace and her dad." Then, she recommended supervised visits as a starting point. I informed her that this was something I had considered as well and planned to ask for at our next court date, which was scheduled in a few days.

The next morning, Grace woke up and said she did not want to see her dad. I asked what it would take for her to be ready to see him. She replied, "Maybe when I'm older."

"What would be different from today, when you are older?"

"When I am older, I will be stronger," she replied. "And I will be able to tell him that if he hurts me again, I won't ever want to see him again."

When I asked her how she was feeling right now, she said, "I'm just not ready now, Mom."

"Do you feel comfortable telling your dad that?"

She immediately said no. "If I tell him, he will be sad."

Hearing her say this broke my heart. I couldn't imagine being in her shoes, thinking that if she was just big enough and strong enough, she would be able to change the outcome and stand up for herself. Children her age should not be thinking in those terms, but unfortunately, it was our reality. It was interesting to see her worry so much about hurting her dad's feelings if she was honest with him, despite the way he had made her feel over the years.

A few days later, Grace approached me and said she missed seeing her dad. I offered to arrange something with him for her. She told me she was too scared. I offered a safer option and suggested Facetime. She refused, saying she was too scared she would get yelled at.

Over the next days, Grace continued to mention missing her dad, but anytime I offered a solution or to find a way for her to have contact with Johnny while feeling safe, she rejected the idea.

On one occasion, she told me she wanted to wait until she was in grade four. I asked what difference that would make. She again said she'd be stronger and older, but then added that she wanted to take Taekwondo, so she could fight back, if he tried to hurt her.

When Johnny FaceTimed Grace a few days later, it did not go well. I was putting laundry away in my room, staying within earshot so I'd have a clear understanding of how the conversation went and stood ready to intervene if I had to.

Johnny said, "You never apologized for what you did the other day. Don't you see how excited I was to see you?" I moved closer to the stairs, so I could hear the conversation clearer. He continued, "What you did at school the other day was uncalled for. You never once said you were sorry."

I looked down to the second floor, where Grace was sitting on the couch in the living room. She gazed up at me and then sheepishly apologized. Next, her body folded into the couch; it appeared as though she felt worthless and ashamed. What she feared became the conversation.

I walked over and told her she did not have to apologize for what had happened. My blood was boiling. *How could this man say something like that to her? Why can't he take accountability for what he's done? He's the reason she feels this way, yet he has the audacity to blame her!*

I wanted to say something to him, but the weight of "don't cause a scene" was heavy. I didn't want the courts to think I was preventing Johnny access, because they were adamant that both parents needed to have contact with her when they were with the other parent. In hindsight, I wish I'd fought harder, but the system was stacked against me. I was still building myself up, too.

Grace ran upstairs to her room, upset, as Johnny said, "I'm coming to pick you up on Tuesday, and you better not cause a scene." When the phone conversation ended, she said in a panic, "Mom, I can't go with him. I'm too scared."

Later that night, she could not fall asleep. She blamed herself, repeatedly saying, "I should have just gone with him that day. Then, he wouldn't be doing this to me." She paced the hallway, coming out of her room numerous times. She said she was worried, and that her dad made her feel like it's all her fault. We had conversations about how this was not her fault, and that it's an adult's job to make children feel safe. I'm not sure she understood the message fully, but it would be a message I had to repeat for years to come.

The next day, I received a message from Johnny saying he would be at the police station, waiting for me to bring Grace. I explained it was not in the best interest of Grace right now to force time together. At 7:27 p.m., I received a call from an officer with our local police service, asking me what was going on. My stomach sank. *Of course he called the police on me. Here we go again.*

A few months before this, I was so desperate to find solutions that a friend reached out to me about a private investigator she'd used. She'd suggested I look into that, too. With nothing left to lose, I contacted the investigator to see what support, if any, he could provide. Then, I met the investigator at his house. He suggested I make a timeline to help him understand what had happened from start to finish, so I did. This timeline actually came in handy when I was on the phone with this officer.

I told him, "This has nothing to do with me withholding her. It has everything to do with the fact that he has caused her to feel scared and traumatized. I want them to have a relationship, but I am not going to continue to traumatize her and force her to spend time with him when she is feeling this way. No parent would." I also informed him that the school was involved, and even the school counselor asked Johnny to seek professional help. They'd said Grace should attend additional counseling, as well. The officer seemed receptive, which I was grateful for.

The officer told me he would not make Grace go with her dad today and hoped she got the help she needed. I asked the officer, "What happens after this? What are you going to do with this information?"

He replied, "I will be documenting this and entering it into our system." Before the conversation ended, he added, "Johnny plans on getting Grace tomorrow. That probably won't happen, will it?"

I said, "No. Nothing has changed. We have a child who is fearful of her father due to what has happened, and you can clearly hear the distress in her voice in the incident of him dragging her out of my car that I recorded last August. It is not very trauma-informed to put her through this all the time and ask her, time and time again, why she does not want to go to her dad's."

What baffled me the most was, despite my disclosing the audio recording, not a single officer asked to listen to it or seemed the least bit interested in learning more. I never understood why. I also informed the officer before this about this ongoing issue of the police responding and having conversations with Grace and me. I expressed my frustration about the abuse being disclosed, yet nothing being done.

I say to the officer, "It's not going to make Grace believe that police are there to protect her. She may stop telling her story one day." I was proud of myself for saying that I did, though he didn't respond. I kept thinking, *If the police don't see anything wrong with this, how is anyone else going to see anything wrong?* I felt so defeated, but I was going to keep fighting.

A few days later, Grace said to me, "Mom, my dad really tried to kill me that day."

I can't imagine how she is feeling. As a mom, we feel things deeply, especially when it relates to our children, and it's ten-times worse when we feel like we can't do anything about it.

Later that night, as Grace was getting ready for bed, she started to worry about sleep. She had troubles sleeping and came out of her room numerous times, saying, "I keep having nightmares." I asked her what about. "Something happens to you, so I get kidnapped and left all alone." She added how she had nightmares every night.

The next day, she said she misses her dad. I asked if she would like to see him. She said, "Yes, but I am too scared he will hurt me." I asked if she would go with him tomorrow if he came to pick her up. She began to cry, pleading, "Please don't let him try to come pick me up. I'm too scared!"

I called the Domestic Violence Action Team (DVAT) for advice, because I was at a loss of what to do. I so badly wanted to keep my daughter safe, but I didn't want to get into trouble and be deemed as someone who was "withholding" our child.

Grace said to me later that day, "If my dad wants to see me, he needs to agree to supervised visits to earn my trust back." I was proud of her for recognizing this and establishing her boundaries, but I was not sure how this would go, if I were to bring it up. This had been discussed at some point, but there was never any follow through during any of our court appearances.

A few days before Christmas, Grace and I were driving to my parents' house so I could go to work while school was closed for the break. As we are driving, Grace randomly said, "I don't know why I'm not allowed to talk about you at my dad's house. Rosie is there, but she is not my mom. I should be able to talk about you there." I agreed. She continued, "I told my dad that Rosie was not my stepmom, and he got mad and threw me in my room."

I asked how did he throw her into her room. She replied, "He grabbed my shoulder like you would grab a doll and threw me in my room." Her words were quite descriptive.

After work, I returned to my parents to pick up Grace. My grandma (Grace's great-grandma) watched Grace for the day while I was at work. My grandma was living with my parents at the time, as she'd just moved back from Manitoba after the loss of our grandpa. Grace spent quite a bit of time with her.

That day, I visited with my grandma for a bit and caught up on how Grace had been. She said Grace was quite aggressive toward her and had yelled at her. "My feelings were a bit hurt, because of the way she was treating me today."

I knew this wasn't typical behavior from Grace, but I didn't like hearing about how she was treating my grandma. We know children become products of their environment, but this was not how I wanted her to treat people.

Once Grace and I got back to our house, I attempted to have a conversation with her about her behavior. She became defensive and said she didn't want to talk about it. I knew it was not the time to have this discussion, but I wanted her to know it was not okay to treat our grandma that way. I knew deep down something more was going on for her, but at her age, it was likely hard to articulate. She would feel like she was getting in trouble for her outbursts. It was a delicate balance, holding her accountable, while recognizing she was trying to express her feelings, even if it wasn't in a healthy way.

# Chapter 19

## The Doctor's Note

We attended the doctor's appointment on January 14, 2021. Fortunately, our family doctor was an incredible human. He truly listened and had a ton of compassion for his patients. We weren't just a number to him.

I explained to him what was going on, and his facial expression said more than his words ever could. He asked Grace if he could examine her. She nodded yes.

I told him about the abuse Grace has disclosed to me and others, including the incident when her father had dragged her out of my vehicle and the countless sleepless nights.

Grace was still quite young at this time, around eight years of age, but she was able to answer the few questions he asked her. My doctor provided me with a note:

*It has been divulged to me that Grace has been experiencing physical abuse at the hands of her father. She is experiencing anxiety attacks as a result of these abuses. She has also discussed suicide ideation. It is my professional opinion that a No Contact order between Grace and her father be instated.*

*Grace needs ongoing professional help and counseling and is awaiting an assessment by a child psychiatrist. This No Contact Order should be in place until Grace has received the appropriate treatment. Please contact me if you should require further information.*

While I appreciated my doctor's efforts, what I found interesting was, even in this instance, it was about Grace getting the help she needed. *What about the abusers getting the help they need, so they don't continue to inflict harm on others?* Don't get me wrong, help for her was necessary. But *what was expected of him?*

It turned out this letter didn't do much for us, but I stored it with all of my documentation, nonetheless. Nobody seemed to bat an eye that we now had a family doctor recommending no visitation.

# Chapter 20

## "We Could Arrest You..."

At 9:00 p.m. that evening, an officer from our local police service showed up at my house, which surprised me. To myself, I thought, *Now what?*

I knew this officer with the downtown policing unit from working in the downtown core. I felt relieved. Maybe, just maybe, he would listen to me and help me navigate this situation.

In my doorway, he said, "We received a call from Johnny indicating you did not return Grace today."

My blood started to boil, and my heart was racing. Trying to keep my cool, I explained the history to him, including the abuse that had occurred and why my child did not want to see her father. Grace was standing at the top of the stairway and I pointed up to her, telling the officer, "Grace is right there. Why don't you have a conversation with her and ask why she doesn't want to go?" I described the last interaction between Grace and Johnny, when he blamed her and made her apologize for not going with him, when he tried to take her from school. "Furthermore," I said, "I've offered to set up FaceTime conversations with her, but she has declined."

The officer said, "You know, Chelsey, this is the fifth time we have responded to this situation. We could arrest you." My heart started racing faster.

On one hand, I was afraid of what might happen, if I retaliated. *Am I going to be arrested if I say something? Or will he arrest me and take me away right on the spot? What grounds does he have? For protecting my child? Where will Grace go, if I do get taken away?* On the other hand, I was so fucking tired of trying to explain and plead for someone to help me. I just wanted to let loose.

I decided to remain calm yet firm, and I said, "How many more women and children are going to die by domestic violence before you guys choose to do something about it? I've been documenting this for over ten years, and you have not done anything with it."

He stood in my doorway, pompously, with his arms crossed, leaning up against my door frame, and said nothing.

I continued, "I have audio recordings of Johnny dragging Grace out of my vehicle, and her screaming and begging for her life. So loud, his neighbors came out and asked if we were okay. Not one of you have asked to hear that."

Finally, he said, "Did you get the neighbor witnesses' information or statement?"

I asked, "Why would I get that? It's your job to investigate. Grace is traumatized, and she's being retraumatized through having to tell her story over and over again. Soon, she is not going to trust police. It's no wonder people don't come forward." I wasn't done yet. "Johnny continues to find roundabout ways to gain access to Grace, despite her being very clear with her messaging. She does not want to see him, and she does not feel safe. Nobody is listening to the fact that she *does not feel safe.* Do you find any of this concerning?" No response. "Children's Services has been called, too."

Then, he sighed and asked what I hoped for, in the future. *Like I haven't just told him.*

I said, "What I want is for Johnny to get the help he needs, so that he can create a safe space for Grace and him to build a relationship. I want him to be a healthy parent and to parent in a healthy manner. I want them to have a relationship, but not at the expense of her mental health."

I described for him the interaction at the police station, when Johnny wanted Grace to be removed from my vehicle and put into his. I said, "Grace told the officer that she felt scared, and when the officer asked why, she told him because her dad abused her."

This officer disagreed. "No. He said in his report that Grace would not disclose why she felt unsafe."

That was an outright lie. *How could that officer omit such important information from his report?* I told the officer in my doorway that was a lie, that I was standing right there when the conversation took place and heard the entire thing.

The officer didn't seem bothered by this. I felt like everyone was trying to avoid or dance around the fact that this was domestic violence. Perhaps the officers didn't want to do the work associated with domestic violence. Maybe they were lazy. But if there's one sure way to prevent homicides, it's to do proper domestic violence investigations.

I was furious, feeling so small when the officer told me this. *I just want to scream.*

The officer sighed again and asked me to send him the audio recording. "Now I have a bunch of paperwork to do when I get back to the office," he added.

I thought to myself, *That is literally your job and what you get paid good money to do.*

"Do you want this to be investigated?"

I replied, "Yes."

He explained I would have to bring Grace down to the station. As if this was some type of scare tactic or would deter me from following through. I thought, *Isn't this your job, to investigate whether I want you to or not? I wonder if they ask people charged with a crime, whether they want an investigation or not.*

I then asked, "Is the station even open right now?"

"It should be open." The station was usually only open until 7:00 p.m. for walk-in hours, so it was clear he wasn't aware.

I then asked, "Why won't you have the conversation with Grace now? She's right here."

"If you want to open an investigation, you have to call dispatch."

*What the hell? You're an officer, standing in my doorway, responding to a call. Now,* I *have to call dispatch? This makes no sense.* One barrier after another.

I told him I had already tried the dispatch approach over the summer. He said, "That report was from July 2020."

I told him I spoke to the sergeant in charge who was working that day, since I was concerned about the abuse I'd witnessed, along with what Grace disclosed. The sergeant on duty minimized my call, saying, "You know, sometimes kids just don't like the rules at their other parent's house, because one parent lets them play Xbox all day, while the other one doesn't."

I had called about the abuse, which was specific to this situation and had nothing to do with rules. The sergeant's final comment was, "Do you want to open an investigation? Or is this a child who was upset at her parents?"

I'd felt like nobody believed me. I was scared to open an investigation because the police and legal systems felt like they were stacked against me. All I wanted to do was keep my child safe and be an advocate. I felt like I was getting nowhere and was being bullied and made to feel stupid by every officer that I talked to. When I hung up the phone, I had very little clarity around how to proceed.

I was getting madder by the minute, though. I used the Department of Justice's definition of abuse, domestic violence, and behaviors of children, then the Government of Alberta's definition of child abuse.

The officer in my doorway said, "Is there anything Johnny can be charged with under the criminal code?"

*Are you fucking kidding me? It's your job as a police officer to know the criminal code, not mine!*

I replied, "I'm not sure, but even if it's not criminal in nature, there is still enough evidence that abuse has occurred!" For whatever it was worth, I added's Grace sentiment that she only wanted to her see her dad once she was older, so that she'd be bigger and stronger and could fight back, if necessary.

The officer said, "Well, that's unrealistic." I asked him what he meant by that. "She may never be able to do that." As he left, his final comment was, "You'll hear from me tomorrow after 6:00 p.m. I am on nights."

He'd also promised to send the audio recording to the domestic violence team with their police service. That seemed like the right unit to deal with this issue. *At least there is something I can hold onto,* I thought. *Maybe I am getting somewhere.*

I didn't hear from him the next day. In fact, I never heard from him again. Nor did any officer ever follow up with me.

After the officer left, Grace began to panic. "Are you going to go to jail?" she asked.

Although I was scared, I comforted her and told her no, I wouldn't go to jail. Though I did think, *I didn't get arrested this time, but when would be the next time?*

A few days later, on Christmas day, Grace had as nightmare and crawled into bed with me. The next morning, I asked her what her nightmare was about. She replied, "My dad was hurting people. Everyone was killed, and I was left alone."

# Chapter 21

## The Trauma Becomes More Visible

A few days after Christmas, Johnny asked to FaceTime Grace, but she didn't want to. Johnny replied via text message, "Okay. I love and miss you, Grace."

Later that night, Grace and I were playing Monopoly. When she struggled to figure out what 10+5 was, I attempted to help her, but she went from 0 to 100 real quick. She was so overwhelmed with emotions, she yelled, saying she was under a lot of stress and could not think.

My heart broke for her. I felt so helpless. I so badly wanted to fix this for her and make all of her worries, nightmares, and fears disappear, but I knew that was impossible. It was not something I could immediately take away, no matter how badly I wanted to. During these tense moments, it was hard not to get frustrated, because these situations and emotions triggered me, too, in more ways than I initially realized.

We were both traumatized and our bodies were reacting. My rational mind knew that reacting would not get us anywhere and would only make things worse. I did my best to control myself and walk away until she had deescalated and was able to have conversations with me. Later that night, as we were getting ready for bed, Grace asked me to tell her dad that she loved him.

I asked her why couldn't she be the one to tell him that. She replied, "I don't want to talk to him. I don't think I will ever be strong enough. I should have just gone that day, so this wouldn't have happened."

I asked her what she thought would have happened if she went. She replied, "I don't know."

In the days that followed, Johnny sent text messages for Grace to my phone, saying he loved her. During the holidays, the messages were focused on the gifts waiting for her at his house. I thought these must be so confusing for her, because his actions and words did not align. I wondered whether Grace saw the same patterns of behavior that I did and wondered what was going on in her little mind.

A few days later, she was playing with her toys as I observed from afar. She turned in my direction and said, "Mom, I'm supposed to slap you in the face" numerous times.

*What?* I was concerned but also curious where this came from. I tried to remain calm, as I knew deep down this wasn't her, that it was coming from somewhere.

We may question why our children want to express those feelings to someone who has harmed them. I did, too, despite knowing what I do about trauma. It's important to identify what trauma is and how the trauma bond can show up in relationships. Without getting too academic, it's important to understand what trauma is.

Trauma çomes from the Greek word *trauma,* which means "wound." (Rousseau, D. n.d.) It is an emotional response to a terrible event, like an accident, crime, natural disaster, physical or emotional abuse, neglect, experiencing or witnessing violence, death of a loved one, and more. (Rousseau, D. n.d.)

Dr. Gabor Maté echoes this definition when he says trauma is an internalized event. Two people can experience the same thing, but the outcomes can be vastly different, because of the way we experience the trauma.

Bessel Van der Kolk notes, "Trauma is not the story of something that happened back then. It's the current imprint of that pain, horror, and fear living inside people." According to the American Psychological Association (2025), trauma is defined as any disturbing experience that results in significant fear, helplessness, dissociation, confusion, or other disruptive feelings intense enough to have a long-lasting negative effect on a person's attitudes, behavior, and other aspects of functioning.

It's important to consider the role trauma plays in attachment and the correlation with attachment theory. According to the Canadian Department of Justice (2023), trauma-coerced attachment, also known as trauma bonding, is focused on the dynamic relationship between coercive control tactics, intermittent rewards and punishment, and exploitation of the power imbalance between victim and perpetrator. Victims who have experienced this type of trauma bond suffer emotional, physical, and mental exploitation, which can impact their safety and wellbeing. Furthermore, trauma-coerced attachment is a powerful relationship that is dynamic and constantly changing, and the attachment can last long after the relationship ends. It compels the victim to protect the perpetrator and submit to continued exploitation, even when the victim has every reason not to.

I wish judges were able to recognize this for what it is and not force parental contact at the expense of children who have experienced trauma.

One day, my friend and I were visiting when she asked, "Have you noticed Grace chewing her fingers and her hair a lot recently?"

I hadn't given it much thought because of everything else going on, but that question hit me square in the face. After some reflection, I recognized she was right. Grace was constantly putting her hair in her mouth and chewing on the skin around her fingernails. There were times when her poor fingers looked raw.

Whenever I asked her if they hurt, she always said no. But I wasn't always sure I believed her. Still, I didn't want to make her feel like I was coercing her to believe or feel something she wasn't.

According to the Victim Service Unit with the Edmonton Police Service, typical physiological symptoms of trauma in children aged seven to eleven are sleep disturbances, nightmares, and night terrors. They describe emotional behavioral reactions as irritability, disobedience, school phobia, and aggressive behaviors.

Signs were being displayed right in front of me. I could no longer ignore them. *How come nobody else pays attention to this or notices these red flags?*

# Chapter 22

## Another Year, Another Battle

We were only a few days into 2022 when Johnny asked to FaceTime with Grace. We still had not resumed our regular parenting schedule from the 2018 order, given everything that had happened. The relationship between Grace and Johnny had continued to fracture over time.

I knew I should go back to court, but the process was so daunting. I kept holding onto hope that something would give. What that something was, I wasn't sure or at whose expense. During their FaceTime conversation, I overheard Johnny tell Grace, "When you are ready, you can come home [referring to his house]. We have lots of presents here for you."

Grace asked to see them, so he showed her then said, "You have even more presents at your grandpa's house."

During the call, Grace asked me if she could go to her dad's house on the following Saturday, if he wasn't working. Johnny confirmed he was not working. After the call, I was curious as to what made Grace change her mind about seeing Johnny, since she had been adamant about not wanting to go there.

Grace replied, "We will be with other family members, and I won't have to stay long." I would become quite familiar with this new pattern of behavior, where she navigated how to feel safe around her father.

That night, Grace came into my room because she'd had a nightmare. The following morning, I asked what her nightmare was about. She said, "My dad tried to hurt me."

A few days later, Grace attended counseling with the school counselor. The counselor had promised to speak with Johnny and attempt to get his consent. It wasn't an easy battle, but over time, the counselor was successful.

Grace continued to put hair in her mouth. Later that night, I woke up from a deep sleep to find Grace standing in my doorway. When I asked what was wrong, she said, "I heard someone at my window."

I walked her back to her room and took a look outside of her window. There was nothing there. I reassured her there was nothing there, that it may have been the wind, and that we were safe. She came into my room a few more times that night, saying she was scared, and I had to tuck her back in. This was the first of her many sleepless nights.

A few nights later, Grace ended up in my bed in the middle of the night, saying she'd had a nightmare. The following morning, as I always did, I asked what her nightmare was about. She said, "I had a nightmare that my dad crawled up to my bedroom window and took me from my bedroom."

We had numerous conversations after this about how her window was pretty high off the ground, on the third floor of our house, so it would be hard for anyone to gain access. But Grace remained adamant that her dad would bring a ladder and climb up. I reassured her, if that were to happen, I would call the police. Grace replied, "The police never come." The relationship breakdown between Grace and the police and her lack of trust in them was justified, at this point.

During one of our conversations, Grace became upset. When I asked what was wrong, she said, "I miss my dad." When I reassured her we could see him on Saturday, she began to cry and put her head down. She wouldn't tell me why, so I asked if she was scared. She started to cry harder and said, "Yes!"

"You can always change your mind, if you don't feel like you are ready," I told her.

"I'm scared of hurting my dad's feelings."

I hate that she was so worried about hurting his feelings, when she had been through hell and back. I wouldn't typically tell someone to disregard another's feelings, but this situation was different.

"You don't have to worry about hurting his feelings. He's an adult. You need to worry about your own feelings, especially if you're feeling scared."

Then she opened up. "My dad tells me, if I don't eat all of my food, he will shove it down my throat." This was not the first time she had mentioned this to me. Initially, I didn't think much of it, but after hearing it repeatedly, I figured there must be more truth to this story. *Why would she lie about something like that?*

Grace continued to worry that her dad was going to climb up her window and take her, leading to more sleepless nights or her having a hard time falling asleep. Eventually, I recorded her concerns on my cell phone, hoping someday, someone would listen. However, nobody chose to listen to this video, either or ask me for it when I mentioned it.

Grace had a gap in her blinds where one of our dogs had torn it, trying to look out her window. Because of this gap between above the window frame, she often tried to tape her blinds and put things in her window to block any visual access inside her room, and so she couldn't see outside.

One day, she said to me, "My dreams are all over my bed and walls, and I can't get rid of them."

I wasn't sure what she meant by that, but I didn't ask too many questions. I just wanted to find a way to make this stop. As curious as I was, I didn't want to overwhelm her. We agreed to put up another dream catcher, to see if it would help. I also suggested we smudge her room in the morning, and she agreed.

The following night, Grace ended up in my room, saying she'd had nightmares. This was on a day when Grace and Johnny had FaceTimed. During the conversation, Johnny had told Grace that Santa left a note at his house, asking if she wanted guitar lessons. Grace had nodded her head yes.

I thought this was strange, as Grace had never asked about playing guitar. I'd keep quiet.

Johnny then said, "If you want guitar lessons, it means you have to start coming home to attend your lessons." *Great. Another manipulation tactic. Why couldn't he just acknowledge the wrongdoings, change his behavior and work to build trust with her again? Why does it always have to be like this? Bribing her with gifts, rather than simply building the relationship.*

Grace appeared excited at the opportunity to play guitar. As I listened, Johnny continued, "It's too cold to ride horses, but we can go see them the next time we see each other." (This was in the beginning of January and, in Canada, that can mean pretty cold temperatures.)

Grace looked a bit disappointed, since she was most excited about horses. Then, Johnny started to tell Grace about his education journey and how busy he was. Most of the conversation was focused around him and what he had going on in his life; Grace appeared to dissociate from the conversation, doing something else, like start to play with toys. Sometimes, she would even act more childish by playing peek-a-boo games or pretending to scuba dive, even removing herself from the conversation by putting the phone down. It was so interesting to watch, but it was also telling a story.

Johnny asked, "Do you have school tomorrow?" Then added, "Mama Sally misses you, so we will go see her, too." Grace did not respond. Before the conversation ended, they made plans for

Saturday, and Johnny indicated he would pick her up at 9:00 a.m., without specifying a location. "I'm excited to see you," he said.

After Grace replied, "Okay," he repeated, "I'm really excited!" It was almost like he was leading the conversation so Grace felt pressured to say more than she wanted to. He continued to repeat, "I'm excited" until she finally responded, "I'm more excited."

At bed time, Grace said to me, "I am worried about my dad." When I asked why, she replied, "I told you already, and I don't want to have to tell my story again and again and again."

I felt bad for continuously asking, but I wanted to remain curious rather than assume I knew the answers. Feelings can change.

Grace came into my room again that night, saying she'd had a nightmare about her dad hurting her. I walked her back to her bedroom, reassuring her she was okay and safe, as I tucked her back into bed. These sleepless nights were becoming exhausting, and I wasn't sleeping well when she was in my room, either. As much as I wanted her to feel safe and comfortable, I knew we couldn't continue on like this.

A few nights later, the same thing happened. This time, her nightmare was about her dad trying to kill her. I asked, "Do you feel okay to go with your dad tomorrow?"

She replied, "I don't know." These were such big emotions and things to process as an eight-year-old. I could only imagine how confusing it all was for her.

On Saturday, Grace is scheduled to be picked up at 9:00 a.m. After making no arrangements, at the last minute, Johnny asked if I could meet him somewhere. As Grace and I left the house, she said, "I'm feeling really nervous." I asked her why. "I'm scared to see my dad."

I told her we could meet him at Tim Hortons, and if she changed her mind, it was okay to do so. I wanted her to trust what she was feeling.

When we arrived, Johnny was nowhere to be found. When he pulled up behind us a few minutes later, Grace began to panic and refused to get out of my vehicle. It was like her body had flooded with a traumatic response and all of her alarm bells were ringing.

Johnny texted, "I'm behind you."

Grace turned around and noticed that her dad was no longer there. With a sigh of relief, she said, "He left."

I texted him, "She feels unsafe," to which he responded, "I went through the drive thru to get something." I told this to Grace.

Moments later, he pulled up next to my vehicle, aligning his window with Grace's window in the back. She was slouched in the back seat, avoiding facing him.

When I rolled my window down, Grace sat up, and Johnny said firmly, "Is she coming?"

I again told him, "She doesn't feel safe."

Grace still refused to roll her window down or look in Johnny's direction. As he drove off, he waved and said, "Bye."

Grace started to cry. "I hurt his feelings. He is crying."

I said, "You are also crying, and you can't worry about him right now. You need to honor what you are feeling."

Later, Johnny texted me to ask if he could pick Grace up tomorrow. I explained that her body was responding traumatically and suggested he look into counseling, so he could rebuild trust with her. He disagreed. Grace then asked me if her dad could bring her presents to our house. I told her he wouldn't do that, as those were gifts his family bought for her, so they would stay at his house.

The next day, I received a text from Johnny asking if Grace wanted to go to the dog park with him, and then he would bring her back to my house right after. I asked Grace, and she agreed to go. She got ready and left shortly after.

A little while later, I received a call from Grace asking if she could go get her gifts from her grandpa on the reserve. I replied, "As long as you feel okay with it."

She said, "I do." Later that day, she came home. When I asked how her visit went, she replied, "Good" and went about her day.

At bed time, though, she began to panic, and cry. She said she was scared her dad was going to take her from her bedroom window. After she had calmed down, she told me that her dad had apologized to her. I asked her how that made her feel. She said she still felt scared and didn't trust him.

"That's okay to feel that way. It's your dad's job to build that trust between you two."

This led to another difficult night of sleep for both of us. It took Grace about two hours to fall asleep and then, she did not stay asleep. She was in my room again soon, complaining of another nightmare. This nighttime routine was becoming as familiar as any daytime routine.

Frustrated yet compassionate, I asked Grace what her nightmare was about this time. She replied, "My dad was hurting me."

Then next morning, Grace complained of a stomach ache, saying she felt anxious and that she was going to throw up. I let her stay home in the morning and drove her to school at lunch. According to Victim Services with Edmonton Police Service, some of the physiological reactions from trauma are vomiting, indigestion, and nausea. *Go figure.*

A few days later, Grace and I were out on a dog walk, enjoying the weather and each other's company. Out of the blue, she said to me, "I feel like you don't want me to see my dad."

I asked her where that came from, as it was not true. She said, "I don't know. I just feel that way."

I explained to her, as I had many times before, that I wanted her to have a relationship with her dad and for them to spend time together, but I wanted it to be a positive experience for her. I explained that watching her get scared, have panic attacks, miss school, and have trouble sleeping, along with everything else that had been going on, was hard and not healthy.

It's funny. As parents, when we try to keep our kids safe and despite our best efforts, our children see it differently. I had never withheld or denied her access to her father, but it was hard not to wonder what was going on in her little mind or if this messaging had been given to her somewhere else.

If you guessed the following night would be any different, guess again. Our bed time ritual ended up taking hours, because Grace had a panic attack. She had difficulty breathing and was waving her hands around abruptly while crying hysterically. It was so hard to watch this, and I felt so helpless.

All I could think was to remain calm and let her process this in whatever way she needed to, while keeping her breathing. I encouraged her to breathe, to regulate her nervous system. She said, "I'm trying," but her poor little body was on overdrive. Again, she said, "Bad dreams are all over my room and on my bed. I can't sleep." She continued, "My dad is going to sneak up and take me."

Again, I reassured her that he wouldn't come to our house. "He is not welcome here." She continued to cry, waving her hands in a flapping motion. I suggested we make a doctor's appointment tomorrow, so we could talk about the nightmares.

Finally, I did something I never thought I would do. I moved Grace's mattress into my room on my bedroom floor, so she didn't feel like she was alone. Hopefully this way, we could both get some sleep. After this exhausting nightly routine, I still had to try to function throughout the day at work, which was difficult to say the least. This entire experience was taking a toll on me, mentally, emotionally, and physically. Something had to change.

The following day, I made a doctor's appointment for Grace. She was scheduled in for the following day.

# Chapter 23

## Verbal Escalations and Intimidation

A few months later, Grace woke up from a dream saying she'd had another nightmare. I asked her what it was about. She replied, "My dad locked me in a closet. I asked Rosie to call the police. I woke up, and I'm not sure what happened next."

Months later, Grace and I were driving home when my phone rang. Johnny's name was on caller ID. I hesitated to answer, but Grace could also see my screen, and I didn't want her to think I was ignoring him.

He messaged me, "You think I am going to beat the shit out of you. I'm not going to beat the shit out of you." This was so random, but the feelings that flooded my body were not.

Familiarity. Fear. At the pit of my stomach. I felt at a loss for words. I did think, *One day, he is going to cause significant harm to us.* Grace was in the back seat and heard every word loud and clear.

He didn't stop there. "All you do is whine to the police and play the victim. Are you going to dwell on this forever?"

I replied, "Don't talk to me like that." I informed him that Grace was in the backseat and could hear him. He didn't care. He continued on for a while longer before changing the subject and asked if Grace could sleep at the Sundance with him, and even that was coming up soon. Grace said she didn't want to, as it would cause her to miss camp, and she loved camp.

Johnny became frustrated that Grace did not want to go with him. For some reason, I felt it was important to remind him of the incident when he'd dragged her out of my vehicle plus other things he had said to her that had caused her to feel this way. I felt like a broken record; this was hardly the first time I had explained this to him. I felt like it went in one ear and out the other. This upset him even more.

He began to speak to me in a condescending tone, which was quite triggering for me. "You don't know what abuse is. You can't dwell on that." He continued, "My mom would make me talk about it. I try to make Grace talk about it, and she refuses."

I said, "That's probably because she does not feel safe. She isn't going to open up and talk about those things with you." I continued, "I know Grace asked you to go to counseling with her. If that means you could rebuild trust and a relationship with her, I'm not sure why you are refusing." He did not provide a reason.

Johnny said, "Recording the incident of me dragging Grace out of your car is manipulation on your end." He continued, "You need to apologize to my mom for what you did to her that day."

I was confused. She was the one who had showed up at my house that night, attempting to take Grace and sending horrible text messages. I hadn't spoken to his mom since that night. I reminded him of the text messages she'd sent me, calling me a victim, and that I should be teaching my daughter to respect her dad. Plus, the fact that they had stood on my doorstep for hours on end, sending hateful messages and ringing my doorbell repeatedly.

This reminder was not well received by Johnny. I hung up the phone.

Looking back, I engaged in that conversation far longer than I should have. He called me back twice. I ignored them both. My nervous system could not handle any more of that today, nor did Grace need to be a witness to it.

This conflict was far from over. As we continued our drive home, Grace said from the backseat, "You should answer the phone when my dad calls, because if you don't, I'm scared he's going to get mad at me."

After our separation, I tried to maintain relationships with most of Johnny's family members for Grace's sake. They were her family, too. I took Grace to one of her cousin's birthday parties, which was held at one of the local spray parks. I knew some of his family, including his partner, Rosie, might show up with the children. They were cousins, as well. I was there for Grace, and that's all that mattered.

I was hopeful things would go well, and it turned out there were no issues. However, I still felt uneasy about the situation. Johnny's mom arrived at the birthday party not long after we did. I felt nervousness rush over me. It had been quite some time since I'd seen her, and my last interaction was a year ago, when she'd been sending me mean text messages from my doorstep.

I didn't want them to know I was fearful, so I did my best to keep my cool. I was within earshot of them when I heard Grace's grandma call her over and say, "What, you aren't going to say hi to us?"

It always blew my mind that this family put so much pressure and blame on Grace, when she was a child. Plus, they had behaved poorly, which had caused Grace to feel the way she did around them. There was no accountability for those who'd caused harm or fear to Grace. This was the biggest challenge of all. If there is no accountability, you cannot change behaviors.

The next day, as Grace and I were getting ready, she said to me, "Yesterday at the birthday party, my grandma asked me why you brought me to the party. She said, 'It should be your own family that brings you to these birthday parties.'"

I thought, *What a strange thing to say to a child, especially because I am her family. I am her mom.* What was even odder about this was that Johnny had texted me earlier that day to say his partner could not watch Grace, so could I just bring her to the party.

# Chapter 24

## A New Relationship, Parking Lot Fights, and the Same ol' Chaos

Johnny had been enrolled in a school about twelve hours north of our home community. He traveled back and forth between home and school, since he was also employed. When he returned from school after summer, Grace spent a bit more time with him. The more time she spent with him, the worse her attitude became toward me.

When I started to date again, I met someone named Robert who lived in Calgary, approximately two hours away from where I lived. He had two children and owned a business. There was much more opportunity in Calgary, so the potential to move there at some point was something we discussed, but not for my immediate future.

One day when out for a walk, Grace brought up her concerns about moving to Calgary. I told her it was not something she had to worry about right now, since it was not happening anytime soon. And even if we did move, we would come back to our hometown often.

Grace said, "My dad is asking a lot of questions. Some, I don't know what they mean." When I asked her if she would be willing to tell me, she said, "I don't want you to talk to him about it."

I hated that she felt she had to hide things or wasn't able to be fully honest and transparent about things, because of a fear of what might happen. I promised I wouldn't say anything.

She then said, "My dad told me to go live with my new dad."

Though frustrated, because I was so tired of the poor messaging, I said, "Your dad shouldn't be saying things like that to you. He should be happy that I found someone who cares about you."

About fifteen minutes later, Grace said, "My dad called Robert an ugly freak. Every time I talk about Robert, my dad rolls his eyes." She continued, "I love Robert, but not in the same way that his daughter loves him."

This made total sense, since he was not her dad. There was no expectation that she'd feel any particular way toward him. There were no expectations on my end that she tell Robert she loved him or call him anything other than what she was comfortable with.

"My dad told me that my siblings don't even recognize me anymore." Over the past few years, Johnny had expanded his own family by having two more children with his partner, Rosie.

Grace had attended her sister's first birthday party at a local indoor playground. After the party, as Grace and I were driving home, she began to unpack her experience.

"The birthday party was full of drama." When I asked her what had happened, she said, "Mama picked a fight with my auntie. They got into a fight over something, and Mama started yelling at Auntie." She said her aunt left shortly after.

I couldn't help but think how embarrassing this had to be, not only Grace, but for the other children in attendance. The writing was on the wall: why would a child want to spend time in a toxic environment like that?

The following day, Grace, my mom, and I drove to Humpty's Restaurant, so my mom could purchase a gift card for someone. As we pulled into the parking lot, I noticed Grace's great-aunt beside her vehicle. I was excited to see her, as was my mom, because we adored her. There had never been any issues between us, even after I left the relationship with Johnny.

My mom parked beside her, and we started to chat and catch up. About ten minutes later, Johnny's sister pulled up next to us. My stomach flipped. I was so scared. I tried to keep calm for Grace, as I continued to talk to their aunt.

My mom went into the restaurant to purchase the gift card while I remained in the van, talking to the great-aunt through the window. Grace was in the backseat, playing with her toys, totally checked out of the conversation between me and her great-aunt.

Moments later, Johnny's sister got out of her vehicle and demanded Grace get out of the van. Grace's facial expression said more than her mouth did. She reluctantly opened the sliding door and stepped outside. As she did, Johnny's sister began to interrogate her. Grace was only ten years old at the time, so you can imagine how terrified she was.

Johnny's sister said, "Why are you hiding from us, *huh*? Because someone tells you that we are abusive?" She continued, "Why weren't you at the birthday party today? Your dad was there."

Grace stood there sheepishly, her head down. My heart was breaking, yet my blood was boiling. I was terrified to get out of the vehicle for fear of what might happen. I felt like I was frozen in time. Paralyzed. But I knew I had to do something. I had to be strategic in my approach, to keep us all safe.

His sister continued to berate Grace in a condescending tone. "You need to spend more time with your family. Someone tells you that we are abusive, don't they?"

Finally, Grace's great-aunt spoke up, saying, "That's enough." She tried to get the sister to stop, but there was no stopping her. Their aunt went silent and remained at the back of our vehicle.

Johnny's sister held up a bag of candy. "This is from the birthday party yesterday. Can I give this to you? Or is this abusive, too?"

I'd had enough of the interrogation. Through the driver's window, I said loudly, "Perhaps the way you are behaving is exactly why Grace doesn't want to spend time with you guys."

Johnny's sister walked to the front of our van and gestured me out of the vehicle, saying, "Get out here."

There was no way I was getting out of our vehicle, for fear she would try to fight me. I had no idea how to fight, and that was the last thing I wanted Grace to witness. This was bad enough.

My mom came out of Humpty's moments later, not knowing what was going on. Grace's great-aunt engaged in small talk with my mom, apologizing for what had just happened, though my mom was oblivious, confused by the apologies.

Their aunt then told his sister to knock it off as they were leaving soon, which I assumed was back to Edmonton, where they both lived. My mom got into the vehicle, and we drove away.

*Holy shit.* It took a while for my nervous system to regulate. I was so tired of these upsetting encounters.

As we drove, I checked in with Grace, who seemed to be doing better than I was or at least didn't show any concern. *Why are they able to act so irrationally and continue to use fear to intimidate us,* I wondered, *yet nothing is ever done to stop that?* I documented this incident and added it to the ten years of documentation I had on file, but I was really unsure what the point was. It didn't seem to serve me well at all.

About a month later, Grace had plans to see her dad. Even though she had made plans, she expressed feeling nervous. I asked her if she had shared those feelings with her dad. She said, "No, because my dad told me before, if I kept feeling this way, he will take us back to court."

Once again, I reassured her she did not have to worry about that stuff. She replied, "If I don't go, my dad will call the police on us again. I don't want the police to come again, because I don't want my dad to go to jail."

*Imagine being ten years old and having to worry about this stuff on a regular basis.*

The next day, Johnny came to pick Grace up. As he arrived, she began to panic, saying, "I don't want to go." Frustrated, I asked her why she'd made plans to go with him, if she didn't want to go. Looking back, I am not happy with my own frustration, but I felt like I had no control over the outcomes. The last thing I wanted was more drama, fighting, and police involvement, only to be blamed for the situation. *Maybe this will be the time I get hauled to jail, depending on how the officer responds.*

I asked her if she would tell her dad that she was scared, because as much as I knew I was her voice oftentimes, I still wanted him to hear it from her. I was tired of being blamed for everything and accused of withholding her, making things up, etc. I knew she didn't feel safe, telling him, so it was unrealistic for me to ask her that. But in the moment, I felt complete overwhelm, frustration, and sadness.

Johnny was supposed to take Grace to a powwow, which was not common, as I was usually the one to get her ready and take her to powwows. When he came over, Johnny told Grace he had already registered her. After talking with Johnny outside, she came inside moments later in a panic.

"I can't go with him," she said. When I asked her why, she replied, "I'm not comfortable." I was confused and again asked why she had arranged to hang out with him if she felt uncomfortable. In hindsight, that was silly. But again, these situations were just as challenging for me as they were for her.

Grace kept looking out the window, as though checking to see if he was still there. Johnny hadn't left. He was sitting in his car outside of our house. "I can't go outside and tell him I don't want to go. I'm too scared. If I go out, he will pull me into his vehicle." She continued, "I don't want what happened on your birthday to happen again, Mom."

Moments later, Johnny came to the door and rang the doorbell repeatedly. I was scared to open the door, but I felt like I had to. I didn't want police coming again. Grace was far too dysregulated to engage in a conversation with him or anyone, at this point. She began to panic again, knowing he was at the door. She ran toward the kitchen, where she was not visible from the door.

Johnny called me, demanding, "Come outside and talk to me." I didn't want a scene in my neighborhood, either, so I made the difficult choice to open the door. I asked Grace if she wanted to come out with me, to which she immediately said, "No." The look on her face was something I will never forget. As I approached the door, Grace said repeatedly, "No, no, no, no, no, no, Mom. He is going to try to take me into the car."

I went outside to meet Johnny and closed the door behind me. "Grace is too scared to come out."

He said, "Why? I've never done anything to her." The complete denial was unfathomable.

I shrugged my shoulders and said nothing. I'd explained to him numerous times and was sick and tired of repeating myself.

"You're just going to shrug your shoulders?"

I replied, "You don't know why she is scared and won't go with you? You do know why she is scared. I don't know why you don't attempt counseling, so you can work on yourself and navigate these difficulties in a safe setting, so you can have a healthy relationship again."

"If we are going to counseling, then we are all going, because you don't understand."

I said, "I do understand, but it's not up to me to fix the relationship between you two. It's yours." He told me it was mine.

I took this opportunity to inform him about the incident from the other day, when his sister berated Grace and me in the parking lot. He said he was unaware. A part of me believed him, but I'll never know, and that didn't really matter. What mattered to me was that he and his family continued to create unsafe situations for us, especially Grace, and it was taking a toll on our mental health and wellbeing.

I continued to meet with resistance during the conversation. He said, "You have no idea what me and my family have been through."

While I admit I may not know everything, Johnny had shared quite a bit with me when we were together, and I had witnessed a few situations. His mother also had shared about the abuse she'd experienced, during our time together. While these stories are not mine to share, I will say, even if they experienced abuse or trauma, they also had the opportunity to change the narrative and how they showed up and became active participants in their healing. We are all responsible for our own healing journey. As much as I have compassion for what they went through, it did not give them permission to treat us that way, nor was it an excuse or a free pass for Grace and me to have to accept the treatment as such. We deserved better, and I was going to fight to make sure it happened.

I don't know why I tried to explain anything further to him, but I did. "You can break the cycle and create a safe place for Grace, so she doesn't have to feel like this anymore."

He replied, "I am going to give you advice. I am doing my practicum in our community, and I have encountered people there who know you. What you have done to me, you have done to them."

I asked him to clarify that, as I had no idea what he was talking about.

He smirked and said with condescension, "What you have done to me, you have done to others, like calling the police. You have done that to them."

I was so confused, because the only person whom I'd gotten the police involved with was him.

He continued, "You already lost once in court. I don't want to have to put you back through that again, but if I have to, I will."

*Was this a threat?* I got a sinking feeling in the pit of my stomach. *Fuck, what's next?*

He wasn't done. "The judge already sided with me and made no changes." Johnny was referring back to old parenting orders, which was another indication that I needed to find a way to get an updated order to reflect our current status.

But I was so intimidated by the process, I found myself stalling, even when I knew it was the right thing to do.

I replied, "The order needs to be revisited anyway." I also reminded him of the incident when he dragged Grace out of my vehicle.

"That's not abuse," he said. When I became triggered, he began to laugh, as though it was absurd to think this was abuse. This triggered me even more.

I disengaged and went into my house, locking the door behind me.

He yelled, "*Hey*!" as I closed the door.

My nervous system needed a break. Inside, I heard Grace talking to someone on the phone. The voice on the other end was my partner, Robert. She hung up the phone when she saw me.

I later learned she had called him when I stepped outside to talk to Johnny, as she was scared her dad was going to beat me up or kill me.

Grace said, "I tried to record some of the conversation, but I couldn't."

I later learned that my mom also received a call from Grace that day, telling her, "I'm scared my dad is going to kill my mom."

# Chapter 25

## A Step in the Right Direction

It took a few years to get to this point when there was finally some movement around my voice being heard. *Far too long.* I was feeling alone, lost, unheard, and with nowhere to turn throughout this process. Every professional seemed to pass the buck. I so badly wanted someone to believe me and to help me make the pain and madness end. I was tired of playing Johnny's game of power and control, which forced me to navigate his manipulation tactics. But finally, we took a giant step forward, although before I could make true progress, I had to learn some tough lessons.

In 2018, when I first made my application to the courts for a parenting order, I had been expected to serve Johnny with the court paperwork. It's crazy that the courts make you do this on your own, but otherwise, you have to pay a commissionaire to do it for you, and there is a cost for each attempt. Based on Johnny's and my history, I was too scared to do it on my own. I didn't know what would happen if I showed up on his doorstep, especially if I went alone. I didn't want to put myself at risk.

I also didn't have the support of my family or friends in this regard: they were also scared of Johnny. I didn't have many male friends who lived in the same city, due to Johnny's various power and control tactics in our relationship.

During this time, I worked closely with a police officer, cocreating a program together that focused on reconnecting to their culture vulnerable Indigenous people who were experiencing homelessness. We spent a lot of time together while building this program, so naturally, we learned about each other. He was aware of what I was going through and offered to serve Johnny the documents for me. He said he would go in plain clothes, while off duty. I was so grateful. Little did I know the drama this would cause, not only for me, but for the officer, as well.

The officer's offer to help came from a good place, and it was helpful, because it kept me safe, too. I wasn't making much money as a single mom with no child support. I had enough to pay my bills, but I didn't have additional funds to pay a commissionaire. And who knew how many attempts they would need before actually serving him, at $50-$75 for each attempt.

The officer was able to serve Johnny the papers; however, Johnny didn't appreciate it and was determined to make that known. Johnny ended up filing a complaint with our local police service, indicating that the officer was abusing his power. As far as I knew, the complaint did not go anywhere, since the officer had made the right decision and the complaint made by Johnny was unfounded. But this was not something that officer deserved. If Johnny could make anyone's life hell, he was determined to do it.

In December 2019, I went on leave from work due to a psychological injury that resulted in a PTSD (Post Traumatic Stress Disorder) diagnosis, after a traumatic event I experienced while at work, I took ten months off from work through Workers Compensation and spent those months engaged in intense therapy and trauma work.

In October 2020, my restrictions from work were lifted and I was deemed eligible to return to working in my field. In November 2020, I became the manager of the Drug Treatment Court in my community. This program worked with justice-involved individuals who were looking at one to five years in custody for drug-related offences. It was a job I loved dearly. We did incredible work, and I will never forget the lessons I learned and the connections I made, all because of this program. It sparked a passion within me that I didn't know existed.

Due to the structure of the program, the nature of our work, and the population we served, we worked as a multi-disciplinary team. Our team consisted of judges, crown prosecutors, duty counsel, police (municipal and RCMP), a treatment team, and a probation officer.

I share this story for a few reasons. One, because I remember one of our clients who was charged with domestic violence and was at risk of being terminated from our program. We navigated this situation, and he ended up staying in the program and graduating. However, I was curious about his situation and how this individual had been charged with domestic violence for keying his ex's vehicle. My own personal experiences, like when my ex followed me home, refused to leave, and harassed us for hours had led to nothing being done by the system. Literally nothing. I needed this to make sense.

I didn't like to blend my professional and personal life, but this was something I couldn't ignore any longer. I needed answers. I mustered up the courage to put my pride aside and seek clarification from the local police Liaison for our program. I trusted him enough that what I said to him would stay between us. Despite my previous experiences, I felt safe about approaching him with my questions.

I won't lie: I was super-nervous, because I still carried the stigma of being a professional in this field while also being a victim of domestic violence, with court battles, and subject to ongoing manipulation and power and control tactics.

As I approached the officer, I explained my situation, and why I was confused as to their approach to our client's situation, yet I had received no answers or support from police when I was followed home.

He appeared just as shocked as I was. He said it should have been dealt with and considered a criminal offence. He offered to connect me to the family violence unit, which I welcomed with open arms.

I thought, maybe with this type of connection, I would actually get somewhere, or at least get an answer. This turned out to be wishful thinking.

About a week or so later, I spoke to the sergeant of the family violence unit. I explained my situation to him. *For the 150th time, it felt like.* I was met with silence, followed by a response I will never forget.

"We probably could have charged him with harassment, but we don't typically charge for historical stuff."

Silence. There was nothing left to say. I, too, was quiet. Part of me was digesting this information, while another part of me wanted to scream. I felt defeated yet again. Looking back, there is so much more I wish I'd said during that conversation. Instead, I gave up and accepted what he said as truth.

I thought to myself, *Yeah, right, you guys charge for historical sexual assaults all the time.* But I didn't say anything. I no longer had faith in this police service or police in general.

In the spring or summer of 2022, we had a dinner with our entire drug treatment court team. I was fortunate to have met one of our judges many years ago through a volunteer opportunity. She knew some of my story from back then, as I had already been struggling with Johnny and his abusive behaviors, and been looking to go through the court process. She was also present when my phone had rung repeatedly during meetings, with Johnny saying he was outside of the building, yet nowhere to be found. I didn't want to say too much at that time, as I like to keep my personal life private, but sometimes, when opportunities present themselves, you have to take them. Especially when you feel the system is stacked against you.

As we the group grew smaller around the table, the judged asked, "How are things going with Grace, her dad, and all of that?"

I explained where things were at and some of the experiences I'd had with the police, judges, and lawyers. She was flabbergasted. Our RCMP liaison, sitting next to her, happened to be the Domestic Violence Coordinator for Southern Alberta. Her face said more than her words. When she could finally speak, she said, "Are you kidding me?"

I replied, "I wish I was."

The RCMP liaison asked me if she could speak to our local police service on my behalf. I agreed. Although I wasn't feeling hopeful that anything would be done, based on my experiences, I didn't want to turn down the opportunity to try. Maybe, if they heard it from another police service, they would take it more seriously. At the very least, I felt validated by her, and that was something I had not felt in a very long time.

A few days later, I received a call from the RCMP officer. She told me she had made contact with the family violence unit with our local police service, and I should expect to hear from them soon. A few days later, I received a call from an officer from the family violence unit with our local police service. Although that initial conversation was brief and it took a month or so before anything happened, we ultimately scheduled a time to meet and for us to be interviewed.

I picked Grace up from school and explained where we were going. As much as Grace wanted all of the turmoil and chaos between her and her dad to stop, she became nervous and asked a million questions as we walked to my vehicle. I did my best to reassure her that this was part of the process and something we needed to do.

When Grace and I arrived at the police station, we spoke to the officer at the front and were asked to take a seat while they let the officer know we were there. My body flooded with shame. *How the hell did I ever end up here, in this situation,* I wondered. *I hope I don't run into anyone I know. I'm so embarrassed.*

Due to interview protocol, Grace and I were split up. She waited in an interview room in the front, and I was taken back to another room that was equipped with technology for audio recording purposes. My interview was an hour long. I worried what Grace was doing and whether she was okay, if anyone was checking on her or if she'd been left in that room alone. She said they didn't check in, maybe because a sign on the door said the room was occupied. But she was so young at the time, it's surprising.

When I finished my interview, I went into Grace's waiting room, and she went back to interview with the officer. It was such an emotional experience for me, but I finally felt heard. I hoped Grace would feel the same way.

After Grace completed her interview, she was ready to head out, like she could not get out fast enough. I stayed back for a minute and thanked the officer, feeling quite emotional. I wanted him to have some context about my past experiences with other officers and how difficult this process had been.

He encouraged me to file a complaint against those who'd responded poorly. I didn't feel it was worth my time or energy, as I still didn't trust the system. It felt like all they did was protect one another with very little oversight or accountability. Since I was fighting enough battles on my own, I didn't think I could add any more to my plate, especially a fight against such a big, bureaucratic system.

Months later, our local police service became a known service in the media, but for all the wrong reasons. They were performing quite poorly, and the service was at risk of being dismantled on a provincial level by the justice minister. After some consideration, I decided to take this opportunity to write a letter to the justice minister about my experience. I felt like I had a right and responsibility to share my experience.

I received a reply letter from the justice minister, informing me that I needed to go through the Police Commission. I gave up then, because I didn't trust their commission to address this without their biases. *They will protect their own.* As time went on, our local police service ended up hiring a new police chief, and the rest is history. They are still an operating service today, but I wouldn't say its operations and poor performance have changed much, based on my experience.

In the family violence unit, the officer assigned to our case informed me that the next steps were for him to consult with the domestic violence crown, to see if these charges would stick. He said, "I feel confident they will. Based on Grace's disclosure, we can charge Johnny with assault with a weapon." I didn't know the full extent of Grace's police interview, since I was not in the room or privy to all of the information, but the officer said, "Grace spoke really well during the interview and provided great information."

I felt a small glimmer of hope but would take whatever kind of hope I could get.

A week or so later, I received a call from the officer assigned to our case. He informed me that the crown believed there was enough evidence and information, based on Grace's disclosure, to lay a charge. The officer informed me of next steps.

He said, "We will be serving Johnny with an undertaking." In plain language, the officer explained that Johnny was being charged with assault with a weapon, and there would be a peace bond (or protection order) put into place between him, Grace, and me. Victim services would be in touch with me shortly. "You will be provided with updates on court appearances and will receive a copy of the undertaking, as well."

One of the stipulations was that Johnny was not to be within fifty meters of either of us. I was scared of what would happen, but to my surprise, he left us alone.

I can't tell you how good this felt. *Finally.* Someone believed us. I felt such a sense of relief, even if it was only for a little while. My fight, determination, and resilience had paid off. I could breathe…

Over the next several months, I received updates as court went on, and the crown made semi-regular contact with me as necessary.

Peace bonds are generally in place for a year, and this was a year of peace for the both of us. Because of the space it provided, it allowed us to engage in our own healing process. During that year of the peace bond, Johnny showed up at a few powwows and ran directly into us, so he knew we were there. As per the peace bond, he should have left, but it appeared he was above the law, so he remained at the events. I could have called it in to police, but based on my past experiences, it was not worth it. The police likely wouldn't do anything, anyway. I did inform the crown of this, but it didn't seem to matter much there, either.

One day about six months later, I received a call from the crown. He proposed the idea of reunification counseling. I went silent, needing a moment to digest what this meant, especially for Grace. Personally, I had mixed feelings about this option; however, I knew it wasn't about me. It was about what was best for Grace. Despite what Johnny thought, I wasn't out to ruin his life. But I *did* want him to be a good dad for Grace, as she deserved that.

I agreed to reunification counseling, although Grace was quite hesitant. I was hopeful I made the right choice for her, even if she didn't see it at the time. The crown found a counselor who had a good reputation for working with domestic violence files and court-ordered clients, so they said. I was a bit skeptical but leaned into the process and took the crown's word for it, because I felt like I could trust him. In all of my interactions and conversations with the crown, I could tell he truly cared and wanted not only to protect Grace, but to ensure we did what was best for her.

The crown said, "Chelsey, I have an obligation not only to protect Grace, but also the other children in that house [her siblings]. If something happens later on where we had to protect the other children and we failed to protect Grace, that wouldn't sit well with me."

We made arrangements with the counselor to start the counseling process over the next few weeks. The peace bond was still in place, so Johnny and Grace would be able to see each other in the counseling office, during the time of their sessions, *for now.*

*Here goes nothing,* I thought.

Leaning in. Trusting the process. Hoping for the best.

We had our first session scheduled during a summer evening in 2023. Grace was reluctant to get into the vehicle, indicating she did not want to go. The anticipation built on the drive there, and it only grew worse as we got closer to counseling office. When we arrived, Grace started to panic. She saw her dad's car parked on the street, and that was enough to set her off. She began crying.

Still a few minutes before the appointment, and things were not going well. I had one hell of a time getting Grace out of my vehicle. Once she did, we approached the door to go inside of the office. Grace froze and refused to take another step. I decided I wasn't going to push it any further. I couldn't. Grace grabbed onto the brick wall outside of the building, crying hysterically.

I called the office and explained the situation, letting them know we were outside, but Grace was refusing to go inside. The counselor came outside to speak with us.

He could see how upset she was. He agreed that in-person was not going to happen today and suggested maybe we try a phone session next time, instead. Grace calmed down a bit, once she heard she didn't have to go in, and agreed to a phone call next time. We scheduled something for the following week or two.

Grace and I were supposed to be camping with my partner, Robert and his children, near Red Deer during the time of the appointment, but I thought we could do both, since we had phone access. I thought it might be good to have the distraction of having fun out there after the session, so Grace could go about being a kid again. I was very wrong.

We had been camping for a few days before the call, and things were going well. The weather was beautiful, the kids had fun, swimming, fishing, eating unlimited ice cream, and boating. The day the call was scheduled, everything changed.

Grace was a mess. The conversation was to take place via phone call, so she and I sat in the trailer, awaiting the call. Johnny was in the office with the counselor for the phone call. The conversation started off okay, but you could cut the tension with a knife.

Grace was asked questions, and she just sat there, her little body frozen. She looked at me as though not knowing how to respond. I didn't want to tell her what to say or how to feel, so it was a very difficult position to be in. I just sat with her, attempting to comfort her with my presence. This felt like a lot of pressure for her, and it killed me to watch.

Grace was quite emotional for the whole session. She could barely talk, and when she did, it was minimal. And it impacted the rest of the day. She wasn't herself. My partner didn't know how to handle it, either. He was divorced, but their divorce and coparenting relationship were amicable, nothing like mine.

On this particular camping trip, he'd had friends come out for the night. I am sure we didn't make a good impression. Following the session, Grace made constant outbursts and disrespectful behavior that was even a bit much for me, as the parent. But it was out of my control. There was nothing I could do other than just accept it for what it was and ride out the storm. But I was fuming inside, because I was so sick of always having to pick up the pieces of Johnny's wrongdoings.

Over time, things slowly improved to the point where the sessions moved to in-person. Things seemed to be going well, Grace appeared a bit happier and more content, more willing to engage in sessions. I received brief updates from the counselor. Since I was always the one to pick Grace up after sessions, I could visibly see the difference. This was all I wanted for her. It made my heart so happy.

Grace chatted briefly about the sessions with her dad. I asked how she was feeling after each one, and she always answered, "Good." She appeared to be rebuilding some trust. *A step in the right direction.*

By November, we were nearing the one-year term of the peace bond, so the crown and I had a conversation about how things were going.

The crown said to me, "I've noticed a shift in Johnny's behavior, from when he first showed up in court to now. In the first few appearances, he was pompous and arrogant. Now, he is calmer and showing more emotion."

*Wow,* I thought. *Could this be the turning point? What we actually needed to get back on track? What a terrible way to get there, but hey, let's see how this proceeds. Despite how shitty this has been, maybe Grace will get the dad she deserves.*

The crown asked me, "What do you want to do with the charges?"

I had no idea I had any say in the matter, so we discussed my options and what was ultimately best for Grace. I felt a ton of pressure and responsibility to make the *right* decision, even when I wasn't 100% sure what that was.

I told the crown, "I would like to talk to Grace about how she feels first, before making a decision."

The crown agreed and said he would follow up in a few days. Later that day, Grace and I discussed how she was feeling and how she would feel if she would be able to have more contact with Johnny outside of counseling sessions.

Grace said she was feeling more comfortable about having interactions with her dad. I was struggling with the idea of the peace bond being dropped, and I wasn't sure if Grace knew what that would mean for her, either. At her age, it was not something she could comprehend.

I didn't think she was ready to go back and forth between our homes again, though I assumed that was exactly what Johnny would ask for, as soon as the peace bond was no longer in place. I felt torn between my own feelings about the situation and the pressure Grace might feel to make a decision. There was a lot at stake.

Based on the information I had and my conversation with Grace, I made the decision to stay the charges. This meant Johnny would not be convicted of the assault with a weapon charge. The crown told me, if anything were to happen within one year of the charges being stayed, it could be brought back into court.

This was reassuring to me, but I was hopeful we wouldn't have to go down this path again. The crown also shared with me that, in court that day, when Johnny found out the charges were stayed, he became very emotional and appeared to be grateful.

He continued, "Johnny's lawyer also read him the riot act, saying this better not happen again, as he'd been given another chance to make things right." This message provided even more hope.

I had no idea the impact or implications this decision on staying charges would have on me in years to come, or the blame it would carry. I don't want to give advice, because everyone's situation is different, but if I could suggest anything, it would be to strongly consider what staying charges actually means for you and your situation. Play the tape forward. It may sound good in theory, but if there are no changes to behavior, you likely won't get so lucky or have any follow-up afterward.

# Chapter 26

## Here's to New Beginnings... *or So I Thought*

The charges against Johnny were stayed. Things were quiet for us for a time after that.

Due to confidentiality, the specific information that crowns can share with you, even as a victim, is limited. The crown was able to tell me that Johnny was successful in his individual counseling. I have no idea what or how they determined success in counseling as it relates to domestic violence; it's something I may never know. I respected what little I knew, based on the information provided to me, and I remained hopeful.

Johnny immediately stopped attending counseling with Grace as soon as the charges were stayed and the peace bond was removed. This didn't sit well with me, but I remained hopeful that all of that was in the past. He knew the severity and impact of his behaviors. But I should have buckled up, because things were only about to get worse.

We entered 2024 softly. Not much happened in the first few months. While I felt at ease, in the back of my mind I was waiting for the other shoe to drop. *Could it really be this good forever?* On one hand, I thought maybe it had been a tough lesson for Johnny to learn and a pivotal moment for both him and Grace. But the other part of me knew the history and patterns of behaviors. I knew, to change any behavior requires an individual first to take responsibility for what they have done, then it takes time, ongoing work, and consistency.

In March 2024, Grace began to have in-person visits with her dad again. One day, she came home from a visit, crying. Concerned, I asked what was wrong. She said, "My dad said, if I don't start sleeping there, he's not going to sign the papers for me to go to Disneyland."

We had plans to go to Disneyland in May, as I was attending a work conference a block away in Anaheim, and I thought this would be a prime opportunity to provide Grace with a fun experience. I had never been, though I always wanted to go as a child. Grace was growing up, so she might only think Disneyland was cool for another year or two, and it's a rare chance to travel to California. My mom had done a lot for me, being my primary coparent throughout these tumultuous times, so I wanted to bring her along, too, and show my appreciation to her. I was in a solid financial place, too, so I could give this to her and thank her for all of her help and support over the years.

Also, what a cool place to take a girls' trip: California! And the most magical place on Earth.

Grace continued, "My dad kept saying your mom tells you stuff." When I asked what she meant, she said, "I told my dad my mom doesn't tell me anything."

Johnny kept repeating himself then changed the subject, saying "Your sister misses you."

Grace also shared that her dad had a road range incident that made her uncomfortable. I asked her to tell me more about that. She said, "We were driving to go somewhere when the car in front of us slammed their brakes on. My dad rolled down the window and began yelling at the driver, saying 'Fuck you' to them and giving them the middle finger." Every light they stopped at afterward, her dad engaged in the same behavior. Grace said, "I felt bad for the other driver. I mouthed *sorry* to them." She was very emotional all evening and quite sensitive to any conversation we had for the rest of the night.

I felt defeated yet again. After all that we had just been through, especially in the past year, now Johnny appeared to be falling into old patterns of behavior.

I was very tired of playing this game. I still didn't have a final court order granted, and the peace bond had just been dropped. Given everything that had happened since our last court order, I didn't feel it was appropriate for us to resume the old parenting schedule. Because of our current situation, I needed Johnny's permission to travel with Grace. I didn't want his permission, since he always seemed to find a way to interfere and make the process difficult.

A few years prior, Johnny had made it difficult for me to travel with Grace. I hated that he still got to have this power and control over our lives, but especially over Grace's, potentially preventing her from experiencing other parts of the world. There was no way I was going to let Grace miss out on opportunities. *I guess it's back to fighting. Back to court we go.*

I made another application to go before a judge and get the court's approval for travel, since I wasn't going to get it from him and time was of the essence. We were leaving in a few weeks. It's not like you can just make applications and get before a judge in a day or two. I knew I had to move quickly, despite how much I wanted to avoid the courts.

When I made my very first court appearance, I had support of this wonderful court liaison, and I was hopeful she would be assigned to me again. I also figured, after everything that had happened, plus with our last court order being from six years ago, it was time to update the court order anyway. I might as well ask for everything we needed, so I could get it all over with. In my application, I requested that I be able to travel without his permission, and that Grace be able to spend time with her dad when she felt safe to do so, not forced on a rotation that had been outlined back in our 2018 order.

I attended the Resolution Services office in our local court house to make my application. I was fortunate enough to get the same liaison who'd helped me with my initial application. Within a week or two, we were back before a judge in docket court. The court worker explained why we were there.

When the judge looked at Johnny, his facial expression and tone of voice indicated to me that he was blown away at Johnny's behavior, his comments made to Grace, and the reason for the application. The judge said to Johnny, "Did you say that to her?" referring to the comments he'd made to Grace about having to sleep at his house before he would sign the papers for her to travel.

Johnny stumbled on his words, attempting to parrot what he'd said to Grace, and then started blaming me, saying I was alienating Grace.

The judge added, "That is not something you ever say to a child!" Then asked, "Did you say that or not?" His messaging was stern.

Next, there was an argument, with Johnny being quite disrespectful toward the judge. I was surprised he was permitted to speak that way and argue back; I've seen that type of behavior shut down in other court rooms.

The judge ordered Grace to get her own legal counsel, someone to be a voice for her, to eliminate the "he said, she said" between Johnny and me. *Finally*, I thought. This is something I had wanted for quite some time.

Johnny was not overly receptive to this suggestion and initially rejected it. He then repeated how I was alienating Grace from him.

The judge asked, "Why would you not want your daughter to have her own representation to speak on her behalf?" Johnny remains resistant. I think this caught the judge off guard, too. The judge looked at Johnny and said, "You're telling me you would deny Grace the ability to have a neutral party involved who can speak on behalf of your daughter, so you can eliminate the 'he said, she said' stuff that is going on right now?"

Perhaps feeling backed into a corner, Johnny finally agreed.

Grace was appointed a lawyer who would be her voice moving forward, but it would be some time before they would meet. I had never dealt before with Legal Aid or navigated the systems on how to access a child lawyer, so this was a new process and experience for me. When all was said and done, and after a few phone calls, Grace had a lawyer assigned. I was later informed that we'd gotten the best child lawyer in the city. A small victory. At this point, we were taking those wherever we could.

The judge granted me the opportunity to travel with Grace and ordered Johnny to sign the papers. We had a great time in Disneyland and made a ton of memories. Grace got to go to Target for the first time, which was one of the highlights for her, as well as eating at Raising Cane's. It's funny what we Canadians get excited about, when we go to the United States. I have to admit, the food was pretty good. Another little break from the chaos at home.

About a week or so after our court date, Grace and Johnny made plans to hang out on the weekend. But when Grace hadn't heard anything from her dad, she sent him a text message to follow up. Johnny responded, "I am going to Calgary with my family."

We were sitting in my parents' living room during this conversation, and I could see her heart break in her facial expression and the tone of voice. She said, "My dad made other plans."

How heartbreaking it must have been for Grace to be told by her own father that the family was going to Calgary. This sent a strong message that she was not a part of that family. Despite how she felt, she and her dad made plans to spend time together the day after he was back.

A few days later, Grace said, "I'm not sure if I am going with my dad. Maybe I will text him and see." She ended up spending the day with him. When she returned home, she described how her dad had had another road range incident. This time, another driver slowed down to allow a pedestrian to cross in a marked crosswalk.

Grace said, "My dad began yelling at the vehicle, saying, 'Fuck you! I have kids in my vehicle.' And the man said back, 'Kids? *You're* the one that's freaking out.'" Grace said she felt quite embarrassed by this and sank low in her seat.

About a month later, Grace and her dad were supposed to spend more time together. Grace followed up with him to see what their plans were. I hated that she had to be the one to follow up and make the plans each time.

Johnny told her he had a big test to study for, so he couldn't spend time with her that weekend. He suggested they make plans for the following weekend. Grace began to cry, saying, "I wish I had a dad who loved me and wanted to spend time with me."

My heart was breaking, but I knew he was making his bed, and someday, he would have to sleep in it.

A few weeks later, Johnny picked Grace up from school, and they spent some time together. A few days after that, when she was at her friend's house who lived down the street from her dad, she mentioned being happy she'd gotten to see her sister for a bit and chat briefly with her dad. A few days after that, her dad sent me a message asking if he could pick her up from school a few days that week. When I told Grace her dad wanted to do that, she indicated she did not want him picking her up from school.

During the final month of school before summer holidays, we were starting to wind down. Summer break couldn't come soon enough for Grace. I love slow mornings, when I can drink my coffee in peace and look out my living room window. This was something I looked forward to every weekend.

At 7:38 a.m. one Saturday morning, I was sitting on my couch in my living room and could hear Grace on the phone in her bedroom. I thought this was odd, as it was quite early and she was not usually up or so talkative at that hour. I wondered, *Who the heck can she be talking to at this time?*

A few minutes later, she came out of her room and down the stairs, saying, "Papa Les died. My dad just called and said he had bad news. Papa passed away this morning. He was sick with cancer. He asked me if I needed anything. I told him no, so he hung up the phone."

This enraged me. *How do you do that to a child?* She was quite close to her papa and her grandma, when the relationship was good. After her grandma showed up at our house, trying to take her, plus the comments she'd made in community or at family events, their relationship had broken down and was essentially non-existent. But her papa never had any part in that. Still, Grace hadn't been able to speak with her papa for the past few years, given the family dynamics.

Grace had not been made aware of how sick he was, and she asked why nobody had said anything to her sooner, so she could say goodbye. This upset her for many months to come. The way the call came in was so cold. Maybe there is no ideal way or timing to inform someone of a death in the family, to drop that hard truth on our daughter so early in the morning, especially given the fractured relationships, was not how I would have done it. And then to expect a young girl to know what she needed in that moment before just hanging up the phone, with no further conversation... I felt there was some other motive behind Johnny's call, beyond just informing her of the news.

Nine days later, Johnny told me he wanted to pick Grace up on June 23 and 24. Her papa's wake was on June 23 and the funeral was on June 24. Grace fought with me, telling me she did not want to go. I encouraged her to go, since it could give her some closure that she didn't yet have. I believed, if she didn't go, she might regret it.

She wasn't interested in hearing what I had to say, but I still hoped it would help change her mind. We ended up compromising. She agreed to go to the wake, and if she felt like she could not attend the funeral the following day, at least she would be able to say goodbye and attend one of the events.

I went to drop her off shortly after 3:00 p.m. on the day of the wake, but she refused to get out of my car. It took some time, but she eventually did. I reminded her she could just go to the wake and then decide if the funeral was something she wanted to do. At least she'd showed up for this.

Grace sent me a text message shortly after I dropped her off at her dad's. "My dad isn't here. He's at work."

I can't say for certain, but part of me thought she'd been tricked throughout this process. It was a highly emotional time for her. Why wasn't he there? He knew how much Grace loved her papa. But he couldn't be bothered to show up and be there for her? If it was such a big deal, why wasn't he there?

Grace had grown quite close to her papa over the years, but this pissed Johnny off. We'd had heated arguments about that. I think children should call their adult relatives or family members what they want to call them (within reason), and that a name shouldn't be forced upon them by a parent because of their own issues. But Johnny did have issues, so he'd been adamant that Grace *not* call Les "Papa," because he was not her biological grandpa.

I'd always said, since she identified him as Papa, she should be able to call him that. This was yet another reason I was so grateful to get out of that relationship with Johnny. These fights felt so petty and small, plus this was just a personal thing for him, not a legitimate argument for what Grace should or shouldn't do.

The next day was the funeral. Johnny and Grace began arguing via text message that morning. She had valid points. She told her dad, "I went to the wake. You didn't show up. I don't want to go to the funeral. It's too hard for me."

Johnny replied, "You need to put your feelings aside and be there for your grandma." After a few hours of back-and-forth text messages, Grace eventually went.

Rosie showed up at my house to get her. When Rosie arrived, Grace began to panic, crying hysterically and saying, "I don't want to go."

When I look back at this time, I think, *Grace is the child in all of this. Who was ever there in that family to support her in her moments of darkness, sadness, grief, etc.? Nobody. Yet she was expected to behave like an adult to others?*

During the summer months, Grace decided to spend a night at her dad's house. He had moved his family about twenty minutes outside of our community. I thought this was strange, since he was working on the reserve, which was about forty-five to fifty minutes away from the community, in the opposite direction. I couldn't help but wonder if he was isolating Rosie and their kids because abuse was occurring in that home.

I heard through mutual friends that when Johnny and Rosie split a few years ago, the reason she left was because of abuse. I don't know the details and I didn't probe, but I wouldn't be surprised, given my own experience. Nothing changes if nothing changes.

Grace said her dad wasn't home that night. She said he worked Friday to Saturday and would be home in the morning, but he never showed up. Grace said, "I asked Rosie where my dad was. She said she didn't know."

Later that afternoon, Grace was dropped off at my friend's house while I was at this friend's daughter's birthday party. According to the schedule from Johnny, he was not scheduled to work that day. So, this was strange. Maybe he had picked up overtime, I thought. But if you are planning to have your child at your house, you should be there to spend time with them. I didn't love the fact Rosie was doing most of the transportation of Grace, but I wasn't about to pick petty battles when I had bigger fish to fry.

A few weeks later, Grace spent more time with her dad. One of the days she came home, she said, "My dad told me I should be carrying a pocket knife with me." When I asked why, she said, "My dad said I should have one on me at all times, for safety."

I thought this was bizarre. Our community is not so unsafe that she needed a weapon. In Canada, a standard pocket knife is considered a utility tool and not a weapon, but it can be legally classified as a weapon if used or intended for self-defence, intimidation, or harm, and many retailers in our province would not sell one to someone under the age of eighteen. There are many other ways to keep ourselves safe without carrying weapons. Grace was eleven years old, far too young for this kind of advice.

# Chapter 27

# The Court Battle Continues

The initial application I'd made to the courts to travel with Grace without Johnny's permission and to update our parenting order sparked a lengthy court battle that would draw out for far longer than I ever could have anticipated. Initially, I thought using the court worker from resolution services was enough for me, since she had been so helpful to me previously. However, I later learned some hard lessons and needed to make some changes to my approach.

I made my application to amend the parenting order in April 2024, hoping it would reflect everything that had occurred since our initial parenting order and align with our current reality. In my updated application, I provided historical information and indicated I had made numerous attempts to speak to Johnny and get him to sign a travel request form, so I could travel with Grace to Anaheim later this month and take her to Disneyland as part of my work trip.

Johnny had told Grace he would not sign the papers for her to go until she slept at his house, and he continued to refuse to respond to my email requests. I also requested in my application that Grace be able to attend counseling without his consent, as her previous counselor had moved and was no longer seeing my daughter.

Also important in my request was for Grace to be able to choose when she was to see her dad, based on her feeling safe to do so, meaning we would no longer have to abide by the strict parenting schedule outlined in the original order. Finally, since child support still had not been addressed after all these years, I decided to include that as part of this application, as well. We were scheduled to be back in docket court to review my application on May 9, 2024.

When we went before the judge that day, I had the family court worker from Resolution Services support me. This felt like such a relief, since she was able to better articulate what I was asking for than I was. Any time I was in a room with Johnny, my ability to emotionally regulate felt hijacked. The judge gave Johnny a stern talking to and asked him why he'd told Grace that he would not sign the papers for her to travel until she slept there, adding how unreasonable that was.

In true Johnny fashion, he mimicked the judge and justified his behaviors. During this appearance, Grace was appointed her own lawyer, to be a voice for her, rather than the "he said, she said" between Johnny and me, as the judge called it.

Johnny was reluctant about the idea. The judge said, "Why would you not want your daughter to have someone represent her as a neutral party?"

Johnny didn't have much of an answer. He was directed to sign the travel papers for us that day, as well, which he did. The fight wasn't over, though: this was only a temporary fix.

We were scheduled for a Judicial Dispute Resolution (JDR) in June 2024. I felt relieved and confident I could get past this hump. Based on everything that had happened, including all of my documentation plus Grace getting older and the fact that my application was not unreasonable, I figure this would be an easy process to navigate.

Grace had met with her court-appointed lawyer and provided her with background information and instructions on how she wanted to proceed. When I walked into our first JDR without a lawyer, Johnny was sitting in the room with support from Native Counseling Services. I didn't think this was fair, since it was just supposed to be the two of us with the judge and with Grace's lawyer, who represented Grace, since she was too young to be sitting in that room. Quite frankly, I felt blindsided and alone.

Prior to our JDR, the court worker had asked me to let her know the outcome of the JDR, indicating she was not able to attend with me. I thought this would be a one-and-done-type deal. I was mistaken. After the JDR, I followed up with her and inquired as to why she wasn't allowed in the JDR, but Native Counseling Services court workers were there.

She said, "That's not typical, for any court workers to sit in JDRs. That was not appropriate."

*I knew my gut was telling me something felt wrong.* I learned in the JDR that the court worker representing Johnny was a relative of his. I recognize, in Indigenous communities, most people are related in some way, but I felt like there was still bias present. I felted backed into a corner, giving him an advantage. *Who was going to advocate for me?*

When we all sat down, my anxiety was at an all-time high. Being forced to sit in a room with your abuser is one of the most uncomfortable, unsafe, and inappropriate things the courts make you do. But that's not all. Despite how much work you have put into yourself to heal from past traumas and abuse, nothing takes away that feeling of having to sit with your abuser, as all of the old feelings bubble up to the surface.

When the judge walked into the room, I felt a sense of relief. She was a woman, which made me think she would have compassion and understanding. What was coincidental was she had been the lawyer who'd done the paperwork when Johnny and I sold our house, years ago. Johnny had been quite difficult during that time, too.

During the sale process, I hadn't wanted to disclose my address at the time, so she and I had waited until he left the room, so I could sign the paperwork and provide my ID, to verify my identity.

As I was signing the papers, the lawyer (now our judge) had said to me, "That guy is a real asshole."

When she walked into the JDR room, I wondered if she remembered us at all. I doubted it, though: she had seen dozens upon dozens of cases since that time.

After introduction and an explanation of how the JDR would go, the "process" began.

Our JDR was three and a half hours long. The majority of the JDR was focused on the Indigenous culture and how the judge could be more involved. She asked many questions. While that was great and a long time coming, based on the history and current reality of relationships between Indigenous people, the justice system, and mass incarceration of Indigenous people in Canada, I did not believe this room was the time or place for these discussions to take place.

It was a complete waste of time, and something that caused my nerves to ratchet to an all-time high. None of this talk served the purpose of why we were there in the first place. We didn't get very far into deciding anything that day, because of how infatuated the judge was with Johnny's culture. Because the conversations appeared to be oriented toward him, his career, and his culture, he drank the Kool-Aid and was on his best behaviour. He took the opportunity to talk about being part of the sacred society he belonged to, and he came across as holier than thou, which only sparked the judge's curiosity and desire to be a part of it all.

To me, it felt as though the pendulum had swung in a completely different direction. From the court's mistreating Indigenous people to being blinded and dazzled by culture.

During the JDR, Johnny took the opportunity to claim that I was ruining his reputation and trying to ruin his career; that was why I charged him back in 2022. What happened next is something I will never forget.

After listening to Johnny, the judge turned to me, made eye contact, and said, "You really hurt his feelings when you charged him."

I could not believe what I just heard. My mind was flooded with internal thoughts. *That is not how that works. What about the amount of grief Grace and I have had to deal with? What about the bed wetting, the trauma, nightmares, lack of sleep, and everything else we have endured? Doesn't that matter?*

The only thing really discussed were Grace's instructions to her lawyer. She had said she was willing to spend one night with her dad at the Sundance, which was scheduled for later that summer. The Sundance is a time of renewal. It is a sacred ceremony held in high regard in their culture; it occurs on the reserve each year. It is a beautiful experience, something you need to experience to understand. It's not really my place to speak about what takes place there or any of its practices, so I won't go into much more detail than that.

I was in support of Grace going, since it was a part of her culture and something she had identified as an event she would go to, in order to spend time with her dad, and would feel safe in doing so. It aligned with what I'd asked for in the court order, as well. During the JDR, we decided on a date when Grace would go. This was put in the interim court order. Depending on how it went, that would determine next steps. We would schedule another JDR at a later date, likely in the fall.

Before the overnight at the Sundance, Grace started having a rough time. By the beginning of August, she refused to sleep in her own room. She was again scared her dad would climb up to her window and take her in the middle of the night.

I talked to my parents about this, and we brainstormed ideas about what I could do to make her feel safer. A few days later, my dad installed cameras at our house. Grace had said that might help her, and I was very hopeful it would. Little did I know how much more safety and comfort they would provide me, as well.

Unfortunately, nighttime remained difficult. Even though our cameras were operational, Grace refused to sleep in her room. For one week straight, she asked me every day, "Are the cameras recording?" I assured her they were.

One night, there was a knock on our door. Grace immediately began to panic and cry. "Is it my dad? Is he coming to get me?"

Later, she told me, "My dad said, if he picks me up for Sundance, I cannot fuss, and I can't talk about you, Mom."

What a strange thing to say to a child. I never understood why she was not allowed to talk to me or about me when she was with her dad. I keep documenting, but there was not much else I could do.

This was taking a toll on me. Not only was I dealing with my own emotions and deep feelings of trauma because of the constant exposure, I was also taking on Grace's pain, while trying to help her navigate all of her fears and big feelings. Not long after this, I began having tremendous issues sleeping at night. I would wake up feeling anxious, worrying about what was going to happen next. Fear of the unknown crept in.

I guess I was always kind of walking on eggshells, waiting for the other shoe to drop. I worried Johnny would wreck my property or would hurt me or Grace. It was the most unstable and unsafe I had ever felt in my life, despite all of the earlier difficult, traumatic experiences I had gone through.

One evening, I notice a vehicle parked outside of my house. I had become hypervigilant over time, so I was super-aware of my environment, and I'd started to question everything. I didn't want to sound the alarms, so I kept note and waited. A few days later, the car was still there. As far as I could tell, it hadn't moved at all. Vehicles aren't supposed to park in front of my house; there is a No Parking sign, so that emergency vehicles can get through.

I shared my concern with a few friends who worked in law enforcement. They encouraged me to get the license plate number, so they could find out more information, if they needed to. The next day, I saw someone sitting in the driver's seat, eating. I watched him for a bit to see where he went or what he was up to. I felt a bit weird about this, but this was for my safety.

I even started to have regular chest pains. I wasn't sure how much longer I could take the stress and this living in constant turmoil. It felt like it was never going to end.

# Chapter 28

## Broken Bones, Broken Hearts, and Broken Systems

The summer of 2024 was one of the most difficult chapters of my life.

My relationship with Robert ended in late 2023. While it wasn't all bad, there were some red flags that had started to surface during the course of our relationship, specifically around power and control and his attempts to minimize me and my knowledge. I knew that was something I did not deserve or want to experience again.

He also expressed concerns about men looking at me at the gym, telling me I was oblivious to that. He had even prevented me from attending the gym a few times, saying I wasn't allowed to go, even when we were on vacation and going to the gym together. Other times, he told me I prioritized the gym over being a mom, and I felt myself slipping into old patterns of justifying my behavior when I didn't need to. Other times, he would try to minimize my knowledge, whether dismissing my academic credentials or my passion for knowledge that led me to reading many books.

He would say things like, "I don't need to read stupid books like that to find those answers."

He would tell me that my knowledge in leadership was "hippy," and he didn't want me sharing my knowledge with his team. He also attacked my parenting style and sometimes who I was as a person. The straw that broke the camel's back was ultimately untrue.

I met Vinny through work about a year before Robert and I broke up. Because we were both in relationships at the time, we started as colleagues that evolved into a friendship. Over time, Vinny and I both became single and ended up exploring what a relationship could look like.

Vinny was the first guy I'd felt seen by, someone I could be authentic with. He cared about the knowledge I had, my research, what I had to say, my thought process, and recognized the passion for the work I did. He came to many of my presentations, so I felt really supported. Our relationship felt genuine and natural. It was everything I could have asked for, and he was what I was looking for in a partner.

Eventually, it developed into a relationship, and we started dating in May 2024. I felt I could be very honest with him, and my fear of abandonment did not take control, so I showed up as the most authentic version of myself. This was new, after my childhood trauma.

Vinny was a sergeant with the RCMP, which was a bit concerning for me in the beginning, as RCMP officers are expected to move locations every four years or so. While not so much anymore, this was something I held in the back of my mind, because I wasn't sure what it would look like if he were to move. I couldn't just pack up our life and follow him.

Vinny was at a point in his career where he could have stayed, because he was closing in on retirement after putting in his time at the RCMP and in the military. He had children, but they lived in in another province with their mom.

This was perfect for me, because, quite frankly, I didn't want to date someone with children. I know, I had a child, but I had no strong desire to have more than one. As women, I think we need to become comfortable saying that. We shouldn't have to live in a world where society's expectations are that we have multiple children and become stay-at-home moms. If that's what you choose to do, that's totally okay, but this need not be every woman's narrative.

What I'd learned in my relationship with Robert was that blending families was quite difficult, and I wasn't sure I wanted to do that again, either. So, Vinny and I had very honest conversations about what our relationship would look like. I was very up front and candid about my desire to stay where I lived until my daughter was at least an adult.

Vinny said, "I'm okay with that. I love policing here and in this community."

We also talked about potentially going overseas once Grace was an adult. He extended an invitation for her to join us, if she chose to do so. I was still concerned, in the back of my mind, he might need to relocate, so I asked what would happen if he was reassigned.

He said, "I would tell them no. And if anything, I can retire and do consulting," adding, "I'll figure it out." Although I had a lot of misgivings, I trusted and believed him.

I was so proud of myself for speaking my truth, leaning into my values, and not "chasing" a guy for fear of him leaving me. This was such new territory for me, but I felt so empowered!

Vinny had been policing in a neighboring community for the year or so before we met. He'd shuffled to fill in at a few other places and then landed back in that community. He still owned a house nearby his previous posting and was in the process of selling. (The RCMP will pay for housing for a period of time, if you are relocated, but eventually, you are expected to purchase something on your own.) He said he was excited to look for houses in and around my community, and we had lots of conversation about what this could look like.

One day, he asked, "Do you want to come look for houses with me? I want your input."

Things felt like they were moving faster speed than most relationships, but because he was older and we were older, I thought, since we knew what we wanted, why waste time. We had agreed, after we'd been together for a year, I would move in with him. I wasn't ready to sell my house and go all in off the hop, and I'm sure glad I didn't.

We looked at many houses, and it was such a fun experience! I love looking at houses and dreaming of possibilities. We saw some really nasty houses, too, but overall, it was a good experience. Vinny could have looked at places closer to the mountains, just so he remained within fifty kilometers of his detachment. However, he chose to look closer to my community, so my commute would be shorter.

A few weeks later, we found an acreage and decided it was worth his putting an offer on it. It was thirty minutes away from my community, which was doable. I was so excited about the future. It felt like a dream come true, and that all of the hurt and pain I had gone through had led me here.

By early June 2024, he'd bought the acreage and was set to move in August. Meanwhile, he was still living in his rental with the RCMP. One time, when I was over visiting, we were chatting about how our days had been. It was so nice, being able to do this with someone, engaging in meaningful conversations. I used to dream of coming home from work and being able to decompress with someone. It felt like I'd finally found this.

Policing in that community was pretty intense. There were added stressors, because chief and council members would call at all hours of the night. Sometimes, people would complain about their family members being arrested. Other times, it was to talk about other things. Sometimes, I was present for some of these calls and knew this would probably put me in a state of burnout, if I was in his shoes.

After we ate dinner, we were sitting on the couch, continuing our conversation, when he said to me, "I've been experiencing chest pains. Policing in this area is really tough."

I immediately thought back to our conversation about how he loved policing in this community and how he would figure it out, but his body was sending a different message. A stronger one. I remained calm and tried not to jump to assumptions, but I could feel my anxious abandonment wounds surface within me.

As a partner, I cared for him and worried about his health. A heart is nothing to mess with. I asked, "Do you think you can continue to police here for the next five years, given the toll it's taking on your health?"

He had an immediate tough-guy response. "Oh yes, absolutely. I love policing here."

But I think my question weighed heavier than he initially let on. The energy in the room grew a bit weird, after that. Even a little uncomfortable. My heart sank, and I immediately assumed the worst. *I thought I was over this.* My old abandonment wounds were surfacing, the feeling of a heart break looming. For some reason, I didn't think I'd have to experience that again, especially with him.

We continued the conversation for a little while longer, my head on his lap. I looked up at him then gazed into the distance and asked, "What does this mean for us?"

He said, "I don't want you to think like that. We will figure it out."

I wanted to believe him, but I didn't want to suppress my own feelings anymore. I said, "I don't want another failed relationship." My heart felt like it was going to beat out of my chest.

He played with my hair and said, "Aww, Chels, don't say things like that."

But I couldn't help it. This was becoming very real for me, and deep down I was scared.

I eventually left and went home for the evening. After that evening, Vinny became very distant and ended up ghosting me for a day or so. I resorted to old patterns and essentially begged him to communicate with me and tell me what was going on. I hated who I was becoming in this process, but I wanted answers. *Didn't I deserve that?*

When he did finally communicate, he was very short with me, and his response times lagged. This was so different from how he'd typically been. I knew something was off. He went from being super-responsive, with detailed, thoughtful responses, even driving forty-five minutes a day to come see me, to essentially nothing.

This went on for approximately two weeks. My gut was telling me something was seriously wrong, but my mind refused to believe it. I was holding on to hope, a familiar reaction I had tried so hard to break. Yet I found myself here again.

In the beginning of July, Vinny was supposed to come with me to my friend's birthday. They camp every year, and I was excited for him to officially meet them. I was always the single friend, so this year, I was happy to finally have someone I could bring around and be proud of. I texted him that morning, when we were supposed to head out to the campground. He did not respond for quite some time.

Finally, he replied, "I'll see how I feel." He never showed up or even bothered to communicate with me. It felt like I was dying a slow, painful death.

I didn't want to burden him or worry myself silly anymore. My heart and gut knew something was off. My gut has never been wrong, but I always try to convince myself otherwise and give people the benefit of the doubt. While this approach is not necessarily bad, I was tired of giving everyone the benefit of the doubt while sacrificing my own wellness.

Eventually, he sent me a text. It felt like a good conversation, based on the silent couple of weeks. But also, pretty surface-level. He wrote, "I don't think I can give you what you need. I'm not being a very good partner." He added every excuse someone can come up with when they can't speak their truth or take responsibility for what is really going on.

I finally had a phone conversation with him later that night, and we ended up talking for a few hours. Part of me was still grasping at straws, and I felt a bit desperate.

He said, "I'll look for postings in Southern Alberta, but nobody is moving. They are all in their positions, waiting to retire." I felt hopeful when he said that. *Maybe this isn't the end.*

Over the following days, he was still distant toward me. Finally, I ripped off the Band-Aid and mustered the courage to send him a text message. I had nothing to lose.

I wrote, "I cannot fight for someone who isn't willing to fight for me." I wrote much more, but I deleted all of those messages and my history with him, because it was too much for me to hold onto, with my phone as a constant reminder of what was.

He responded awhile later. "The RCMP is relocating me, and I'll be moving in the next month or so. I am not sure I want to continue to invest in something if I am moving."

My heart was shattered. I'd felt this coming, but I'd still hopeful for a different outcome. This was the greatest heartbreak I'd ever felt.

I cried for days on end, literally. I had never felt a break like this one. I was so proud of myself for owning who I was and bringing my best, most honest, and authentic self forward. Even though it still hurt. Even though this was the outcome, something I never wanted.

What hurt the most was that *he never left*. It's two years later, and he is still policing in that community. The hardest part of this entire situation was accepting that I will never have an answer as to why we broke up. I've had to learn to be okay with that. Some people just cannot meet me at these depths. Bottom line: *he promised me a life he wasn't capable of giving me.*

During our relationship, Vinny knew my situation with Johnny. I was initially worried he would judge me for it, based on his profession, but he appeared to love me through it all, until he didn't. He told me once, "I wish your stuff was in RCMP country, because we have so many checks and balances when it comes to domestic violence." *Hmm,* I'd thought. I wish I did, too. Maybe he was right. After all, Vinny works for them. He would know.

Fast forward to a year later, and my file ended up in RCMP country. I learned firsthand how they may have written procedures around domestic abuse, but the implementation of those policies and daily practice were incongruent. It depended on the officer responding and the discretion they used. I often thought back and wished I could have told Vinny how broken his beloved RCMP policies and practices were, but that is something I just have to take with me. Fortunately, I've been able to explain that to other RCMP members in my life.

This chapter of my life consisted of broken bones, too. *Like it couldn't get any worse.*

After I mended my heart (or a large part of it, anyway), I was working with our mentor on a provincial framework for mentors in drug treatment court. We were scheduled to travel to different communities across our province that had drug courts, where we'd engage in the interview process, collect data, and create a framework and guidelines for mentors.

When it was time for me to head to Edmonton to interview that court, our mentor lived there, so I was going to meet her there. I had plans to pack, hit the gym, and then make the five-hour trek to Edmonton.

I was almost packed but needed to grab a few more things, like my gratitude journal and another book. My hands were full as I walked up the stairs. My house has five levels, and my room is on the top floor. As I headed up the last flight of stairs, I tripped. *Going up.* Not only did I trip and fall, I broke my foot in the process. I didn't know it initially, though. I thought I had sprained or twisted it, because that's what it felt like, bringing me back to my childhood, when a sprained ankle seemed to be a yearly event.

It became swollen almost immediately. I sat on the stairs and cried. Grace went to get ice and called my dad. No answer. When he called back, he asked, "What's up?" After I told him, he said, "Do I need to come?"

I said no, I should be okay. "I am putting ice on it, and I should be good to go in a bit." I sat on my stairs, icing my foot and ankle for a while, and then went on my way… to the gym. Probably not the smartest choice, but that's where I was headed. I was adamant to get a workout in before the drive.

I hobbled around the gym, finished my workout, and then got into my vehicle to head to Edmonton. I'd planned my route for the fastest way out of the city and started to drive. I had my luggage and everything with me, so there was no need to go back home for anything.

I was only two minutes away from the gym when I received a text message from Grace. "I think I broke my nose." *You've got to be frickin' kidding me.*

I called her. "What happened?"

She said, "I was at the pool with my friend, and she came up from underneath the water and smashed me in the face with her head. My nose was bleeding really bad."

I asked her if she needed me to come look at it. She sent me a picture, and it didn't look so good. *I guess I'm not heading to Edmonton. I'm going west, instead.*

I headed back to the westside and picked Grace up from her friend's house. I called 811, the number to health link, and asked whether she needed medical attention, since I had no idea what to do in this situation. I'd never broken my nose.

The nurse said, "If it bled and looks out of place, you need to go to the emergency room."

So, I cancelled my Edmonton plans and headed to the hospital, instead. The nurse estimated a thirty-minute wait, which didn't sound too bad for an emergency room. We left right away for the ten-to-fifteen-minute drive.

As soon as we walked through the ER doors and I scanned the waiting room, I saw it was full. I thought, *There is no way this is a thirty-minute wait.* I spoke to the nurse at the triage desk who said, "Are you sure you want to be here?"

With a smile, I replied, "Listen, if I don't have to be here, we will gladly leave. 811 told us to come because of her nose."

She said, "You can probably leave, but I'd like to get a second opinion, just in case." She disappeared from the desk. When she returned moments later, she told us, "Another nurse will be up in a minute to provide his opinion."

The second nurse came and looked at Grace's nose. "Oh yeah, you want to get that looked at."

So, we sat in the waiting room for hours before getting taken back to a room. We were there a total of five and a half hours. Our room was at the end of the busy hallway, unfortunately stuck beside someone who was violently throwing up and making terrible noises. They sounded like they were in a lot of pain. Listening to that for hours was not a fun experience, but you never know what you're going to get in that place. If anyone has ever spent a significant amount of time in the ER, you know what I am talking about.

Finally, a doctor came in, did a quick assessment, and said, "Do you want me to adjust her nose?"

I looked at Grace, who looked back at me, terrified. I asked him, "Is that something you think you should do? I don't know anything about this."

He did absolutely nothing, just said, "We should wait for the swelling to go down before we do anything."

I thought, *What the hell…? We waited* this *long just for* this*?*

While we were waiting for the doctor, to kill time, I made a post on social media showing my foot, which looked like I had a third ankle on the top of my foot. I was working with a very knowledgeable Olympic weightlifting coach at the time who replied, "Dude, your foot is broken."

"I can still walk on it. Can you walk on broken bones?"

"Yes, you can," he wrote. "Go get that checked out."

Ironically, there we were, in the hospital. *How convenient.* Though Grace's doctor had a bit of an attitude, I thought it would be great to ask him about my foot, too. Once he finished assessing Grace, I asked, "Hey, does my foot look weird to you?

He replied, "No, but if you want me to look at it, you have to go back through triage and wait in the waiting room."

My immediate thought was, *Absolutely not. I'm not waiting another five-plus hours. I'll come back another time.*

The following day, I again looked at the wait times and again it said under thirty minutes. I hobbled back to the ER and found the waiting room was empty. I thought, *Perfect! I'll be in and out of here in no time.*

I was put into a room in the back relatively quickly, but then I remained stuck there for another five hours. I watched investigators with the police go back, and inmates being wheeled in on stretchers. *Great. They'll get priority over me.* The nosey part of me wondered what had happened, though.

Finally, someone I knew was put in the room next to me. She explained how she'd broken her ankle walking her dog earlier that morning. She got lucky: she was given crutches and a cast and then left before me. At least I killed some time, visiting with her.

Finally, I was assessed and directed to get an X-ray. Once that was completed, I was put back into my room to wait for the doctor to see me. When he came, he said, "We have your results." At the viewing station, he pointed to the bone on my X-ray and explained, "You have a small break in your metatarsal bone."

I asked, "Okay, so, what do I do for it?"

His response: "Walk it off."

"Really?" I asked. "No air cast or anything"

"Nope," he said again. "Just walk. Air casts won't do much for you, given where the break is."

So, walking away is what I did. I hobbled back to my vehicle, thinking to myself, *What a waste of time.* At least I got confirmation, but there was no real outcome. So, I kept walking and living my life. One hobble at a time.

At a follow-up appointment with my family doctor four to six weeks later, she told me, "Your foot isn't broken."

I was confused. "The doctor showed me the X-ray and explained to me what was broken."

She said, "No, it's not broken. See?" She turned her computer toward me. There was no X-ray, just a written report. It blew my mind. I asked for an ultrasound, to be sure there was no ligament damage, which she did think I may have.

Long story short, I fought with the medical system over my own health needs, and then I followed rehab protocol from my coach, which was far more helpful. A year later, I had a follow-up MRI that confirmed there was no sign of any damage, which was great. I healed up fine.

This part of my life wouldn't be complete without ending with broken systems.

On July 31, 2024, Grace was scheduled to spend the night at the Sundance with her dad. She began to panic, saying, "I'm scared my auntie is going to beat my mama up."

This seemed like an odd thing to say, but it had to be coming from somewhere. I knew there had been historical violence between Johnny's family members, along with poor behavior, so it didn't seem totally impossible. I wanted this to be a good, safe experience for Grace, so I decided to ask Johnny about it.

He claimed to be unaware and said, "I'll ask Grace."

Rosie picked up Grace from my parents' house a little while later. I stayed with them for a bit then headed to the gym. Less than an hour later, my mom started receiving text messages from Grace. (She could not text my iPhone but could reach my mom's android.)

In one message, Grace said, "My dad is yelling and blaming my mom for everything."

Johnny had taken Grace to his house, dropped her off, and headed out to the reserve on his own. While I was still at my parents', he called me, yelling and very accusatory. He demanded, "Why does Grace not want to be there?"

My mom was still texting with Grace, who told her Rosie was going to bring her back to my parents' home. I was a bit confused as to all the moving parts, but what became clear was Grace was planning her exit, but trying to be strategic.

I remained on the phone with Johnny, trying to put the pieces together. He continued, "You are coming to get Grace."

I said, "I am not coming to get her. I was told Rosie was bringing her to me."

Angrily, he said, "*What*? The courts aren't going to like this. You are breaching this order. You are supposed to make her stay here."

I replied, "Johnny, if my daughter feels unsafe somewhere and is being screamed at, I will never make her stay. And I am sure you would do the same thing."

He said, "No, I would tell her she needs to respect her parent and I'd make her stay."

I reminded him of their history and that he needed to remember that. He got mad, saying, "I got charged because you are a liar, a manipulator, and always playing the victim."

I hung up the phone.

Grace called me shortly after and said, "My dad asked me for better reasons why I don't want to be there or sleep there. He said feeling unsafe was not a good-enough reason."

I felt so enraged yet so helpless. I wanted to go and get her, but I knew it wasn't safe for me to do so. I needed to protect myself, so I could continue to protect her. *At what cost* kept replaying in my mind. Johnny must have turned his vehicle around and gone back home to get her. He did not let Rosie bring Grace to me, so she ended up being taken to the reserve, instead.

The power and control dynamics of how this played out made me sick to my stomach. I felt like, no matter how hard I racked my brain, I could think of nothing to do. So, I went to the gym and tried to plan my next move that would keep us both safe.

While I was at the gym, text messages from my mom kept blowing up my phone. She sent screen shots of text messages from Grace, along with photos of her crying. From what I could gather, on the car ride out to the reserve, Johnny continued to berate Grace, which is what had prompted the text messages and photos to my mom and then to me.

I remember being on the bench, doing single arm rows, thinking to myself, *What the fuck am I going to do? What can I do?* The police didn't believe me, and I didn't want to go through that again. I still had the lingering fear, *Could they actually arrest me? Then what happens to Grace? I can't go to jail.* I keep working out, but the thoughts weighing on my mind became too much for me. I knew the courts would continue to blame me, and if I did anything, Johnny would have reasons to say, "See! I told you she interferes with my parenting time."

After our last JDR, with the judge who was so obsessed with Johnny and the culture, there was no way I felt safe. I felt so trapped. No matter what I did, I was fucked. *I need to take care of Grace. But how!?*

Around dinner time, more text messages came rolling in. "Mama, my dad is yelling at me. I'm crying. He's blaming stuff on my mom, and I am telling him why do you always blame my mom?"

My own mother was also feeling trapped and helpless. She asked her, "Are you going to be okay?"

The conversation continued follows (including the spelling as Grace wrote it, so grammatical errors to be expected):

Grace: *"mama, my dad is yelling at me. I'm crying because he's blaming stuff on my mom and I'm telling him why do you always blame my mom."*
My mom: *"oh no Grace, are you going to be okay?"*
Grace: *"idk, tell my mom tho but don't let her tell my dad."*
My mom: *"if you're not feeling safe, go to the police tipi."*
Grace: *"I'm not at Sundance. Did you tell my mom."*
My mom: *"But when you are. Yes I did."*
Grace: *"ok did she text back, I'm really scared to go to Sundance."*
Grace: *Sends a photo of herself crying.*
Grace: *"Rosie's going later but still. I wanna go back to my mom's where I feel safe."*
My mom: *"ummm what do we do?"*
Grace: *"idk but I am scared"*
Grace: *sends another photo of her crying.*
My mom: *"what happened"*
Grace: *"he was yelling. He doesn't want me to go to the powwow."*
My mom: *"oh man"*
Grace: *"yeah he said u can miss one powwow for once and I told him I want to dance and he told me so ur choosing dancing over family like I never said that"*
My mom: *"geez, will you be okay out there?"*
Grace: *"my mom will get me soon."*
My mom: *"she is?"*
Grace: *"yeah when my dad leaves. Cause only mama and Rosie will be there."*
My mom: *"oh, will they let you leave?"*
Grace: *"yeah maybe. I hope I'm just really nervous right now."*
My mom: *"this is not good."*
Grace: *"yah but he's talking to Rosie" next text "mama tell my mom he's gone."*

My mom: *"Diamond city I imagine."*
Grace: *"yeah u will see a white truck and Rosies' car"*
My mom: *"okay I will tell her."*
Grace: *"I told her and she told me I get it, yes I will bring you there." (in relation to Grace and Rosie's conversation).*
my mom: *"okay"*
Grace: *"now my dad is making me spend the whole day with him"*
My mom: *"what"*
Grace: *"yeah but I can't do this. I can't do this." "Tell my mom I need her to come get me pls."*
*"wait don't but can you tell her to tell my lawyer. I'm sad."*
My mom: *"Okay what should your mom do?"*
Grace: *"he's calling my lawyer." Next text "he's calling her."*
Grace: *"he's blaming my mom now"*
My mom: *"but why her?"*
Grace: *"idk" "he told me that my mom is threatening to pick me up"*
My mom: *"omg you asked her to cause you were scared"*
Grace: *"ik"*
Grace: *"He's talking about my mom but I am going to ask Papa Jake to bring me and he told the girl that my mom was saying that it's an unhealthy place to be."*

I was still in town and went to my friend's house to get my nails done. Afterward, we had plans to hang out in her pool. I briefly mentioned what was going on and how I felt really stressed and unsure of what to do. She was at a loss for words, too.

While I was getting my nails done, Grace called and asked what she should do, since she was still feeling unsafe. I told her to go to the police tipi and ask for an officer. Grace called me back a little while later to say there were no police at the tipi. I told her to find someone around there and ask for an officer.

She followed my directions and called me back five to ten minutes later, saying she'd asked a lady there where the police were. The lady had pointed to a male officer and said, "There is one, but he is off duty. What do you need the police for?"

Grace replied, "I am feeling unsafe because of my dad, and I want to go home." She indicated there had been previous abuse and he was continuing to yell at her and make her feel unsafe.

The lady told Grace, "The police will have to open an investigation, if that's true. Otherwise, you have to go back to your dad."

When she told me this, I was livid. *Who was that person to tell her that?* That was unacceptable. All I could think to do next was, since Grace was on the reserve, to call my friend who was an inspector with the tribal police.

My emotions were heightened, and my body began to shake. As soon as my friend picked up the phone, my tears started flowing, and I could barely make out my words. I explained what was happening and told him I was at a loss for what to do, plus I did not like the response this random lady gave to Grace at the tipi. He was also concerned and told me he would send an officer down to talk to Grace right away. I stayed by my phone.

The officer assigned to go speak to Grace was someone I had hung out with in my teenage years. Cue the stigma, but I felt hopeful, too, since I knew he was kind and would be able to speak to Grace in a good way. The drawback was that Johnny also knew the officer from childhood. My friend reassured me that this was a good officer to deal with the situation.

I made some calls to Grace to inform her and help her be ready to meet the officer when he arrived at the police tipi.

About five hours after this whole crisis began, the police were finally able to speak to Grace, and she was in a different state of mind. *Five hours is a long time.* The responding officer called me to say, "I met with Grace. When I asked her if she was okay, she told me she was and was going to see the horses. Unfortunately, there is not much more that I can do at this time."

This was not the outcome I'd anticipated, but what else can you do, when so much time has lapsed? The officer added, "There is not much we can do from here, but I can go have a conversation with Johnny about what's gone on."

I was a bit worried about the outcome of this, as I knew Johnny hated the police.

Grace eventually went back to the camp and told us the police were talking to her dad. Grace said, "I heard my grandpa tell my dad he should just let me go back home." It was evident Johnny did not support that idea. This was more about power and control.

After the officer spoke with Johnny, he again called me. "I had a conversation with Johnny. He said that Grace will be brought home by 9:00 p.m. tonight. I will draft up a report and send it to you.

Shortly after, Grace called. "Mom, I'm scared my dad is going to hurt you." When I asked why, she said, "He was saying bad things about you and that he could lose his job because of you."

9:00 p.m. rolled around, and Grace was still not home. I connected with her, and she informed me she would be sleeping at her dad's tonight, as the other children were too tired and Rosie was unable to give Grace a ride home.

*Was this another one of their manipulation tactics? They'd lied. To the* police. *Where was the accountability in this?*

The next morning, I spoke to Grace at 9:46 a.m. and asked her what the plan was and when she thought she would be brought home. "I don't know. My dad is still sleeping, but Rosie should be home within the next thirty minutes. She could bring me."

I missed calls from Grace at 9:49 a.m. and 9:50 a.m. I called her back at 10:07 a.m. No answer. She called me back a few minutes later, twice. But Grace was still not brought home.

At 12:05 p.m., I received a call from her again, asking if I could go pick her up.

I drove to the community where Johnny and his family had recently moved, which is about fifteen minutes from where I live. I had no idea where I was going, but I did my best to follow Grace's directions.

As I was driving, my mind was racing. *He is going to be so mad when I get there. Is this safe? What's going to happen? Will he cause a scene? Am I going to be able to find the house okay? I hope she comes out, and we can get the heck out of there.*

I arrive at 12:22 p.m. with no idea where their house was. I parked adjacent to the park, a short distance from their house, where I could still see. (Though later, I learned I was nowhere near the correct house.)

At 12:25 p.m., I receive a text message from Johnny. "You cannot pick up Grace without talking to me first."

I responded, "You're sleeping."

He said, "This is my time with her, and it's stated in the court order. You come to my house, I am calling the cops."

I reminded him she was to have been brought home last night.

This only escalated the situation. He responded, "I don't have to explain anything to you. I don't have to communicate with you when you call the cops on me when I am at Sundance during my time with my daughter."

I explained, I was there to pick her up, because we had to go to Calgary later that day.

Johnny then said, "I called the officer where Grace's lawyer works and spoke to the assistant about your actions and how you are undermining my time with Grace. If you show up at my house, I'm calling the cops."

I replied, "Go ahead. I am here to pick Grace up as per her request."

He said, "You're harassing me when it's my time with her. It says nothing about you picking her up without me knowing, and you are not supposed to be texting with Grace and talking behind my back when she is at home with me."

I responded, "I came here to pick her up as she requested."

"Not requested by me."

Johnny's words via text messages were making me feel like he was gaslighting me, but I had very little control of the situation. I didn't know what to do.

I tried to remain calm and plan next steps on how to navigate the situation. I messaged Johnny to say Grace had the right to contact me and ask to be picked up. It was also in our order that Grace needed to have communication with her parents when she was with the other. He stopped responding.

I made numerous attempts to call Grace. I was becoming increasingly worried as each minute passed. *Is she safe? What is going on? Why hasn't she come out of the house?* (Remember, I thought I had a visual on the correct house.) I had visions of her running out of the house and getting into my vehicle then us leaving.

I felt sick to my stomach. Something didn't feel right. *Where the hell is she? Why isn't she answering?* All of these thoughts raced through my mind, a million miles a minute. *What if he killed her?*

I was sitting alone in my vehicle, terrified. Too scared to go to the residence.

I decided to call the RCMP liaison with whom I worked closely. I hated blending my personal life with my professional life, and in some way, I felt a bit pitiful, but I had to put all of that aside, as this was my daughter's safety, which meant more than anything.

For some reason, I made myself believe it wasn't serious enough to call for a wellbeing check. Maybe that was because of the way the system made me feel: oppressed. Nobody seemed to believe me when I expressed my safety concerns. This added to more self-doubt and gaslighting myself.

I called the liaison, and she answered. *Thank God.* I explained what had happened. She reassured me, "You did the right thing. There is nothing you can get into trouble for. You absolutely need to call and ask for a wellbeing check. Your daughter is inside of a home with an abuser and not making contact."

When we hung up the phone, I called the complaint line and spoke with RCMP dispatch.

At 1:37 p.m., I received a call from Johnny telling me, "Stop calling Grace. I am with her."

I could hear her crying in the background, saying, "Mom." This made me feel even more uneasy in the depths of my stomach. It felt like a scene from a horror movie.

I said, "I can hear her crying, Johnny. Just let her go."

He said, "She's fine. She's not dying."

*What the fuck was that supposed to mean? Why is she crying for me like that?* The cry was one of despair. I knew something wasn't right. This is the most helpless and hopeless I'd felt in a long time, if ever.

He proceeded to tell me, "You are not allowed to talk to her when she is with me," followed by, "You called the cops on me yesterday, you fucking psycho."

I hung up the phone. I knew Grace was in the background and could hear this conversation. She deserved more than this.

Scared, worried, and frustrated, I was still waiting for police. I called my dad and explained what was going on. When Johnny and I were together, he and my dad had had a good relationship. Many times, when issues surfaced during our relationship, I'd felt like my dad took Johnny's side more than mine, even when it was not really about taking sides.

My dad said he would try to call Johnny. When he called me back, he said, "Johnny didn't answer, so I left him a voicemail." Johnny would later tell the courts that my dad was harassing him, yet Johnny returned my dad's call, and they spoke at length.

During the conversation, my dad suggested to Johnny, "If Grace doesn't want to be there, let her go. Bring her home. This is doing more harm than good to your relationship."

Johnny appeared to be furious. He kept referring back to the court order and his parenting time, however this date and time was not specified in any order. He was actually in breach of the order, because there is a condition in there that indicates, when Grace is with either parent, she must have the ability to communicate with the other parent via text or phone calls, and he took that away from her.

My dad continued, "Grace is a human being, not something you own."

Johnny said, "Grace has a way of manipulating Chelsey and making the situation worse."

"I want you to have a relationship with your daughter, but trying to raise her through a court order will do more harm than good."

Johnny bit back, "I have more information on you than you'll ever know." He continued, "I have other children to raise," then spoke harshly to my dad about the way he'd raised me and his own children. He continued, "Chelsey charged me with assault, and those charges got dropped. I won that. But I could have lost my career. Your daughter has taken me to court seven fucking times, and I've won each time." He continued, "If your daughter wasn't such a psycho bitch, I would have Grace."

The RCMP finally arrived. A male officer met me at the park where I'd been waiting and told me I couldn't actually see the correct house. In fact, I was nowhere near where Johnny lived. I just wanted them to get Grace out of that house, but there was no urgency in their approach. A female officer arrived, too, then the male officer phoned Johnny and got the correct address. The male and female officer left to Johnny's house, while I remained parked where I was.

When the male officer returned, he said, "Johnny said exactly what you said he would. That you are trying to ruin his career."

I had a small hunch that the police protected Johnny because he was a first responder, too. It's not often talked about; like a silent code that isn't broken often. The female officer arrived, so I was talking to both officers from inside my car.

The male officer told me that my police clause was "too weak," that they could not take Grace from Johnny, because he was a guardian, and they don't apprehend from guardians. I thought to myself, *You guys apprehend children from parents all the time with child welfare. What do you mean, you don't do that? Especially when the child is saying she is scared.*

The female officer said, "Johnny was becoming quite aggressive when we spoke to him. We warned him, if he continued to escalate, we would have to come back." She continued, "Johnny asked us if we were saying he was abusive. He is quite difficult to deal with," she added, as if that didn't raise any red flags or cause concern for them.

The female officer said that, when she was speaking to Grace separately, Grace had said she was scared and wanted to go home with me. "Grace disclosed that Johnny threw a metal container into the wall, creating a hole."

I informed the police how Grace had already struggled with suicide ideation, and the last thing I needed was for my daughter to kill herself over this.

The female officer said, "We don't want that, either. If things get worse, you can always call us back."

The male officer chimed in, "Johnny said he will bring Grace home by 7:00 p.m. tonight." Then, they'd left Grace in the residence with him.

I couldn't believe it. After the history, Grace's disclosure, and Johnny's escalated behaviors, even in front of the police, plus everything that had happened today, nothing was done. I wanted to scream.

When the police left, I pulled away, too and started to drive home. Grace texted my mom to say she was going to run away, as she could not breathe. *What else has to happen before we are taken seriously?* I couldn't help but wonder how scared Grace must've been feeling.

At 7:00 p.m., Grace wasn't home. She called me from her dad's phone at 8:06 p.m., asking to be picked up from Sundance. I was frustrated by this request, which felt like another manipulation tactic on his part. *Why is he able to skirt around times and accountability, yet I'm threatened to be arrested for having good reasons why I don't want to force my daughter to go somewhere she feels unsafe.* None of this made sense.

I knew the only way to get Grace home was to go out there and pick her up. I brought my mom with me, so I had a witness, in case anything happened. Upon my arrival, I made numerous attempts to contact Johnny and Grace. There was no answer.

About twenty minutes later, I finally get ahold of Grace. Johnny walked her halfway to my car, keeping his distance. As Grace got into my car, she said she'd left her phone at her dad's and could we go get it. *Now I have to go to that house? What kind of drama is this going to cause, even if they aren't home? Are we even allowed to? I mean, Grace should be able to get her things, but I can only imagine what he will say about this.*

I asked Grace, "Does your dad know we are going to the house?" She said he did.

On the drive from Sundance to her dad's community, I had so many thoughts in my head, but I tried to keep cool and listen to what Grace had to say. It was almost like Grace now had a weight off her shoulders, so she could share freely about what had happened.

She said, "I asked to go outside when you told me that you were there."

"How come you didn't?"

"My dad said you can't take me without talking to him, and he said I could not go outside and he told me to go sit down. I asked him to go home, but he told me no." Grace continued, "I told my dad I was getting rid of my dog. This might be the last time I get to see her. Can I please go?"

For some context to this part of the story, we'd gotten a puppy earlier that year. This was not the best decision, looking back, but at the time, I'd felt I was doing the right thing by finally getting another dog. Grace had been asking for once since we put our other dog down. From that time on, anytime Grace asked to get another dog, I'd always said no. I didn't want to go through the heartbreak again. Now, the conversation looked a bit different. A small voice in the back of my mind questioned whether I was being selfish by denying her request.

Over time, this became a lot of work for me. While Grace did help sometimes, the whole "I'll help you and take care of the dog, I'll walk her, and everything else" narrative slowly faded. Grace's social life became more important, as every teenager's does. She walked the dog with her friends sometimes, but there wasn't consistency, and anyone who has raised high-energy, working dogs knows the requirements and consistent efforts that come with raising them.

The added stress of all of this was taking a toll on my mental health, too. It was just too much. Grace and I had conversations about not having enough time for the dog, that it was unfair, and that we needed to rehome her, to give her the life she deserved. We didn't just want to give her to anyone, so I explored my options. We were supposed to head up to Calgary, to see if she would get along with my uncle's dogs. They might take her, if so.

As Grace pleaded with her dad to be able to go, her request was regularly denied.

Grace switched gear and shared how she felt when her dad threatened to beat my dad up. "After Papa called, my dad told me he never wanted to hit my grandpa more than he did right now. He had a tin box and a metal chair. He took his hand by the baby gate and smashed the wall. Then, he punched the boxes. You could see his fingerprints dented the box that he hit. My dad said, 'I'm so sick of this, because it's happened for two days.' I stood there. I was so scared. My dog ran away and went to hide."

Then Grace said, "My dad threw the tin box in the garbage and sat in one of their chairs at the island and continued to yell at me about how this has happened for two days and how I was in the back of a fucking cop car yesterday." Grace then described another impactful moment for her. "You know what my dad said? He said, good thing my sister wasn't there, because she looks up to him as a hero. If she saw me talking to the cops, she would have been shocked to think her dad isn't a hero."

When I saw you phoning me, I asked my dad if I could answer, and he said no." Grace had messaged her friend earlier, and she told me how her friend was sending her messages back, too, checking in on her. Everyone was worried.

Grace said, within minutes, Rosie attempted to grab Grace's phone from her hand. "We played tug-of-war until I let go. Rosie put it on a table beside her own phone, where I couldn't get it. I was crying." She continued, "My dad went to the bathroom, and then the cops called him."

When the cops talked to Grace and asked how she was feeling, she told me, "I said I didn't know. Then my dad said, 'Tell them, tell them.'"

Johnny then said to the police, "She's not ready to speak with you."

"My dad kept talking to the cops and then they hung up. So, I asked, 'Can they call my mom to get me?' But he didn't respond. My dad sat on the couch across from me and talked to me in a firm tone." [Grace said this with a sarcastic tone and appeared to mimic her dad and his words].

A few minutes later, Grace said, the police were at the door. When Johnny saw the police on his doorstep, he said out loud in an angry tone, "And there's two of them!"

Rosie opened the door. The cops wanted to talk to everyone, so they came inside. Grace said she told the cops, "My lawyer said, if I'm scared or stressed, I need to go to a safe place before I run away, and my safe place is at home with people I trust." Grace added, "The girl cop told me to wait as she went to talk to the other cop with my dad. Then, the officer called me over to them and my dad." Grace walked over. "The police told us there is no reason for them to be here."

Grace said she started crying, saying, "I need a safe place. Then, my dad said, 'See, this is manipulation.' And the police agreed with my dad!"

Once the police left, Grace and her dad sat on the couch. She said she got a nose bleed, which was common when she was stressed. Johnny told her, "Someone could be getting assaulted right now. This is a waste of police time. A kid could actually be getting abused and the cops came for this little thing." He continued, "I have won two times now, and four people agree you're manipulating them."

Grace was full of stories. For our entire sixty-minute drive, she relived the last several hours.

"My dad said the judge will probably give him what he wants because you aren't following the court rules," Grace began, adding how this made her feel really confused and worried what would happen to me.

"My dad called the lawyer's office and lied to them." I asked her to clarify. "He said you were threatening to pick me up, and you didn't even do that. I called you to be picked up. I heard my dad call you a psychopath."

I said, "Yes, he did. I hope that, no matter what happens, you never tolerate that type of treatment from anyone, especially a man."

Returning to the conversation, Grace said, "My dad said, 'See, the police always take my side. Even the officer from the tribal police took my side yesterday. Your mom doesn't even know what abuse is. Look at my lip, look at mama's legs. Your mom doesn't know.'"

On the drive out to Sundance, Grace was asked by her dad, "Why don't you remember things? You say you forget, but you remember so clearly the day I dragged you out of the vehicle." He then told her she needs to explain to him what stress is. When she didn't respond, he continued, "Your mom is going to say I abused her when I put my hand on her shoulder to try to talk to her when she was changing your diaper."

I continued to drive, keeping my eyes on the road. Thankfully, Grace couldn't see any of my facial expressions.

Grace shared how, on their way out to Sundance, they stopped at Subway to get some food for the drive. When they placed their order, Johnny became upset about something and started getting angry at the person making their sandwiches.

Grace said, "My dad asked them, 'What did you say?' in an angry tone." Grace was confused at first, but she later found out he was mad because he thought the Subway staff said something about him in their language that he did not understand.

Grace said, "I felt embarrassed. I stood in the corner and said to myself, *Great*." As they were making their way out of town, Grace's dad pulled up to a vehicle and started yelling at the person to learn how to drive and made a comment about "All of these immigrants." Grace said she felt really embarrassed.

After the police had spoken to Johnny at their tipi, Grace said she overheard a conversation between her dad and her grandpa (Johnny's father). "I heard my grandpa tell my dad that he could not control me. But I didn't hear what my dad said."

We finally arrived at Johnny's house to get Grace's belongings. I waited in the vehicle with my mom while she went in to get her stuff. I was still ruminating on what Johnny would say about us going to his house, but Grace needed her things and should be able to get them. Moments later, Grace came out with her stuff, and we drove home.

It felt so good to be home.

The following day, Johnny called my dad, telling him, it was none of his fucking business, getting involved, adding, "The police will never believe Chelsey. I always win."

"As if my daughter's life was some game, or this was some sick experiment," my dad told me.

Fast forward to about a week later, during the first weekend of August 2024, Grace and I were at a powwow all weekend. I received a text from Johnny asking if Grace could go to the Sundance with him, as they had some responsibility to fulfill. He asked this last minute, giving me less than twenty-four hours' notice, and we had plans to be at the powwow all weekend. Plus, that was where Grace wanted to be.

I informed him he needed to give reasonable notice, like it said in the court order.

He responded, "I knew you would ruin this moment for me and my daughter. You know Sundance changes every minute. You know what you are doing. I understand you wish you could be a part of this, but it's for family only, and besides, you know when Sundance is. You knew what days Grace needed to be here. But in the end, I knew this would happen. You would pull a stunt like this. I understand you wish you could take part in these things, but it's for family only and you can't be involved, so you make sure Grace can't be involved. I really don't know why, jealousy maybe, selfishness. Only you know why you do these crazy things. I'm sorry you're always the victim. I'll pray for you."

I stopped engaging as it was evident we weren't going to get anywhere with the conversation.

He continued to text me later that day. "You know, tomorrow is a big day. I would like to pick Grace up in the morning." I didn't respond but received another text after midnight saying, "Rosie will be there at 8:30 a.m. to pick her up. Parade starts at 10."

I told him tomorrow did not work.

The next day, he asked me to drop Grace off. I responded, "No, I told you it wasn't going to work."

I was exhausted. No matter what I said, it did not land for Johnny.

The next day, he sent another message. "What time are we picking Grace up, or are you dropping her off?" Followed by, "You will be in contempt of our most recent JDR, if you continue to ignore me and refuse to communicate."

I continued to ignore him, but I couldn't ignore my feelings of overwhelm and anxiety as they built up. *Is he going to show up at my house? Will another incident occur? I can't take much more of this. When will it stop?*

He continued, "As per our JDR, I will be there to pick her up in the morning. If you do not follow the JDR, you are in contempt of the judge's orders. We will be there at 10:00 a.m. to pick her up."

I did not respond. I couldn't. My nervous system couldn't handle any more of the chaos, the threatening behavior, and the unpredictability. I was at my breaking point.

I didn't know what to do. I felt extremely worried in anticipation of what the next day would bring. It's like feeling trapped and wanting to run, but having nowhere to go. Feeling like the court controls your entire life.

Grace didn't want to go with Johnny, *and* she was scared to stay at home in case he came to get her. I was scheduled to go to work and wasn't sure where Grace could go, as children were not supposed to come to work with us due to the nature of our job. I eventually brought her to work with me, until I could come up with another plan.

# Chapter 29
# The EPO

On August 6, 2024, a day or two after the repeated text messages, I made an application for an Emergency Protection Order (EPO). To be eligible for an EPO, the parties must be family members, parents of the children involved, and provide a reason as to why this application is being made. I started my application at 12:08 p.m. that day, and my EPO was granted by 4:00 p.m. that same afternoon.

This was such a difficult process to go through. I had no idea you could get EPOs, and the police don't really tell you about them, nor were they helpful in this matter only days prior, even though they had the ability to start the process. It wasn't something they even offered me, when I'd called them for the wellbeing check a week prior.

When I spoke to the DTC RCMP liaison, she informed me that the responding officers should have completed a FVIR (Family Violence Investigative Report) assessment. This was news to me, but I can confirm no assessment was completed. Despite me saying the right things to the right people, like, "He has access to weapons. There is a history of domestic violence…." I said all the right things every time, as directed to me by the Domestic Violence Action Team, but it never seemed to matter.

A year or so later, I took a deep dive into the Alberta Policing Standards and came to realize that not a single officer who had responded to any of our calls had completed any type of assessment or followed any of these standards. *Make it make sense. What are those in place for, then?*

With the help of some friends, I was able to make an application for an EPO. I was so nervous and worried about the outcome. I had never done something like this before and had very little faith in the system, but I knew, no matter what, I had to keep trying and keep fighting. I was scared of judgment and embarrassment, and I anticipated another let down.

My friend asked her husband who worked for our local police service how to go about making the application. He told us, "You can apply online." So, I went to her office and sat with her and another friend. Together, we made the application.

A few hours later, I received an email from their email address indicating that, because it was during business hours, I had to go to the courthouse to make an application. You can only apply online if it's after hours. I went down to the courthouse a few hours later to complete the application.

Much to my surprise, I went before a judge that same day. As I made the application at the Court of Kings Bench desk, they informed me who my judge would be. The name didn't ring a bell. I was directed to sit outside of the courtroom until I was called in.

As I was standing in line to complete my application, one of the defense lawyers I'd worked closely with was standing behind me. He said, "Hey, Chelsey."

I replied, "Hi!" but I felt so ashamed to be there. I was sure he could hear my conversation with the clerk.

I was called in a few minutes later, took a seat in the courtroom, and waited for the judge. When she walked in, I noticed she was Indigenous.

*Fuck,* I thought. *She is going to rule in his favor, because she is Indigenous and so is my ex.*

I was asked to take the stand and share what had happened and the reason for my application. I was an emotional wreck as I told my story. My body was shaking, I was crying, and I was doing my best to recall everything, so she had all the information necessary to make an informed decision.

I was so overwhelmed and scared, but I kept going. Trembling. Scared of Johnny and what he might do next. Even though I wanted this EPO so badly, it didn't take away my fear around how he would respond, if it was granted.

I was wrong about my assumption about the judge's being Indigenous and her ruling against me. She ruled in my favor and granted the EPO. *Thank God.* What a sense of relief I felt. I had finally gotten the reprieve I was looking for and would get a break from the madness. Except, this was not the end.

As I left the courtroom, I did wonder whether this was what it felt like for people of color to go before a White judge, and their automatic assumption that the judge would not rule in their favor based on the color of their skin. While I recognize the systemic racism in the justice system, this reflection sat deeply with me for quite some time. My experience is an opportunity to challenge our own assumptions and offers learning opportunity, if we are open to it.

From my understanding, the next steps were to have the document filed in the courts, then it would be sent to the police in Johnny's jurisdiction. They would serve him. You'd think that an emergency protection order would be an emergency; that is in the title! It was not.

Officers from our local police service showed up at my house on August 15, 2024, looking for me. I was not home; I was at the gym. Grace was home, though, and the officers approached her. They asked, "Where is your mom?"

Grace was hesitant and scared to answer, as she thought they may be there to take me to jail. But she replied, "At the gym." She constantly lived in fear since that one officer had threatened to arrest me.

Once I got home, Grace told me what had happened. I was concerned about why the police were at my house and why they would ask my daughter where I was. When I called the police to inquire, I spoke to the staff sergeant.

She told me the police had come to see if I had Johnny's address, because they were trying to serve him with the EPO. This was nine days after the EPO was granted!

That struck me as a long time for him to go without being served. They had his address, of course—the RCMP were just at his house, plus, they knew where he worked. Who would have been responsible, if something would have happened between us during those nine days? And what might be happening to other women in similar situations?

On September 6, 2024, we had another JDR. The EPO was finally in place, after almost two weeks after being granted. I felt so uncomfortable and scared for my safety, having to sit in a boardroom with him. I thought it was insane that I had to sit in a room with him, while an EPO was in place. But as I was learning quickly, nothing in the justice system makes sense.

As I sat there, I was filled with emotions. I tried deep breathing and anything else I could think of to compose myself and stop the tears from flowing. *Just hold it together, Chelsey,* I told myself. *You'll be okay.* I was not okay. Eventually, I broke down.

Grace's lawyer was also in the room. There was something comforting about her presence, although she did not represent me. It felt like, at the very least, I had a witness to Johnny's behavior.

When the judge entered the room, she greeted us and then took her seat. I could no longer keep my emotions inside, and I started to cry.

I said, "I don't feel comfortable sitting in here with him, especially because there is an EPO in place. Can I please be excused?"

The judge acknowledged the EPO then said, "I am not comfortable going forward with our meeting today, due to the EPO." She excused me. I wanted to get out of there before anything else happened. Prior to me making my exit, she asked Johnny how he felt about the letter that Grace's lawyer had provided to the courts and to each of us.

The letter laid things out and explained why Grace did not want to go to her dad's, outlining some of the behavior that Johnny had demonstrated during our court interactions and conversations, etc.

Immediately, Johnny bit back, saying the letter was hearsay and biased. He continued, "I told you things would go bad, and of course, they did. Grace started crying and sending pictures to her grandma, and Chelsey started claiming abuse. This is not abuse."

As I left the room, my final words were, "This is domestic violence at its finest."

He just sat there in his chair with a snide smirk on his face. It was so triggering for me. Due to the situation, Grace's lawyer indicated she would attend our next court date on our behalf and adjourn it, since the EPO would still be in place until that time. The next court date for the EPO hearing was scheduled for September 12, 2024.

I had never gone through the EPO process before, so I had no idea what to expect. I was not aware that you had a lawyer appointed to you through legal aid, at no cost to you, as the victim. I was fortunate in this. However, the process was not smooth, and for a moment, I felt like the system had failed me again.

I went to our first EPO hearing on September 12, and the judge asked me where my lawyer was. I was confused. I had not retained one, and I had no idea what they were talking about. Johnny had already retained a private lawyer, who was present via CCTV.

Johnny stood on the other side of the courtroom as our names were called. I stood before the judge, confused, intimidated, and feeling sick to my stomach. Finally, someone appeared via CCTV, and a voice spoke. (For anyone unfamiliar with CCTV, it's a closed-circuit television system providing a virtual option for people to attend court, mostly prisoners.)

The voice said, "I'm here on behalf of my friend, Chelsey." This left me even more confused… *Who*?

The lawyer stated his name and asked that court be adjourned, because we had not had time to connect. Court was adjourned until September 18, a date that holds specific meaning to me, because Johnny and I started dating on that date, back in 2009. It's funny how trauma can impact your memory in many ways, but dates do stick with you.

Although it was a surprise to me, I was happy to have a lawyer, so I wouldn't have to do this on my own. *What a relief.* The lawyer called me after court, and we had a quick discussion. He asked me to send him as much information as possible. I got to work. I had been documenting since 2012. *Finally..., all my work and documentation paid off...* Or so I thought.

I walked into the courtroom on September 18, 2024, feeling pretty confident. My conversations with my lawyer seemed to be going well. Despite his accent and English not being his first language, I trusted he knew enough about my case, and I believed he would represent me well. I was proud of the work I'd put in and everything I was able to provide to my assigned lawyer.

I have to say, during this time, I also had the support of victim services with the RCMP, and I was so incredibly grateful for her support. I don't think I could have gone through all of these court dates and chaos without her. I cannot thank her enough. She was my voice of reason throughout all of this. She was present at every court date and a calm presence for me. I always felt, with her there, I had a bit of a buffer between Johnny and me. It was that extra sense of safety I so badly needed.

When our matter was called, we both walked up to the front of the courtroom and faced the judge. Both of our lawyers were from the Calgary area, so they appeared via CCTV again.

Johnny had hired what appeared to be quite a feisty lawyer, and she ripped our case to shreds. I wish I could explain the feeling I had as I stood there. The confidence I'd had, walking into the room, was stripped away immediately. I felt embarrassed, like there wasn't enough evidence or "proof" that we were victims of violence.

I don't know what case law she threw out there, but it was enough for the judge to rule in her favor. The judge basically said there was no evidence of domestic violence and the EPO was being rescinded.

I was so disappointed with this process and with my lawyer. Despite all of the information I'd provided to him, he focused too much on the historical stuff and not what had led us to getting the EPO after the most recent events. So, he did not help my case at all.

The EPO was dropped. It was all over. I had never felt such a swift kick to the stomach. I walked out of the courtroom with my Victim Services rep, and we went into a side room, where I broke down. I was hysterical and felt numb, as though I'd been frozen in time.

*Now what*? I thought, among many other things, like *Why does this keep happening? Why doesn't anyone believe us or see how abusive this man is? What more needs to happen? Do we need to die?*

Victim services called Grace's school for me. I was in a panic, in survival mode, and I worried that the first step Johnny would take was to go to the school to try to pick up Grace. I didn't want her to have to go through that. Victim Services and I went to pick up Grace from school, to assuage my fears.

I walked into the school and told the front desk why I was there. Victim Services came in with me, as I was having a hard time articulating my points. A few minutes later, I saw Grace walking toward the office, accompanied by the school counselor. I was so grateful she had that support. Part of me worried that I was being irrational, but the larger part of me said we needed to get out of the area. I was so scared for what might happen next.

This was always a game to him, and he would always say he was winning. Yet Grace and I were fearing for our safety.

I needed to come up with a game plan. I didn't feel safe, and I felt like he would be even more mad now, because of what had happened. When we went home, I began to plan as best I could.

The following day, Grace did not want to go to school. She said she was scared Johnny would come get her from there, like he did when she was in elementary school. I took her to work with me, so I could make a game plan. I knew she wasn't supposed to be there, but I wasn't sure what else to do. I let my boss know what I was doing and basically asked for forgiveness for having her there. Although skeptical, I think he was also a little taken back as to what was happening in my life and didn't really know what to do.

Grace sat in my office with me. It wasn't long before I received a call from my Executive Director. She was based out of our main office, located about an hour and a half away. You know how, when someone calls and you're in such a vulnerable state, as soon as they ask you what's wrong or act like they care, it triggers all sorts of emotions and the waterfalls? That's exactly what happened. I broke down. I'd been strong for so long, but I couldn't take it anymore.

She thanked me for being so vulnerable with her and for letting her know what was going on. She then brought up a concern. "I'm worried that you are putting others at risk, too. So, it's probably best if you aren't in the building, either." Cue the shame and embarrassment again. She added, "I want everyone to be safe. Even you two. Pick somewhere you want to go for a few days, and we will pay for you and Grace to go."

I packed up my things, and Grace and I left to head home. I was racking my brain as to where we should go. I wanted to decompress, so I didn't want to go somewhere that was busy and full of chaos, like Calgary, despite it being most familiar to me. I thought of a place I'd always wanted to visit: Radium Hot Springs. I had been in the area a few years prior and fallen in love, but I'd never made it to the hot springs. It was a five-hour drive for us, but that would give us the time we needed to slow down, decompress, and drive through the Columbia Valley. It truly was so beautiful.

As Grace and I were packing, she told me she wanted to die, because she was so tired of going through this with her dad. "I don't deserve to be alive."

Those were some heavy words. If you've ever had your child tell you that, you know it's one of the hardest things to hear.

There was one problem, though. We had not been successful in rehoming our dog months ago, so she was still in our care. This became a barrier for us. We couldn't just pack up and leave. Dogs weren't always allowed in hotels, and I was in no position to be thinking critically. I was merely in survival mode.

In the midst of the scramble, I expressed to Victim Services that I could not leave the city, as I had the dog and many hotels don't allow pets or, if they do, there are additional fees. She called up some of her connections and was able to find somewhere for the dog to go for a period of time, so we could leave the city. We would deal with the rest later, when we returned to town. Grace and I left the city.

This was one of the hardest things I've had to do, and it took a lot of time to work through the guilt and shame I carried over this. Even though I knew it was the right choice and something we'd been working toward, the way it happened so abruptly made it very difficult.

I'm happy to report that, despite the shame, guilt, and emotions both Grace and I had about leaving the dog, we were able to rehome her through the Humane Society. She has been adopted by another family who has all of the time, energy, and stability she needs for a great, loving life.

# Chapter 30

## No Order, No Choice

We packed our bags, loaded the car and headed to Radium for a few days. It was exactly what we needed.

On the drive there, we took our time and decompressed. I drove slower than the speed limit (which is rare) and just soaked up the scenery, engaging in conversation and, in some moments, sharing in silent reflection. As soon as we crossed into British Columbia (BC), the energy shifted. There is something about the smell of the BC air that is so comforting. It feels like home, even though I grew up in Alberta. There's just something about that place. It's hard to put into words, but if you know, you know.

I had the sunroof open, and we soaked it all up. It was beautiful. We stopped at a few different places and pit stops along the way. One of the locations is pictured below. I wanted to share this. It came to hold a lot of meaning for us, and we've traveled to it each summer since then.

On the drive out, I received an email notification from Johnny's lawyer. I didn't read it, but it made me feel sick to my stomach. Anytime an email popped up in my inbox from a lawyer, it made me feel uneasy.

Once we arrived at our destination, I found the courage to open it. Johnny's lawyer said that our leaving town was not going to be appreciated by the judges.

Before we left, I'd sent an email to Grace's lawyer, explaining what was going on and that we were leaving the city for a few days.

Johnny's lawyer tried to frame her email response as though I would get in trouble for fleeing the city and "evading" or something like that. If I was actually trying to flee, I wouldn't have told anyone we were leaving, especially not Grace's lawyer.

Grace and I woke up the following morning feeling well rested. She said to me, "I feel safe here. This is the first time I've had a good sleep in a long time."

Those words felt so good to hear. I felt safe, too.

From the bed next to mine, she added, "I know he can't hurt us here."

Although this sentiment was only temporary, I gladly accepted.

Over the next few days, we checked out the hot springs and went ziplining. Ziplining was the highlight for Grace. The way she let go and hung upside down on the final run was as though she was letting go of everything, even just for a moment in time, and embracing what it meant to be free.

Ultimately, it was time to go home. As much as I loved my home, I dreaded going back. I didn't want to face our current reality yet again.

The drive home was just as beautiful. We took our time and made plans to return the following summer. We dreamed of spending time at Windemere Lake, ziplining and bringing my mom. My mom has always been such a support, not only to me, but for Grace, as well. Grace loves when my mom joins us on our adventures.

So, we talked about what that would look like and joked about how funny my mom would be on the zipline. It had been years since she'd done something like that. We talked about the highlights of the trip, and I tried to make the rest of the trek home as positive as possible.

I'm not sure what Grace was thinking or feeling on the way back, because she didn't say much afterward. But we made it home and settled back into our routine.

# Chapter 31

## What's Next?

I don't know what the universe was trying to teach me or how much stronger she needed me to be, but she wasn't done yet.

I returned to work the following week, and Grace went back to school. I was still grieving the lost relationship with Vinny, and working through that heartbreak. As each day passed, it felt a bit easier. I was journalling daily, practicing gratitude, and giving myself grace.

In a journal entry from that time, September 2024, I wrote something that still really hits home for me. "I am so over feeling this way. I am taking my power back." From that point on, it was as though something shifted, and I was committed to my healing journey. I was done feeling sad, and I was tired of sitting in the suck. As we know, healing is not linear; it is a process.

One day at a time.

A few days after we returned home, Grace called to tell me, "I found three bugs in my hair."

*Are you kidding me? Please, Universe, stop punishing me.*

It had been years since we'd had to deal with a lice issue, and I'm going to be honest, I had the help of my friends during the last case, when Grace was younger.

When Grace came home from school, I took a look through her hair and thought I saw something, but it didn't look like lice or what I'd expected it to look like. I pulled it out and thought it looked more like dandruff than anything. I'd seen lice before, but the cases

I'd seen were quite extreme, to the point where the entire front part of the child's head was moving or I could see white specs all over the top of their head.

Since that was more what I was looking for, as I continued to look and pick whatever I found, I said, "I think you're good. I pulled a few out, and I think it's dandruff, not lice." Where I found the "dandruff" was in a weird spot, too; not where lice typically like to hang out. Since those friends had moved out of our neighborhood, I had no one to consult, though, so I was on my own for this one.

Later that day, Grace went to her friend's house a few blocks away. They'd had a sleepover about a week prior, with another girl whom we later found out had a case of lice. I'm not sure if the girls knew at that time, but it definitely became an issue this day. The friend's mom is a hair dresser, and she treated both girls' hair that day then braided their hair. She told the girls, "Leave the braids in until tomorrow."

I was so grateful for that mom for dealing with it, because I just couldn't take much more. Lice alone may not have been a deal breaker, but the amount of baggage I was carrying around was quite heavy and already taking such a toll on my mental health.

Still feeling so frustrated by how the system had failed me, I decided to reach out to someone who had been there for me throughout all of my recent court proceedings; Victim Services.

I felt so desperate. *What was missed? What did I do wrong? What else can I do to get the help we so badly need?*

Victim Services arranged for me to speak to one of the officers on duty who was quite well versed in domestic violence, or so she said. She assured me he would listen, and if anything, he would do something. I had lost all faith in police by this point, but I took her word for it. I had over sixty pages of documentation spanning ten years. I printed it all out and went to meet with this officer at the local RCMP detachment.

The officer introduced himself to me with a formal handshake and then walked me into an interview room. He took out a pen from his front pocket and began to skim my printed notes. He made some small notes on my documents then said, "We could have charged him here. Or maybe even here, too" He kept going, making additional comments and notes by different dates and incidents I had recorded.

He said, "Seems like this guy is kind of an asshole." To me, he added, "This is parenting and what it means to coparent. Have you and your daughter gone to counseling? Have you tried EMDR?"

I told him yes, we both had done counseling; however, the systems were pretty broken, so I could not take Grace to counseling without her dad's consent, and he hadn't made that easy, even refusing to sign on more than one occasion.

After the officer finished reading through all of my documentation, he told me there was nothing they could do, then he opened the door so we could exit the room. Victim Services was waiting outside, in the entryway of the detachment. He asked to speak with her, while I waited in the front foyer.

A few moments later, Victim Services and I walked out of the detachment toward the parking lot. I was quite emotional but had calmed down by the time we got to our vehicles. My sadness and frustration turned to anger.

The Victim Service worker said, "The officer told me during our conversation that you seem really tired." It was left at that.

*No kidding, I am tired.*

Around this time, I also learned that the RCMP never seized Johnny's firearms when they were supposed to, during our EPO. The RCMP officer told Victim Services they were not aware they were supposed to seize weapons, despite it being written in bold letters on the order. Two weeks later, they allowed Johnny to walk into the station with his firearms and turn them in to police. The irony of this, enter the RCMP detachment, there is a large sticker/sign on the door that says no weapons allowed past that point. *Except when you are given privileges and are a fellow first responder, apparently.*

If something were to have happened to us during that time and we'd been killed with those firearms, who would be accountable? It's a question I desperately want answers to.

# Chapter 32

## I Feel Like Such a Burden

I often felt like such a burden on my friends and family. All of this chaos was going on in my life, and it felt like that was all I could talk about, *because it consumed me*. I wanted to isolate and dissociate from everyone, but I knew, deep down, that was not healthy, either, nor would it serve me well in the long run. I needed to continue to find joy in the little moments and focus on those things. This was easier said than done but a non-negotiable for me, at this point.

I couldn't help but think, *I don't need to show up as some battered, pitiful woman. I can present as well as I do and be exactly who I am, while also being a victim."* Domestic violence doesn't discriminate, and victims don't look a certain way. These comments were the definition of insanity, but they show just how skewed people's perceptions are about what a domestic violence victim looks like.

In journal entries during this time, some of the most difficult times, I expressed how I got through. I can see in them the truth that, once we can move through the pain, there is beauty.

*Mornings are hard for me. I wake up with my heart clenched, it literally hurts, and if I could describe what the brokenness truly felt like, I would. I am holding onto what I thought I had and not what my current reality is. It's still tough, but I guess it's something I need to work on in this healing process.*

*He texts me, and it felt like closure, which was nice, but it was basically saying that he will find peace one day, but this place isn't it and thanked me for the moments. It killed me. Why can't he just choose me and find a way to make it work?*

*I know I'll be okay, but that doesn't take away from the strong emotions I feel. I do well on some days; I cry most of others. I don't know why I feel so alone. I just want someone to come home to. Someone who makes me feel safe. Grace wants someone to fill that void, as well. I don't feel like I have done enough to be a good mom. Sometimes, I feel like I am failing her. I'm not affectionate enough. I can't handle my emotions. Failed relationships make me feel unstable. I have navigated so much tough stuff, but I just never feel like enough, especially when I am grieving. It's a lot on my own.*

*As the days went on, the moments of hurt pass through. I am becoming more at peace. I can't change the situation, but I can understand it for what it is. I am holding onto what I thought I had and not what currently is. That is something I had needed to truly come to terms with. The things he did and the things he said play through my mind. How good he made me feel, and what those words and actions meant. That sense of security and safety I thought I had and so badly longed for. I believed him when he said he wasn't going anywhere and that I was his person.*

*I know I'll move through these feelings, but it will take some time, but man, what an experience this has been. Emotional, painful, thought-provoking, and reflective. I've never experienced a breakup like this before.*

*My friend said something to me the other day, and it stuck with me. Whether it's true or not, sometimes people give you the messages you need to hear at that time. She said to me, "If you really set his soul on fire like he says you did, you are rare. He will never find another like you."*

*Healing isn't linear. It's all over the place, and it's hard. I am tired of the lessons. I want something real, something that someone will fight for, and something that means something to someone.*

Reflecting back on these words, I see how this was something I had to give to myself. I could not count on someone else to make me feel that way. In some ways, I was likely still waiting on someone to give me the safety I longed for since childhood. A place where I could calm my nervous system. *Home.*

Another friend told me I needed to find peace wherever I was, and I did. That lesson taught me I could find that within myself, wherever I was. In my solitude, in the mornings when I write in my gratitude journal with my morning coffee, on my walks, and essentially everywhere I go. But it had to start within.

I was tired of walking around, feeling like I had a dark cloud around me and always talking about all of my situations, the heartbreak, and everything else. I'm sure others would say I talked about other stuff, but I felt like I was drowning in the misery. It was time for me to really make a change, while not ignoring what I was processing.

About two weeks later, I went for a massage. As I entered the room, my massage therapist said, "Girl, you're throwing out all the vibes today. Your energy is so strong!"

"Really?" I asked, thinking to myself, *Maybe I am finally taking my power back.* It felt like a small, subtle shift, but it was obviously something noticeable to others. Little by little, I leaned in.

A few weeks later, Grace and I were at a powwow in the same community where my ex was still policing. I saw him, and it killed me. Just when I thought I had taken my power back, the sight of him made my heart feel like it was being wrung out. It made me miss him and what we could have been. I was so proud of him and even more proud to be with him.

As I watched him walk around in the arbor, I noticed something that struck a deep chord inside of me. One word came to mind: *ego.* He was all about his image. He was married to the RCMP. That was his sole identity, and nothing else mattered. He'd left his children in another province, so what made me think he would stay with me? As long as he looked good and bent over backwards for the service, that's all that mattered to him.

That did not align with my life, and so, as much as my heart was breaking, things were also becoming clearer. There was more misalignment than I'd thought, which made it easier to slowly let go.

It was time to rename experiences and find the peace that I longed for. I deserved a calm presence, and I needed to find that within. This wasn't the first time I would learn to engage in this process, giving familiar spaces and experiences new definitions and positive meanings. I was no longer allowing men to identify places for me. I could no longer avoid. I needed to embrace the discomfort and create a new identity for those spaces I so badly loved.

In between court dates for our JDR, I started to have nightmares again. In one of my dreams, we were back in court, still fighting. Johnny was yelling and being so condescending and abusive toward me. Eventually, the lawyers and judges saw it, but they did not do anything to deescalate. They just sat there in silence. It was as though they were frozen in their tracks and too scared to call it out and shut it down.

I felt so afraid. This feeling was not new to me, but I felt like I couldn't escape it. Not only was it my reality, it was also showing up in my dreams. I was constantly living it.

# Chapter 33

## We Don't Keep Secrets

A few days later, Grace woke me up numerous times throughout the night. She said, "My dad ruined my life."

I was confused and half asleep, so I asked her, "What's going on?"

She said she'd been texting her grandpa's wife, Lucy (she doesn't call her Grandma; she calls her by her first name), asking if they could pick her up to go shopping. Lucy responded, "With everything that is going on, we were told we cannot pick you up."

While crying in my room, Grace begged and pleaded with her via text. She then sent another message. "Please don't listen to my dad. You guys make me happy. My dad is lying to you, please don't listen to him."

I made attempts to contact Grace's grandpa, Jake and his wife, Lucy, to clarify whatever information they had received from Johnny. I told them, "There is no court order that says you cannot speak to or see Grace." I offered to show them the order if they wanted. I continued, "Please continue to spend time with Grace. You are important to her, and she enjoys spending time with you." I never received a response.

My heart was breaking for her. It seemed Johnny would use any angle he could to hurt and punish Grace. It was like, because he could not have access to her, he was going to make sure he cut his entire family off from her, too. The homicidal comment he'd made many years ago reared its head again in my memory. "If I can't have her, nobody should."

I couldn't believe he would go through this much effort to make it so hard for Grace. I was very proud of her for speaking her truth and holding her ground, even when she couldn't control the outcome. I can't wait for her to share her part of this story one day, if she chooses to do so.

I have another journal entry from this autumn. In it, I was questioning what I'd done so wrong in this life to been handed such a shitty deck of cards.

> *I remind myself to breathe, but the uncertainty is too much and making me feel so overwhelmed. I sit here, wondering when he's going to show up or send a message demanding Grace. Hearing Grace say that she told her grandpa's wife she wanted to die was the icing on the cake. How can people think I am making this up? I hope for peace in 2025, when we can live happy, healthy, and to heal. I don't want her to feel like suicide is the only way out.*

Every day, I woke up feeling anxious. I felt so overwhelmed by everything, like I might have a mental breakdown at any minute. I felt like I was a ticking time bomb, which was not the way I wanted to live my life. I decided it was time to retain a lawyer: I needed someone to help me fight this battle, since I could no longer do it on my own. I retained my lawyer on September 24, 2024. I also made an appointment with my counselor; however, I had to wait a couple of weeks before I could see her.

As much as I am a proponent of doing our own healing and inner work, it's hard when the systems continuously place blame on the victims and the children and require them to go to counseling, but the perpetrator or abuser has zero accountability or expectations. Plus, you can't heal in environments that continue to hurt you and a system that continues to expose you to them.

I wrote in my journal, "*One day, we will live a life of peace, and there will be so much joy. This will all be a distant memory.*"

My next appearance in court was scheduled for October 2024. I felt confident about having retained a lawyer. However, I had yet to hear anything from him since our initial meeting. I had little faith in lawyers, after being failed in the past, but after our initial meeting, I got a sense he knew what he was doing after a decade of experience. He came highly recommended, which made me feel better.

I'd provided my lawyer with all of my documentation and what I had done up to the present moment. He was impressed and said I'd basically done all of the work. He said I would pay a small retainer fee, and he could likely complete the case within the retainer fee of $3,000. This sounded good in theory, but I didn't want to put all of my eggs in one basket.

So, I paid my fees and left the office. He left me in the dark until closer to the court date. During this time, I was very worried they would make Grace go back to her dad's house on a rotation and follow the original court order, despite what had happened. I tried to have faith, but it's so hard.

I continued to engage in activities that regulated my nervous system, such as training (I was competing in Olympic weightlifting during this time), spending time in nature, and reminding myself in the little moments to remain present, and that life is still beautiful. I was still writing in a gratitude journal and in my personal journal daily. It's so important to find the things that bring us joy, along with a practice that brings us peace, whatever that looks like to us. No matter how hard it is, we cannot lose ourselves in the process.

Our court date came and went. After court, I walked back to work and into my office. As I walked through the front door, my boss was standing nearby. He looked at me, not sure what state I would be in upon my return. I said, "Well, I'm not crying this time, so that's a good sign." And I chuckled, as I always do (which is likely a coping mechanism for me). I carried on with my day and for the next few weeks, until our next court date, which was scheduled for October 24, 2024.

We walked into the courtroom that day before the same judge who had ordered Grace to have her own legal representation. I was a bit hesitant and extremely nervous, because I'd had various experiences with this particular judge, including when I worked in child welfare. I shared how I was feeling with my lawyer, and he said, "You'll be okay." While those words were somewhat comforting, the system had shown me not to be entirely sure I would be.

Johnny's argument was that I was alienating Grace from him, and he denied that any of the reported abuse had occurred.

The judge said, "We are not talking about a four-year-old child here. She's saying she does not want to go to her dad's, which sounds like a genuine statement. We are not going to force a mother to drag her child by the arm to go, even if it is alienation. Furthermore, we are not forcing a child to go somewhere she does not want to go. She's twelve years old."

I felt a huge sense of relief. Those were the little moments I held onto, hoping they would lead to a bigger breakthrough in the future.

During court, Johnny's lawyers asked that Grace and her dad go to counseling together, and that I be expected to cover the costs. The lawyer asked for more. "Johnny should be allowed to attend her sporting events." This despite Grace having made it clear to her lawyer that she did not want her dad at any events or she would quit. This was also during the time of her suicide ideation, so our current court order had said he could communicate with her via text and that was it.

Just prior to this court date, Grace had met with her lawyer to tell her what she wanted to have happen. However, she'd felt like she could not be honest, that the court was going to make her do things, so she'd said what they thought they wanted to hear, such as, "If the courts make me go to counseling with him, I will." However, after I picked Grace up from that meeting, she completely shut down and said she did not want to see him. It was like depression completely wiped her out, as I watched her shrink in her seat.

After her lawyer meeting, we went to Costco to get groceries. As we walked into the store, she said, "I feel like I have no choice. I am being forced to see my dad, but I don't want to." It was as though she was starting to become fearful, being a puppet of the courts who had to tell them what they wanted to hear, rather than what she wanted for herself.

I encouraged Grace to share this information with her lawyer. I reassured her, "You do have a voice and a choice, much like with anything in life. Even when it doesn't always seem like we do."

When I was debriefing with Victim Services, who'd asked how court went, I shared the conversation Grace and I had had. She encouraged Grace to write a letter to her lawyer, explaining how she felt. I shared this idea with Grace and asked if it was something she would be interested in doing. Grace agreed. I wanted to stay out of it, so I provided Grace the space, pen, and paper to write.

She put it in an envelope when she was done, and I helped her to seal it. I have no idea what was written in the letter, since I wanted it to be in her own words and for her to articulate how she was feeling, without any influence. Victim Services helped facilitate this process and delivered the letter to her lawyer.

The following day, I received a call from my lawyer indicating that Grace's lawyer had changed her tune a bit and felt that the way Johnny treated me was why Grace did not want to go to her dad's. I explained that I was not sure why the abuse was being ignored or minimized. Although he did not beat the shit out of me, we had been exposed to family violence, and the system continued to make us victims of violence.

My lawyer didn't have much to say after that. He did say, "You should have never stayed the charges after the No Contact Order, because it doesn't stay on Johnny's record for having charges." It would just note that they were stayed.

While I can appreciate that now, I was never out there to ruin his life. All I wanted was for him to be a good dad for Grace, because she deserved that. If I'd known he would stop going to counseling all together and continue to terrorize us, then yeah, maybe I would have made a different decision.

My lawyer suggested completing an assessment that came with a hefty price tag: $10,000, paid half-half by Johnny and me. I thought, *I'm already almost ten grand in debt with lawyer fees, and now I'm supposed to keep forking out more money for assessments and continuous fees after that?* My lawyer said he'd initially said no to the assessment and wanted to explore counseling for Grace first.

I don't mind counseling. I think it's a tremendous tool. But why is it that we always have to do the healing, while the abusers can sit back and enjoy the ride with no effort? The system continues to cater to them. If I am being honest, I don't think my lawyer looked at the sixty pages of documentation I provided to him during our initial meeting. I always wondered why I kept all of the documentation I had, as it didn't seem to get me any further: not with police, courts, or help in general. At the very least, though, it came in handy and contributed to a large portion of this memoir!

I had additional paperwork like the undertaking, our no contact order, and other legal documents that provided proof and painted a picture of where we were and how we'd gotten to this point, but it didn't seem to matter much. This was beyond frustrating.

Johnny's lawyer continued to argue the fact that he had never been charged. (Because I had stayed the charges, she could use that in her defense.) What I learned from my time working in the justice system was that just because charges were stayed, dropped, or whatever else can happen in that system, it doesn't mean you just ignore it. There's a reason it's on file. *This only made my desire to fight stronger.*

The justice system contorts and makes you feel crazy. Not only are you gaslit by your ex-partner, the system plays a large role in also making you doubt your perceptions and sanity. Oppressive. *I survived him, now I have to survive the system.* It's like a double-edged sword. Sometimes, I just want to scream from the rooftops: *"YOU AREN'T LISTENING TO ME!"*

Johnny continued to use power and control tactics to make life incredibly difficult for Grace and me. Yet again, he refused to sign a letter for me to travel with Grace. I so badly want to take all of his rights away, but I also knew that would be a daunting task, and I was so sick of fighting in this system. The system gives abusers too much power.

I also still couldn't get her into counseling, since it requires both parents to sign for consent, which he wasn't willing to do. I'd asked for years, and in the application that restarted this whole court battle, again requested that Grace be able to attend counseling without requiring Johnny's permission or signature.

In all of Grace's life, I can recall one healthcare appointment that Johnny took her to, and he couldn't handle it. She was getting a cavity filled and ended up panicking because she didn't like being at the dentist. He has never fulfilled any parental duties and has only isolated and traumatized our daughter more. Yet he still gets to decide what supports she needs and what she does not. The system is so backwards and continues to give power where it doesn't belong.

In November 2024, we were back in court. My lawyer was thirty minutes late, so I began to have a mild panic attack, wondering where he was and worried about what this meant for me, if he didn't show up. I didn't have anything other than his office number, and I didn't want to leave the comfort of my pew in the court room to make attempts to call him. I tried to keep calm, but my mind was going a million miles a minute, worrying, if he didn't show up, would Johnny's team just bulldoze over everything.

My lawyer finally entered the courtroom. Later, he explained he'd totally forgotten about court and had had to throw on a blazer over his jeans (generally forbidden in court), so he looked "somewhat professional." This was such a relief.

During our hearing, Grace's lawyer had her back and provided the courts with a hard no on Grace seeing her dad. She did not want to see him, so forced visitation was not appropriate at this time. Johnny's lawyer kept pushing back, as per usual, continuing to ask for more parenting time and for Johnny to attend Grace's activities.

Parental alienation was still a hot topic and his lawyer's main argument. I watched my lawyer closely and noticed he does not ever play into her tactics. It was quite fascinating to watch him make his arguments on my behalf. That made me trust him more and showed me I had to embrace this learning opportunity, even if I never really grasped his tactics

The judge did not rule in Johnny's favor. Again, the court repeated, "There will be no forcing Grace to go somewhere she doesn't want to go." I couldn't help but wonder, if this was still the message, what the hell were we doing there again?

I woke up the next morning and started to write. As I expressed my feelings of anxiousness, I began to physically sweat. I'd had a bad dream on the night after court, justifying why we were where we were. It felt like a never-ending game and such a joke at this point.

I continued to wonder why domestic violence is so minimized. Why do we say stuff like, "Neither parent is to speak negatively about the other?" Why do we write other conditions in the orders that clearly don't matter or get enforced? Why don't we actually solve the problem and believe what the victims are saying *and* allow some space so the victims can truly heal? Why don't we place more expectations on the abusers?

I often wondered if a female lawyer would have represented me differently, thinking maybe they had a different understanding of domestic violence, but I remained hopeful we were at the end of things. Switching lawyers now would cause a significant delay and a bigger headache for me, so it was best I stay the course.

I still dream of the day when I am out of fight mode. When I can drop my shoulders and exhale. *It's going to feel amazing.* When the nightmares disappear, and I don't wake up sweaty. When instead I wake up feeling excited for a new day. I can't wait to have that soft place to land.

# Chapter 34

# Little Say

I had sent my lawyer the video of Johnny dragging Grace out of my vehicle back in 2020. It had taken four years to get someone to actually listen to this audio recording, but I figured it was better late than never.

My lawyer called to tell me, "That's gold! It demonstrates that you have never withheld Grace from him."

Truth be told, I hate how I showed up in that video. Despite Grace begging and pleading not to go to her dad's, that she didn't want it, I still forced her to go, because I'd felt the weight of the court order over my head. I had to tell her, "You have to… The courts say you have to…," and so on. Anyone can hear in my voice how frustrated I was getting. I hate listening to that video.

Even now, my lawyer said I had almost pushed too far for her to go. *What else was I supposed to do? Risk going to jail?* I felt such immense pressure from the courts and police, I couldn't even do what was best to protect my own child.

My lawyer suggested, "I may ask for a mental health assessment."

I asked, "Why do the abusers literally have no accountability or have to go through assessments, but victims are assessed time and time again?" I didn't get an answer.

On November 27, 2024, we were back in court for our third JDR, before the same judge who had been with us since the beginning (outside of regular court appearances). There are pros and cons to this continuity, but I was hopeful maybe she was starting to recognize patterns of behavior. Johnny hadn't ever been shy about his demeaning behaviors, constantly mimicking and making derogatory remarks in front of the judge and lawyers around the table. But no action had ever been taken to stop him.

This JDR went better than last time, but it was still emotionally draining. The judge opened the session like always. Sounding bubbly and friendly, she said she had a good understanding of what had been going on after briefly reviewing the file. She recognized that the last JDR did not go well, since the EPO was still in place and the sheriffs had to get involved.

Johnny piped up to ask, "What? What sheriffs?"

The judge explained that when things escalate like they did last time, they have a protocol to involve the sheriffs. His body language shifted to defensive, like he was feeling under attack.

He began to say he had done nothing wrong, then he and his lawyer persisted with their same arguments: about parental alienation, that he was not abusive, and all he wanted to do was be there for his daughter.

His lawyer looked around the room and then looked me straight in the eye. She said, "I will say this, and I'm not sure that it will be well received. But you need counseling. You should work on self-awareness."

I did not break eye contact and responded firmly, "I do go to counseling."

She had nothing left to say after that and looked away. Anyone who knows me knows that I am one of the most self-aware people on this Earth, and I have done a tremendous amount of work on myself to get to where I am today. I wasn't going to argue with her or try to prove to her I was who I was. Her comment didn't affect me, but my response did stop them in their tracks.

His lawyer shifted gears. "Chelsey works in the justice system and has too many connections to legal professionals in this community. We would like to move the case to Calgary."

Johnny added, "Chelsey's dad plays hockey with some of the judges here in town, and when Chelsey and I were together, I saw her dad talking to one of them. I don't want to go before that judge anymore."

Their argument didn't stop there. They began to dissect everyone at the table for the Drug Treatment Court program I was managing at the time. Eventually, the judge shut this down and said, "That is criminal court, not family court. And these matters are not moving to Calgary."

Next, Johnny's lawyer asserted that I monitored Grace's phone closely, an incorrect assumption on her part. They claimed, when Johnny tried to get ahold of Grace, I undermined everything he said to her, along with his parenting, and that I interfered with contact.

The judge tried to redirect the conversation back to the issue of visitation. While that was not going to happen between Grace and her dad, the judge did want her to have access to her siblings, especially her younger sister, as they had a relationship. Grace requested that her grandpa be the person to help her have those sibling visits.

Johnny scoffed at that suggestion, laughed, and looked at me. "Really? *That's* the person you'd choose? You know what he was like and what he has done."

I replied, "That is *Grace's* choice, because she feels safe with him, and we need to respect that. It's not about you."

Johnny disagreed, insisting those visits had to be done through his mother. Grace and his mom no longer had a relationship, not since she had showed up at my house years ago. Simply put, his mom was not the person Grace had selected, so I'm not sure why Johnny continued to argue as long as he did.

The energy in the room shifted. It became very tense and awkward as he continued, "Yeah, of course she wants my dad. She just wants him to buy her expensive things." The hate that man has for me was coming through. I don't know if anyone else could sense that, but he was really overbearing in the room that day. He said again, "I've never been abusive. Chelsey always says I'm an aggressive person." He chuckled.

Nothing came from this JDR session. Another wasted afternoon of talking in circles and being blamed. The only thing the lawyers and judge could agree on was that a Practice Note 7 (PN7)-Voice of the Child assessment should be completed to determine what was really going on. *Like I haven't provided enough evidence as to what's been going on.* Our lawyers would discuss this further, as we would with our individual lawyers, as well.

A PN7 is a procedural tool and court guideline used by the Court of King's Bench in Alberta, in family law cases. It governs how independent professionals, such as psychologists or social workers, intervene, evaluate, or assist families during high-conflict divorces or separations involving children.

What grinds my gears is that it's always referred to as "high conflict," whereas, it should be called what it really is: domestic violence or family violence. The voice of the child component to this assessment consists of expert interviews with the child and both parents, including stepparents (if any), to ensure the child's perspectives and feelings are safely presented to the judge.

A few days later, Grace and I went to pick up her distribution. Sometimes, reserves give money to each registered band member. The reasons and allotments vary each time. Johnny historically had collected Grace's money, but after all of this happened, I was curious how I could go about getting that money and putting it into a savings account for her. She lived with me and I had the court documentation to prove that.

I reached out to the reserve, briefly explained the situation, and asked what I needed to do to get the money for Grace. They told me they needed my court documents plus for me to sign one of their forms. *Perfect.* I did that, but then didn't get an answer.

It was a bit of a battle, but with the help from my friend's mom, I was able to speak to one of the managers so that, for the next distribution, I was able to collect it for Grace.

Johnny must have found out we had collected the last distribution, but there was nothing to hide. The money was Grace's, so I'd put it away for her future. On collection this day, I had explained to Grace that, after school, we were going to pick up her distribution.

She asked me, "What if my dad takes my money?"

I told her, "He can't do that. I have documentation to prove it, and we got things figured out."

So, we headed to the friendship center to pick up her money. As we walked inside, we saw Grace's cousin working at the table next to ours. We greeted one another as I approached the staff working at our table.

She looked through her papers and said, "I don't see a check here for her." They looked under my name and Johnny's, too, but still nothing.

Their cousin at the next table said, "It should be under Chelsey's name. She got it last time."

Another lady came over and asked, "What is her dad's name?" After I gave her Johnny's, she said, "Oh, yeah. He wrote us a letter. Her money is in trust."

I kind of smiled and walked away, furious inside. Grace was quite upset and started to cry as we left the building. I thought, *How the hell could he do that? Why does* his *letter override court documents?*

Grace said, "See, Mom? I told you he would take it."

The next day, I sent an email to the band office that oversees this department and explained the situation. Their response was, "He's a band member. You're not."

That guy was really pulling all the strings to make our lives miserable. I followed up with an email to my lawyer, informing him of the situation. At the very least, it contributed evidence to my file of Johnny's ongoing manipulation and interference.

# Chapter 35

## Another Woman Dies by Domestic Violence

I don't watch the news, but my mom and grandma have it on daily. One day, my mom called to tell me about a program discussing domestic violence.

According to the story, in Calgary over the recent 2024 holidays, a man had killed his wife and then himself. The news reporter discussed how these domestic issues continued to be ignored and that people were dying. They said the riskiest time for a woman or anyone fleeing domestic violence is when they are leaving.

Although that's true, I believe, from my personal experience, it is dangerous any time the abusers feel they have lost control. It's been ten years since I left the relationship, and I still fear for my safety and wait for the shoe to drop. I still feel like I am at risk. The more things don't go in Johnny's favor, the more risk we face.

Our government introduced Clare's Law a number of years ago, which is great in theory. Basically, it allows you to go into the police station and inquire about someone's history of abuse, if you are experiencing some unusual, controlling, or manipulating behaviors, or physical abuse. But it begs the question, "What happens if the person has never been charged before or had police involvement? If the charges were stayed, does it show up in the same way as if they weren't?"

Based on my experience, the police don't even seem to lay charges that often, especially for what they may deem as "minor," so what happens in that situation? I understand people can make assumptions and false accusations, but that's not what I am referring to here. Police are too quickly dismissive of cases. This leaves a gap in systems and feeds the reactive approach rather than a proactive one.

Far too many people die by domestic violence every year. In fact, in 2024, 187 women and children were killed violently by some form of intimate partner violence in Canada, with 93% of the accused being male (Paths, 2025). In the United States, 5.4 million reported they had been victims of domestic violence in the past five years, with 80% of victims being women. Domestic violence homicides have more than doubled from 2019 to 2024, increasing from 1,065 to 2,339 (Schecter, Lowe, Ramos, 2025).

I came across a show on TV one day about an investigation conducted by the RCMP on intimate partner violence in British Columbia. The investigation was into a wife who had apparently drowned in a lake near Revelstoke. She was camping with her husband, which was typical of the couple, doing an activity they enjoyed together.

People had started to notice how the husband's behavior appeared "off," among other things. During the investigation, the husband made statements that did not make sense. However, experts validated his story, confirming he did try to get her body out of water.

During the investigation, the police discovered the man had been abusive to his previous wife and children. They also discovered that the deceased wife had provided documents to the RCMP in Westlock, Alberta, which included a written statement about the abuse she was experiencing by her husband. It had been dismissed by the RCMP.

A female RCMP officer was interviewed for the documentary and spoke about how many police get into the field and become police officers because they want to help. She became emotional as she said she wanted justice for the woman who was killed. It would make anyone think. I feel angry when I hear statements like that, because officers have so many opportunities to actually help and change outcomes, but they don't, for whatever reason. Where is the justice when people come forward? It takes so much courage to do that, only to be dismissed by the very people who say they want to create change.

I understand investigations require proper process, and sometimes, there is not enough information. Sometimes, it takes a while to build a case. But intimate partner violence keeps occurring at alarming rates, so many women and children are still dying, yet the systems continue to be reactive instead of proactive. The police need better training, and the criminal code needs a serious upgrade.

I remember what my ex-boyfriend told me about the RCMP and all of the checks and balances they have for domestic violence. Yet when my situation ended up in the hands of the RCMP, they still did nothing. In fact, what they did do was an embarrassment to the RCMP as an organization: by not following protocol, by saying they cannot apprehend from guardians, and by waiting almost two weeks to seize weapons and allowing the abuser to bring them, himself. *With zero consequences.*

Around the same time, another video came out about the Gabby Petito case, on a show called, *American Murder, Gabby Petito*. It was hard to watch and triggering at times, but I stuck it out and finished it. Shows with domestic violence are always hard for me to watch. I started to feel very angry as I watched this program, at the way they handled the investigation and the ways they placed the blame on Gabby. This was all part of victim blaming, which seems to be more common than I think any police service or justice system would like to admit.

The police treated Gabby so poorly and outright assumed that she was the aggressor. The conversations between Gabby, her fiancé, and the police were ridiculous. Sure, many victims do go back to their abusers, and why they do it makes sense, especially without adequate intervention. But it becomes way riskier for the victim, and victims get pretty good at learning how to protect themselves, even in the smallest ways.

After this confrontation between the couple and the officers, the police put the abuser in a hotel room to protect *him*. This shows how police need much more training in trauma and domestic violence. Things need so desperately to change. Even when the fiancé hid out at his parents' house after Gabby's disappearance, the police basically left them alone. They let him get away without talking, sheltering and protecting that whole family.

Fast forward to 2026, there was another case in Calgary. This time, two children died at the hands of their father. There had been a history of domestic violence between the parents. The mother had attempted to warn the police that something was going to happen.

She was at the courthouse, filing an application, because the children's father hadn't returned the children the night prior. She found out while she is in the courthouse that her two children were found dead in a vehicle that her ex-partner brought to the police.

We can and should do better. These deaths are preventable.

# Chapter 36

## 2024 Comes to a Close

We all may have thought 2020 was the worst year of our lives, due to the pandemic, but nothing prepared me for the hell that 2024 had brought.

At Christmas time, I found myself in such a period of reflection. There were so many lessons and opportunities to reflect on. I did a deep dive on the lessons I had learned over the year and looked at what I had learned about myself throughout the process.

When Christmas morning rolled around, I was drinking coffee in the silence of the morning, under the glow of the Christmas tree lights, waiting for Grace to wake up and open presents. It's funny how, when children are young, they can't sleep the night before Christmas, because they are so excited about Santa coming and opening gifts in the morning. As they get older, though, it becomes less exciting. Sleep becomes more important, and roles are reversed. The parents become more excited for the morning than the children are. Or maybe we just get excited to have morning coffee in silence before the chaos.

When she finally woke up and opened her gifts, I drank my coffee as I watched. It's also a weird feeling when you're a single parent and don't have gifts to open. It can feel one-sided and awkward, at times.

Grace looked a bit let down. I asked if she was okay and had gotten what she wanted. Maybe I felt a bit like I'd let her down or hadn't had enough gifts under the tree for her. Previous

Christmases had had far more gifts. As children age, their interests and gift ideas become more expensive, which, depending on a family's financial situation, can look a bit sparser under the tree. I am not sure why I put so much weight on the number of gifts under our tree, but for some reason, on this Christmas, it meant more than it should have.

I had finally heard back from my lawyer recently that he found an assessor to complete the PN7-voice of the child assessment. The assessor agreed on a fee of $10,000, for which I would be responsible for paying half. This didn't help the Christmas spirit, as it was already a difficult year, after spending thousands of dollars on lawyer fees that year. Now, the amount of the assessment weighed over my head, adding additional stress.

Grace said she'd gotten what she wanted and went upstairs to do a "Christmas haul," like all the kids were doing: making videos of everything they got and sharing them with friends. She ended up talking on the phone with her friend, while I was in the kitchen making breakfast.

When she came downstairs and entered the kitchen, she said, "I got more gifts last year." So apparently, this disparity meant something to her this year, too. She started listing off what her friends got as gifts, making me upset. A flood of emotions came over me. I really had tried to give her a good Christmas.

Single parenting is no joke in the best of times, as we all try to make ends meet. Christmas puts additional financial stressors on parents, all while trying to keep the holiday spirit alive. Christmas 2024 was especially triggering for me, and I found myself filled with childhood memories about how stressful Christmas had been. Not necessarily around the number of gifts, but my dad was the only one who worked in our household, growing up. I'd inherited the same stress as my dad felt, along with the perception that Christmas had become more about gifts than anything else. As an adult, I knew better, but children don't necessarily understand that concept.

Grace's lack of gratitude and compassion killed me that morning. Why I expected her to have compassion, I am not sure, but in the moment, that's what hit me.

She said to me, "I hope my dad brings me gifts." When I asked why, she didn't really have an answer, but eventually said, "I wish I had a dad."

My heart broke for her. I had to remove my emotions from this moment, because her behavior that morning was rooted in something more, exactly as she had expressed.

I thought about how miserable my dad used to be at Christmas, mostly due to the financial pressure. He didn't like how the holiday was more about gifts as opposed to gratitude, being with family, etc. I think he had a point, but the way he showed up for Christmas did not always reflect positivity. That impacted me more than I realized, and I can see some of those behaviors in myself each Christmas, no matter how hard I try to show up differently and with a more positive mindset. I see the lessons now, which is the beauty of reflection, but it doesn't mean these core memories don't continue to surface for us.

When I reflected on many things that morning, I also thought about my ability to build healthy relationships with men. Much of this stemmed from my childhood and never feeling like I was good enough for my dad. I'd come to understand, through my own healing journey and counseling, that my dad did the best he could with what he had at the time. I understand now that I must give myself what I needed from him. He may not have said and given me the love I needed, growing up, but in my adult life, I can see why he may have behaved that way based on his own childhood experiences. I know that, now, he is proud of me, at least to some degree. As an adult, I no longer seek his approval and validation, because I trust in where our relationship is right now. It's better than it's ever been.

It wasn't until my mid-twenties that I came to realize how deeply my relationship with my dad had impacted me, along with my desire to have his approval. Once I became aware of this, I was able to make changes in my professional life. However, intimate relationships were always a bit harder.

My abandonment issues surfaced with partners, and I became triggered. I didn't know what it was or what it meant to have a healthy relationship. With that RCMP officer, I felt like I'd found it, but even then, I was proven wrong. I began to wonder if I got in my own way.

I started to ask myself some difficult questions, to see what came up for me. "Why do I struggle to build healthy, strong bonds with intimate partners?" "Do I need to show up differently?" "Does my lack of trust impact my ability to build healthy relationships?" "Am I going for the wrong type of guy?"

These are questions I sit with, but I also came to the realization that I need an emotionally intelligent man who will hold space for me while I navigate these questions. I may have the answers on my own, but things seem to shift when I get into relationships, and that is the part I need to figure out.

I also pondered what it would be like to have someone in my space. I've been on my own for so long, I am not sure I know how to let someone in my space. The question arises, "Will I ever be able to form a healthy attachment or relationship with someone?"

This is a question I carried with me into 2025, while remaining curious as to what I can learn about myself through this process.

# Chapter 37

## Are We Done Yet?

In early January, 2025, when most people are excited for a new year, for me, it was just another year, one riddled with uncertainty. I was hopeful that this battle would be over, but I still didn't have answers or closure.

I received an email from my lawyer asking me if Grace had started counseling yet and if Johnny had attended. While we were waiting on the assessment, it was suggested that Grace and Johnny go to counseling. I told him Grace was still on a waiting list. All of this was making me feel so anxious and frustrated.

It was my understanding that this was separate for each of them, as Grace had no desire to attend counseling with her dad. She always said, "We tried that once, and it didn't work." Things only escalated from there. I'm not sure why I would be privy to knowing whether Johnny had attended. I really didn't care. Despite how badly that man needed counseling, whether he went or not wasn't my concern or business.

I continued to wonder why the courts insist on exposing children to their abusers, further victimizing the child. They wanted so badly to reunify families, while failing to recognize that the adult must be healthy in order for that to happen.

My lawyer also informed me that I needed to top up my retainer fee, because I had used my initial amount. *Great*, I thought. *More money. When will this end?* The system will milk you for as long as you continue to feed it. I'd drained my savings completely for this battle, and we aren't even near the end.

In February, we were back in court yet again for another JDR. In typical fashion, Johnny put on another show. He raised his hands to say, "She's evil. She laid charges on me for no reason. She convinces our child how terrible I am. I shouldn't have to pay child support, because I have a wife and three other children to take care of." Nobody in the room said anything, so he was allowed to continue.

My lawyer waited until Johnny was done, looked at him, and said, "You should worry about putting food in this kid's mouth," referring to Grace.

Johnny continued to claim parental alienation, and his lawyer continued to advocate for essentially forcing parenting time together, where I would have to bring Grace to Johnny's house.

Grace's lawyer exclaimed, "That is not going to happen!"

Johnny continued, "Grace doesn't want to call me Dad anymore, and when she was told to come home for Christmas to open gifts, she told me she was not coming home." He continued to call *his* place *home.* A home should be a place that makes you feel safe. It's not just a physical structure.

Grace had not spent time at her dad's since the summer of 2024, when that incident occurred. This was not something he was willing to accept. Johnny said, "I may as well sell her gifts, since she won't come get them." This denial of his actions that had caused her to be fearful of visiting his home struck me as stubborn ignorance.

I'd always thought, if he wanted to build a relationship, he would first acknowledge his wrongdoings and then make it right by working on himself, so he could show up in the way Grace deserved, not by buying presents as a way to lure her into going there. The one thing I am most proud of, despite wishing Grace didn't have to go through this, are the boundaries and advocacy she created and modelled for herself.

The topic of child support was a sensitive one. Johnny said he shouldn't have to pay, but he soon realized, after my lawyer presented the federal guidelines, that he didn't have a choice. Johnny offered $200 a month. After a lengthy discussion about income and his still getting a break, based on his year prior's income information, he was supposed to pay me over a thousand dollars more each month than he'd offered.

To his offer, my lawyer responded, "That's negligence," and asked for the whole amount, according to the guidelines. Eventually, it was agreed by all parties that Johnny would pay the full amount, based on the previous tax year, giving him a break and lessening the amount that would be due in this current tax year by approximately $200 a month. Back pay was also up for discussion, but that amount would come later, in the final order.

This conversation heightened the tension in the room, but at least Johnny would finally have to pay his portion, after causing so much turmoil and chaos. Still, no amount of money could undo the trauma he had caused.

After the negotiation over child support, Johnny continued to argue about gifts. He lied to the courts, saying, "My dad and his wife brought gifts over to her house, and she refused to open the door. She told my dad to leave the gifts inside the house and gave them her door code."

I thought to myself, *Does he know how crazy this sounds*? If I didn't want to see his parents, why would I give them my door code and allow them access to my house? Here's the truth. There were no issues with the relationship between Johnny's father, wife, Grace, and me. We would have welcomed them with no issues.

We were not home when they showed up at our house, unannounced. My camera notified me about a person at my front door, so I opened the app to see who it was. I saw a woman pacing up and down my front sidewalk, wearing a ribbon skirt. As she turned around to walk back to my front door, I was able to see her face. It was Johnny's stepmother, Lucy.

I spoke to her through my camera, explaining we were not at home but they could leave the gifts inside. I then provided her the door code, as I did not want their gifts left on the step, where they could be stolen. She agreed and left immediately after putting the gifts inside my door. In the camera footage, you could also see that my vehicle was not in the driveway, more proof we were not home).

During the JDR, I gave Johnny Grace's passport application, as she needed to renew it. He was so frustrated about having to pay child support, he did not know where to sign his name on the application form and struggled to find the signature line. I pointed it out for him before he tugged the paper from my reach. Once he'd signed, he threw the paper back at me, in front of the lawyers and judge.

My lawyer then brought up my video of Johnny dragging Grace out of my vehicle and said, "I don't think you want that video played in court."

Johnny chuckled, saying, "Yeah, but is that really abuse?"

A few days later, I met with my lawyer again to sign papers regarding child support. It had taken me almost ten years to get child support. Previous judges would not grant it, always saying things like, "You're technically 50/50" or "Your income is relatively the same." Then, the issue of Johnny contributing to his daughter's expenses while living fully with me was always brushed under the rug.

We had an appointment in court for the official grant of child support order in a few days, so it was important I sign these forms. As I worked on the papers, my lawyer brought up the PN7 assessment again.

He told me, "When you go to meet with the assessor, tell them what Johnny did. You will look like the battered wife."

This did not sit well with me. I was quite surprised we still hadn't completed this assessment, after selecting the assessor months ago.

I shouldn't have to "play" anything. It was aggravating that this was not the first time I'd been told something like this, and I'm sure I am not the only woman who has experienced it. Just because I hold myself together and present well does not mean I am not or haven't been a victim of violence. Society and those who work within the system assume that victims of domestic violence are only poor, pitiful, battered women, crying in a corner. Domestic violence does not discriminate.

When I arrived at the courthouse, as I went through security, I chatted with the sheriffs, who were looking at me, confused. "What are you doing here?" they asked. "It's not Drug Court day."

I smile, nervously. "I know. I'm here for personal matters... Family stuff."

When I began to walk toward courtroom #7, though, I felt more at ease, since this was a familiar room to me, because that's where Drug Treatment Court is held. Those little moments of victory made me feel more at peace.

Johnny was sitting outside the courtroom with his partner, Rosie, plus one of their children, his father, and his father's wife. Alarm bells went off in my head, setting my entire body into fight-or-flight mode. I quickly returned to the sheriffs at security, suddenly feeling like a lost little girl who needed someone to protect her. I told them I am going to hang out with them until my lawyer arrived, because I did not feel safe. It is wild to me how quickly I'd felt unsafe with Johnny in the building.

One sheriff asked, "Are you on our list?"

"What list?" I asked.

He grabbed a paper off their desk and showed me the list of everyone on the docket who had any history of domestic violence. The entire list: just our two names—Johnny and Chelsey.

I said, "Yep, that's us," then expressed how embarrassed and ashamed I was to be in this position.

The sheriff said very calmly, "Don't feel embarrassed. This is pretty common. There is nothing to feel ashamed or embarrassed about." He offered to wait with me outside of the courtroom until my lawyer got there, and I took him up on the offer. I was so grateful for those relationships; they helped to regulate my nervous system and lent me an essential feeling of safety while I waited. We stationed ourselves across from the elevator and engaged in small talk as we waited.

Moments later, when the elevator door opened, a defence counsel who often referred clients to Drug Court stepped out and saw me standing there. Confused, he asked, "Hey, what are you doing here? This isn't a drug court day."

This, again, hit me in the gut. I thought, *This is so embarrassing."*

I kind of chuckled to him and said, "Yeah, I know," hoping he would read the room.

By that point, my lawyer had walked up and was standing with us. The lawyers knew each other, so I think defense counsel knew this was family-court related. Once my lawyer arrived, the sheriff confirmed it was okay for him to leave.

Moments later, Johnny's dad walked by and mumbled something in their native language. I didn't understand what he'd said or whether it was directed at me, but I realized then that any relationship I'd thought I had with him or his wife had fractured and perhaps no longer existed.

At the courtroom, I learned that our judge was actually a friend of mine, one of our Drug Court judges. I said to my lawyer, "I don't think we can do anything today," and explained why.

He said we should be fine, since we were just finalizing the order. As we all walked into the courtroom, I noticed that Johnny and his dad had brought some of their ceremonial stuff with them, including one item that looked like it was his holy blanket.

I thought to myself, *I am not the person you need protection from, nor is this a place for these items.*

When we were called up, the judge indicated she could not proceed with the file due to her conflict of interest. Therefore, another judge would have to sign the order. I'd suspected that.

Thankfully, though, it didn't derail our progress, and we were still able to move forward.

Child support was granted, a definite victory. Finally, a small win out of this process. I could now slowly change the narrative. This would begin my comeback story.

Afterward, I had a conversation with our Drug Court clerk and asked her why the courts continue to expose victims to their abusers. Her response was, "Because we have sheriffs here to keep people safe and to watch for behaviors."

Sure, from an image perspective, I could understand that, but from a lived experience perspective, the fact of sheriffs merely being present didn't actually make someone feel safe. Her remark brought me back to when I was in junior high.

My best friend's mom was dealing with domestic violence and had recently separated from her husband. After court one day, she was dragged down the stairs of the courthouse and toward the staff parking lot at knifepoint by her ex-husband, after some court appearance had not ended well for him.

Her mom's new partner was driving past the courthouse to see if they were still there and witnessed her being dragged down the stairs. When he intervened, the ex-husband slashed his hand between his thumb and finger, leading him to need plastic surgery. I'm not sure if the sheriffs responded to that incident or not, but if they did, they were a little late and didn't guarantee any safety.

Later that month, there was a powwow hosted in our community. As always, Grace and I attended. Johnny was often there with his family; he gave Grace an awkward side hug.

She told me that, as they hugged, he had said to her he loved her, and she'd replied, "Yeah."

Grace was happy to dance with her sister. This was one of the few opportunities she'd had, because of her dad's interference with her ability to see her sister, also facilitated by his father. Other than that brief interaction, I didn't see Johnny make any attempt to see or talk to Grace, nor did I see him watch her dance.

It appeared he had gone home. I couldn't understand why someone would put up such a fight and claim alienation, when he didn't take advantage of the opportunities he did have to engage and build on that relationship. I asked Grace, "Does it bother you?"

She said "No. I just wanted to see my sister."

A few months later, I noticed some cuts on Grace's leg, near her groin area. I was confused how those got there and wondered whether she was engaging in self-harm. With compassion, I asked, "Grace, what are those?"

She looked at me, seeming embarrassed, and said, "Nothing." When I asked again, she confessed that she just wanted the pain to stop and wanted her dad to stop ruining her life, so she'd taken her scissors and cut her legs.

I became increasingly worried this would become a common pattern of coping for her. What I knew about self-harm and cutting was that it is often done by individuals as a way to make the pain stop and to feel like they are in control, even if it's for a little while.

Grace and I had more discussions around self-harm. I was worried I wouldn't be able to leave her home alone, for fear of what she might do to herself. Especially because she had expressed suicide ideation in recent years. But I didn't want her to know how worried I was for her. All I wanted was to keep her safe. Not only from her dad, but from herself, too.

Grace said she wouldn't do it again.

I monitored her closely. I also shared this information with my lawyer and the assessor, once we got to meet with her. This never seemed to be taken very seriously, however.

# Chapter 38

# Culture Can Be Weaponized

The justice system and police have caused significant harm to Indigenous people; there is no denying that. This continues in their practices to this day. Because of systemic racism, there is a lot of pressure to decolonize and embrace culture. While I believe that's important and that culture holds many lessons and important aspects, there are a few considerations I believe the courts, justice system, and programs offering support should attend to.

I recognize this may be an unpopular opinion, but it's important for me to share. From my experience and observations, the pendulum has swung too far the other way. Culture is being mandated and forced down Indigenous people's throats. Many Indigenous people have been traumatized or ostracized by their culture, and the system fails to recognize that. In attempts to correct the system's wrongdoings, they have now put blinders on and forcefully "order" culture. It's so important to respect each individual's journey and allow them to define what they need, even children. Access to culture is important, but what should not be prescribed is whatever the system thinks is best, almost like an automatic fix. For far too long, the system has been recommending what is best yet failing to acknowledge the significant harms that come with it.

Culture should not be emphasized over the safety of our children. Over the course of my JDRs, the same justice had seized on our file, meaning the same judge presided over our case for the duration of proceedings. Our first JDR was three and half hours long, and we spent the entire time talking about how beautiful the culture was, powwows, and how the justice system could become more involved in the culture.

As our JDRs evolved, so did the comments, and not in a good way. Johnny's family has always said that Grace's family should be the ones to make Grace's regalia. I can support that, to a degree. Her first jingle dress was made by her grandma.

Grace entered the powwow circle as a jingle dress dancer at the age of two, but a few years later, she found her love of fancy dance and made the switch. I made all of her beadwork with the help of a former friend. That took tremendous work and many, many hours of learning and unlearning, but eventually, I completed her set.

As she got older, she grew out of regalia. More recently, it was time to get new beadwork. I found someone to bead for us, a distant cousin of Grace and Johnny's, so technically, it was family. As Grace got older, there was not much follow-through by Johnny or his family to get Grace what she needed. Now, with the relationship being as fractured as it was, it was not possible for them to get Grace new regalia. She refused to see them or be measured for much of the regalia.

I paid $500 down for the beadwork, with the remaining $500 to be paid when completed (now been paid in full). I sent Johnny an email to request half of the down payment and said I'd send him the invoice, when I paid the second portion.

He replied, "I can't afford that right now."

It's not like I had a ton of money floating around, especially after losing my job in the fall of last year, but I was determined to make it work, because Grace needed it. Fast forward to the beadwork being complete. I paid the additional $500, then sent Johnny an email with proof of payment and requested he pay his portion. He never responded. This was so typical of him.

In 2024, Johnny joined one of the sacred societies. I thought, *Wow, they really let anyone in, these days.* It felt so strange to me that he could behave the way he does, cause harm to his child, and then be accepted into this society, where they are held to a higher standard and respected as such. It's hard for me to respect someone who does what he's done, despite the "position" he holds.

As he was in the process of joining, a certain protocol had to be followed. It's not my place to speak about that, but Johnny did in a text message, "Grace needs to be painted on this bundle. As the oldest child, she will have responsibility. If she is not present to be painted on the bundle, she won't be able to come around it."

Other times, Johnny and his family would show up to court with their ceremonial items, such as holy blankets and medicine pouches, almost as though they had something to prove.

(While it is not my place to speak on behalf of ceremonial practices or what these bundles entail in specific, I will share that the bundles hold significant meaning to many Indigenous people, and there is protocol that follows each bundle and ceremonial practice.)

Yet he still would not acknowledge his behaviors that had led to Grace not wanting to see him… This was a dangerous game to play, and I didn't feel like his statement was fair to make, nor was his choice to weaponize culture like that, given his wrongdoings.

During one of the JDRs, Johnny's lawyer was adamant that Johnny be the one to get the moccasins made. I replied, "That will not work. Grace doesn't want to see him right now, and she would need to provide Johnny with a tracing of her feet. Moccasins aren't something you whip up or purchase at a store."

His lawyer continued to push for this, until Grace's lawyer finally spoke up. "That is not going to happen right now!"

Johnny's lawyer and even the justice supported the idea that, "Johnny should be the one to get her regalia and things to do with the culture, as it's theirs."

Just because I was White, I was not supposed to support my daughter in her connection to culture? That made no sense to me, either.

Another thing I want the courts to consider is this: just because a parent isn't from the same culture doesn't mean they are not capable of providing and accessing the culture in a respectful, appropriate way. I have spent a lot of time with Indigenous people. While I admit I don't know everything, I have a deep respect and understanding. I have always been respectful and determined that my daughter has a connection and, as she got older, she be allowed to define what that meant to her. She has spent time at Sundance. However, given her dad's behavior during her time there, it has ruined what the Sundance is or could mean to her. The family *and* the courts need to respect that. Forcing Grace to go there will only cause more harm and grow further resentment.

I began my career under the child welfare umbrella. I came to learn about band designates and the role they play in ensuring that Indigenous kids in care have access to their culture, seeing they were not easily adopted by non-Indigenous families. Again, I can respect that role, but as I found myself in my own court battles (even though I was not involved in the child welfare system), I couldn't help but to wonder, *When will they come for me and try to intervene*?

I spent a lot of time worrying that, because I am White, they would find ways to go around the system and force parental contact or even full guardianship, because, in the end, Grace is an Indigenous child. The system was full of surprises.

From my experiences, the question becomes, what are we really striving for and prioritizing? And at what cost?

# Chapter 39

# The Quiet Reward of Doing Right

By spring 2025, it was time to renew my mortgage. Without going into too much detail around the initial fights as part of this process, I share part of my story because it's a reminder that, when you carry integrity and continue to be a good person, despite the shit life throws at you, good things happen.

Johnny and I purchased a house before Grace was born. We also got a line of credit. During our time together, we purchased a fifth wheel with the line of credit. He also purchased a saddle and various other items with that money. I didn't even know how to use or access those funds, but I would later find out that wouldn't matter. During our separation, it was agreed that I would not take any money from the sale of the house and that he was responsible for paying the line of credit. We would both walk away without that debt.

A few years later, I applied for a credit card, which required a credit check. I learned that I did not have a good credit rating. The bank questioned me about that old line of credit. I was confused, since I'd thought it was paid off. I explained to the bank what had happened and said I would talk to Johnny about it.

When I circled back to him, he just said, "I had bills to pay." Meaning, he paid his "bills" without paying the line of credit.

*Great,* I thought. *Now, I'm fucked.* I asked the bank what I could do about it. The lady said, "Nothing really. It's already so far gone, even if you made payments on it, it wouldn't make a difference.

Honestly, just wait a few years. The chances of this bank loaning to you may be slim to none." *Awesome.*

When I moved in with my parents, I paid off all my debts and saved to purchase my own home. I initially went through a different bank than held the line of credit. Of course, my credit score didn't change regardless of the bank, but they were still willing to lend to me if I had a co-signer. My mom agreed to do that for me.

So, when it came up for renewal, I assumed I would renew through that bank plus hopefully pay off some debts I had accrued over the past few years, now that I had some equity in my home. It was stressful, having to do that all on my own, but I was all I had, and I was determined. If anything, the past few years of continuous fighting and advocating had made me one tough cookie, and I was going to figure it all out.

The bank denied me, saying my debt-to-income ratio was too high. I remembered that an old day home provider of Grace's was now a mortgage broker; I had been following her on social media for a while. I wasn't really sure of the difference between a broker and going through the bank, but I had also heard that brokers get access to different rates. I thought it wouldn't hurt to see what a broker could do for me.

I reached out to her and we began to work together. She was able to make serious magic. With her help, I was able to get my credit card and vehicle paid off. From what she said to me, my debt-to-income ratio was not even that bad, and I had even more room to pay stuff off, if I really wanted to. I was so grateful for her. *Another victory!*

Despite the process being a bit difficult and messy, with a lot of back-and-forth communication, we navigated it well. I wanted to see if I could have my mom removed as a co-signer on my mortgage, as well. This required I go through a lawyer, which I knew would come with a fee, but it was worth it.

Fortunately, I was able to have her name taken off the title, and I was very proud of myself for accomplishing this. *I did all of this on my own.* The lawyer's fee was over $1,000. The mortgage broker, during her conversation with the lawyer, even asked him to cut me a deal, since I had been through so much. I wasn't expecting that at all.

On the day I was scheduled to meet with the lawyer, the broker called to tell me he was going to waive his fees entirely, due to my story. I broke down over the phone and started to cry. I couldn't believe it. I wasn't expecting my break to look like this, but maybe this was the break I had been waiting for all along.

After all of the fighting, wondering what it was all for, and how much more I could take, then out of nowhere, this kind soul did this for me. I decided to get him something, despite his asking for nothing in return. I went to the store to get a card and wrote a heartfelt message, sharing a bit more about my struggle and experiences. *I wanted to share my gratitude. He had no idea what this gesture meant to me.*

When I went to meet with him and sign the paperwork, he didn't even want to accept the card, but I made him anyway. He said, "You have given so much to others through your work with Drug Treatment Court, I want to give back to you."

I was truly grateful; my heart felt like it was going to explode. I don't do this work for accolades; I do it because I care about making a difference. Perhaps the ripple effect was felt in this moment. It was a reminder that, even in the shit, good things can still happen. The Universe will reward you in some way; we just have to be open to it. This felt like a new chapter of possibility.

It was also tax season, and I'd assumed I would be getting a tax refund. I also felt the need to take a trip to a tropical destination, one for me and Grace to decompress from all the stress, plus to celebrate our resilience. I booked us a trip to Mexico for April. We had been to Cancun a few years before, but this time, we thought we would try something different and went to Puerto Vallarta.

What a beautiful place. Sure, the ocean wasn't as pretty, but that didn't matter. The decompression of my mind and body was a reward by itself. To be fully present in the moment is not something you can often find in the hustle and bustle of everyday life, especially not during intense moments of stress and uncertainty.

We soaked it all up. Listening to the birds singing their different tunes than what we heard at home and hearing the wind through the palm trees was incomparable. I loved watching the sunset with Grace, seeing her embrace the present, playing in the water and celebrating the little moments together made my heart happy. Her resilience is incredible, and I am grateful to be able to give her this life. I hope she forever remembers the trips we take together.

I sat on the beach, in the warm sunshine. We went for a massage, one of the best I've ever had. We had plans to paddleboard with the dolphins in Bucerias, however, Grace got quite sick, so we had to cancel. As I sat near the ocean with my coffee, I couldn't help but think how grateful I was. How much more I wanted to travel and experience the world. I knew good things are coming. I was so proud of myself for how far I had come, how far *we* had come, and how much I have accomplished. Not to mention the life I was giving Grace, even when it's hard. This was all worth it.

I was so grateful for all of the learning opportunities that led us to being able to travel on our own, doing what we want, living freely on vacation, without a strict structure. *This was the life.*

As I sat on the beach, I couldn't help but to people-watch. I noticed a couple on the beach that made me reflect on what I wanted in a relationship. Recognizing that what you see in a snapshot is not the whole picture, I had no reason to assume anything different about this couple. I want to feel secure in a relationship. I want to know that a man loves me and wants to be with me. Not in the bossy or possessive sense, but someone who truly shows up as much as I do for them. A true partnership. Someone who respects my independence and my story.

# Chapter 40

## Change Begins with a Story

One day, I was chatting with our local Police Liaison for Drug Treatment Court via text message. When he sent me a photo, I was not sure what it was about. All I could make out was that he was taking some type of training for family violence. *Why is he sending me this?* I wondered.

He replied, "I am taking a family violence course for family violence supervisor." This was odd to me, because he was in priority crimes at the time. He continued, "It's a course to help deal with offenders and victims of domestic violence."

I commended him. This was really awesome.

Then he surprised me, writing, "I am taking this course because I know someone who had some really shitty experiences, and I never want to respond the same way officers have responded to you, when I go back to the streets on patrol."

I was blown away. To be honest, it brought a few tears to my eyes. *I feel so emotional lately. Crying over things.* All of the stigma I'd held and how ashamed I was to be a victim plus working in the field. Well, this told me it had been worth it. It was the confirmation I needed that, when we share our stories in a good way, we have tremendous power and influence to make a difference.

As we continued to chat, I mentioned how officers need so much more training around domestic violence and also that the criminal code needs to change. I told him I would be making these recommendations when I finally wrote my book. "If we can create change by even 1%, then that's a win."

He thanked me for being the catalyst for change. *This was only the beginning.*

Sometime soon after, I had a similar story with the RCMP. There was a going-away dinner for me as I left my job as the manager for the drug treatment court to pursue another opportunity (more on that later). The RCMP liaison came down to celebrate. As we sat down for dinner to catch up, she said to me, "Hey, I want you to know that we actually changed our police because of what happened to you with weapons seizures."

I was shocked. "Really!?"

She shared how irate she was when I called her to tell her about the weapons seizures and all of my struggles with the RCMP last summer. Her boss had heard her upset and asked what was going on. Over time, they made some changes to their policy.

She says, "Yes. You can essentially call it the Chelsey Policy without it being called the Chelsey Policy."

I was sitting at a table full of judges, crowns, lawyers, probation officers, and my team, so I tried to hold back my tears. But oh my God was I so proud (and emotional, again). The power of storytelling is real.

I am so grateful to have her in my corner, then and now. Without her support, this change would not have been possible.

# Chapter 41

## A New Opportunity on the Horizon

This chapter is a story about the power of forgiveness. Forgiveness doesn't mean that you necessarily forget. But when we hold onto hurt, anger, and resentment, it only impacts us and our own nervous system. It doesn't affect the other person at all. I share this story because of the profound impact that forgiveness had on my life.

In the spring of 2025, I had a sense something good was about to happen. This was a strange feeling after recent years, which had been nothing but gut punches and waiting for the shoe to drop. I had no idea what it was going to look like, but I just had this *feeling*. I kept it in the back of my mind and kept on living my life.

Come May, I was headhunted by an organization to manage a program inside some of our provincial jails. The person who headhunted me was someone I had gone to junior high with. While we were acquainted and worked alongside each other in similar fields, as adults, our history was not as pretty. She'd been quite nasty to me in school, taunting me in class and calling me "monkey," along with other cruel comments. I remember her sitting behind me in math class, whispering behind my back.

During breaks and at lunch, she and the rest of the popular crowd used to sit in an area called the "skywalk," which was a walkway full of windows that connected the old part of the school to a new part. It was the worst place to walk through, because it felt incredibly long, and you were taunted the whole way. Those girls were awful to me and many other kids.

I had to take the bus to this school from the opposite side of the city, as we didn't have any junior highs on the westside at that time. Some of those girls were on my bus. They'd throw sucker sticks and candy at me, among other things. It got to the point where I no longer felt safe on the bus and would rather make the three-hour walk home than deal with the torture for that thirty-minute bus ride.

I always wondered if she knew the pain she'd caused me, but I figured I would never really know, since we'd never had the chance to talk about it. I wasn't sure I even wanted to know. It was so long ago that I didn't still hold any resentment. More like I was more curious.

As I grew into adulthood, other bullies had shared with me how they had had no idea of their impact on me during that time, and had apologized. This shed a different light on not only my experience but what the bully must have been going through back then. (I hope to share more about this piece of my story in my second book.) I mention this here because, if I had held onto resentment and ignored this woman, despite our careers crossing paths, the following opportunity would not have been presented to me.

One day, this woman sent me a message that their organization was hiring, and she thought I'd be a perfect fit for the job. I was a bit reluctant at first, because I knew it was highly political to some degree, and I was unsure if it was the den I wanted to walk into. The only way I could find out for sure, though, was by requesting to meet with them and ask further questions. So, I did.

I arranged a meeting with the Executive Director and Program Director. The meeting went better than planned, and the opportunity was quite enticing. The executive director asked me excitedly at the end of the meeting, "When can you start?"

I responded with a chuckle, "Oh boy, I don't know. I wasn't looking for a new job. This is something I need to think about." I asked for a few days to think and get back to him by the end of the week.

I called up one of my best friends, who also knew about this opportunity, and went to see her, so she could be my voice of reason as I worked through the pros and cons list. This ended up being an opportunity I couldn't pass up; however, it meant walking away from Drug Treatment Court, a job I absolutely loved and a program I'd proudly contributed to and built in my community.

I was scheduled to attend the national Drug Treatment Court conference in Florida in about a week. I felt bad for going, paid for by my organization, because I knew I was going to pursue this new opportunity. I needed to say something to my current boss; I would feel terrible dropping that bomb on them upon my return. There was a bit of a time crunch as well, as the program director was going on maternity leave soon, and they wanted me to spend some time with her before her departure.

Under pressure, I approached my boss and informed him of what was going on. He supported my decision to leave, since it involved a big increase in pay, and it presented me with opportunities that my current employer could not offer. They told me, because it was such short notice, they could not replace me for the trip to Florida, so I should still go. I will be forever grateful for that agency—they treated me so well.

Long story short, I went to Florida. The other manager and I added a few extra days to the trip so we could relax, go surfing, and act like tourists. It was well worth it. I was feeling so proud of myself, knowing how hard I had worked to get to where I was, and that I had made the right choice. I was really excited to see what I could do in this new role. *Or so I thought.*

I was flooded with so many emotions. Anxious, scared, happy, sad, proud, all in a matter of seconds. It was overwhelming. Change is a good thing, but it can also be hard. I am no stranger to change, but a small voice in the back of my mind whispered, *What if it doesn't work out?*

I silenced that voice and tried to reassure myself that things would be okay and that it's good to take risks. *There is no growth in comfort zones.* But it's far easier to walk away from things when you're miserable than it is to walk away from things you love.

When I think back on my life and everything I have gone through, I am so proud of the life I have created for Grace and me. So many times, I wanted to give up. I contemplated suicide on more than one occasion, and I've struggled with mental health. There was a time when I truly felt it would not get any better.

Just as you spiral, sometimes opportunities present themselves, if we are open to them. It was reassurance that my fight is worth it. Even though my fight was far from over, this was another victory that I was going to accept with open arms. More money. More memories, and the ongoing ability to create an even more stable life for us.

The fight is always worth it.

I was emotional for days leading up to my Drug Treatment Court departure. Instead of ignoring the feelings, I gave myself permission to feel them. I didn't have to be tough all the time. I let the tears fall. As I cooked breakfast and gazed out my window, I was flooded with emotion. This time, it was with feelings of overwhelm, pride, and a little fear of the new. I'd fought so hard in my life, especially in the past few years, and sometimes really struggled to make ends meet financially. There were some weeks when I only had three to five dollars in my bank account and anxiously awaited payday, often going to my parents' house for dinner.

As I let the emotions flow, I embrace acceptance. I am ready to embrace the changes that life has to offer and appreciate the connections I have made on this journey. *I wouldn't be here without them.* I reminded myself that those can remain, that I can continue to nourish all of the relationships I have built. This didn't have to be a final goodbye.

I was finally in a place where I could comfortably engage in conversations with my new boss. I felt this change would be good. I was so excited to share my knowledge with my new team and see what I could do over there. The knowledge and passion I had about offender rehabilitation and best practices in that area were things I was bringing to the table that the organization did not already have. So many funders and grants require organizations to reduce recidivism, yet they have no way of measuring it nor are they measuring the criminogenic needs.

I thought, *This will be so awesome! I can help make these changes within the organization, so they too can speak to how they reduce recidivism. This will allow me to gain so many more connections across the province, too!*

In the back of my mind, as I was preparing for my exit, I was worried about who would take my place as the manager of Drug Treatment Court and what would happen with the program, once I was gone. I had to come to terms with the fact that, after my last day, it would no longer be my responsibility or have my name attached to it. So, I shouldn't stress about it. I sent emails to all of the stakeholders I was connected with, to inform them that I was leaving, tell them where I was going, and give them my contact information. At least I was leaving the program on good terms. That was something to be proud of.

My last court date for Drug Treatment Court was emotional. I was really proud of what we'd created and the people I'd gotten to work alongside, including the clients I was able to work with. One of the justices had some final words for me in court that day, and it broke me, in the best way.

He recognized that I'd built the program into its success today. "You are leaving big shoes to fill. Everyone is going to miss you."

I hadn't ever done something like this before, but I decided to write a card to each participant with words of encouragement, and

I handed them to each individual as I left the courtroom for the final time. The participants were quite upset that I was leaving, with very little notice.

Resiliency served me well during this time. I'd had some tough battles, getting the program to where it needed to be, while working with some difficult stakeholders, but I'd kept fighting, and it had been worth it.

My last day of work was bittersweet. I knew I would miss the team, the clients, and my bosses, but I leaned into the excitement of my next chapter. I kept reminding myself, *This is the right move, and I'm proud of myself for stepping out of my comfort zone and taking the risk, even when the outcome was unknown. I did my due diligence, I made an informed decision and I need to trust that. I need to trust myself.*

The team gave me a card, too, which included heartfelt words. I was surprised to see my boss didn't write in it or say anything to me on my last day. That hurt a bit, but I guess it was kind of his personality.

A new chapter awaited....

# Chapter 42

# A New Chapter Begins

On my first day at my new job, lots of things felt familiar, because I was accustomed to working inside our correctional institutions. But there was also lots of new terrain for me to navigate and learn, including the staff and their personalities. I came to learn something new about myself during this process, as well: I don't love being the newest staff member and feeling like a fish out of water. This was the first time I'd felt like this. Perhaps my body knew that something was off from the very first day. But how was I to know? Only time would tell.

One of my former staff members worked there, and although there was a supervisor between us, I was still the manager with oversight of the entire program. Things did not end well between us in our prior place of employment; this was another factor that had made me hesitate about moving over to this organization. I'd been very honest with my new boss about the difficulties we'd had. My boss had reassured me, if anything should arise in this current environment, they would do a proper investigation. They assured me I wouldn't have to do much of the disciplinary stuff with her, either, as that would be the role of her supervisor. This staff member had filed a complaint against me that was uncalled for and unfounded, as confirmed when human resources conducted their investigation. But her dislike of me was strong, and she'd influenced other stakeholders to think the same way.

As I settled into my role and onto the unit, I recognized a former Drug Treatment Court participant with whom I had worked and, unfortunately, had had to kick out of our program. It was great to see him doing well and have a catch-up. I was also approached by many people from the jail who were excited to see me there. Some gave me the biggest hug and shared how happy they were to have me. That felt good. Even though I felt like a fish out of water in this role, I still had those relationships and felt things were going to work out. I learned quite quickly that my alliance was with corrections staff, and I never felt like I belonged within the organization where I'd just been hired. A part of me felt tricked, but this wasn't something I could have known, prior to making the switch.

During the early days of my new employment, I was reading a book called *The Power Code*. In it was this quote: "Don't use power as fear. Use it as excitement." I loved it so much, I wrote it in my journal.

This book reframes the way we as women define power and how we can use power *to,* not power *over.* I thought this was a great perspective and something I wanted to carry with me as I moved forward. Rather than having power over others or situations, we have power to... This could be power to create change or different systems or anything else needed for the situation before us. It's having a more positive connotation of power, rather than how many males think of it, which is to demand or be in control. That reminds me of being in an abusive relationship. Instead, it's to have the power *to* face difficulties and rise above.

This connected to my own experiences, in that I wanted to take my power back from an abusive relationship and also to create systems change. Little did I know, my new workplace would end up having many of the same challenges of being in an abusive relationship, that I would be made to play small and silence myself, making me feel as though I did not have what it takes.

When I first started this position, I felt like a celebrity and a token child. I guess you could compare it to love bombing. My director took me around and introduced me to others, both virtually and in person. He bragged about the work I'd done with Drug Treatment Court, along with the knowledge I was bringing to their organization. After about a month into my employment, however, those dynamics changed, and very quickly I was being bullied by not one, but two of the directors, both of whom were male.

By the end of August, I had cried more at work than I ever had before, even during my previous employment when I'd been struggling with PTSD. I knew this feeling all too well. I felt trapped. I regretted leaving Drug Treatment Court and kept beating myself up a bit for making the decision to leave. *How could I be so foolish?* I couldn't believe the way I was being treated.

I went to the poor casework supervisor from the jail and cried in his office more than I care to admit. He was always so welcoming and willing to hear me vent, but I always wondered what was going on in the back of his mind, since jail doesn't really handle "emotional" well. I don't think I ever shared with him how grateful I was for his being a safe place for me during that time.

It was hard to get through the days. One day, my mom and I were talking, and she said to me, "Chelsey, I haven't seen you like this in a very long time. You have to do something."

I was trying to get past my probationary period, so I could take a leave for mental health. But I was hanging on by a thread. I resented going to work, and I hated being there. It was such an awful feeling.

I reached out for advice from the program director, who was on maternity leave. She said, "Remain open to learning. They are probably intimidated by you, because you are a strong woman, and they don't like that."

*Interesting,* I thought. I wasn't about to apologize for being a strong woman, though.

I didn't feel valued at all. Nothing I said and no suggestions I had or ideas I shared mattered. I felt bullied by the two directors, especially because I was not in recovery. They would often speak to me like I had no idea what I was talking about. Sometimes, it was as though they had dry-drunk mentalities. They were sober, but their thinking patterns were very much still of the criminal and addictive mindset.

During my initial conversation with the executive director and program director, I asked them if it would be an issue, my not being in recovery from addiction. They were quick to assure me no, that they needed some "normal" people working with them. But what I was feeling and the way I was being spoken to did not align with what they said. I felt really alone. I didn't align with all of those in recovery.

I reflected back on my time in Drug Treatment Court. Our program had a mentor attached to our team, someone who was in recovery and had gone through the program. They walked alongside the clients in a different way and served as the bridge between clients and case workers, at times. It was an essential role for our program. I thought about how she and I didn't have any of these issues, working together, so, my problems in the job still boggled my mind.

I often found myself in reflection, but not the peaceful type of reflection; more the anxious kind. "Why is this happening? What about this situation is so different?" I never really landed on an answer and could not figure it out. All I could deduce was how that mentor I'd worked with had a lot more commitment to personal development, and she did not see things from one single perspective, especially when it came to recovery and its modalities.

I knew there had to be a lesson in this, but I wasn't sure how much of it I could take. The constant negative comments and belittling of my ideas or of what I'd thought I was brought on board to do was getting to be too much.

Then, one day, I had a meeting with the director of operations, who told me that I was feeling intimidated. This caught me off guard and left me very confused. He continued, "You're intimidated by our COO."

I replied, "But there's nothing that intimidates me about that person."

He said, "Well, maybe that's a me thing. But I am very intimidated by her."

"Yeah, you might me, but I am not. I have no problem sitting in rooms with judges and crown prosecutors, and I am not intimidated. They are just people to me."

He didn't have much else to say after that. I still have no idea why he projected his own shit onto me, but it seemed to be a common theme as time went on.

Another incident occurred with this same man not long after. Four of us were talking in a meeting about the ministers coming to town to do tours of the units. Suddenly, this guy said in a disparaging tone, "When you find your voice, Chelsey."

I was blown away. Never had I been spoken to like this in a workplace before. I kind of chuckled to myself, because anyone who knows me knows that I *do* have a voice *and* I know how to use it, especially for good. I didn't say much, though, as I didn't see the point.

I'd been hired as the manager of quality assurance, which meant I was to ensure the programs were aligned with quality and evidence-based practice. I was soon told, however, that I was not able to touch any of the programs or make changes to them (yet). Even though, previously, I'd been asked to look at all of the sessions they were facilitating, to ensure there was alignment and consistency across all programs.

I was so confused. *What was I supposed to do, if I couldn't touch the programs?*

Over time, I became quite emotional in meetings with my director. Finally, one day, I told him, "There is a misalignment between my values and the values of the organization, including the way I have been treated."

He said, "You just can't touch programs and make those changes now. But you may be able to do it later."

I was very confused. It felt like I was being gaslighted and manipulated every time we engaged in conversation. Every day, it was something different. This feeling was overwhelmingly similar to my relationship with Johnny. I was trying to plan my exit, but I felt even more confined here than I had, leaving my ex-partner. My income depended on this job, and there were not a ton of job opportunities in this field in our community that paid more than entry-level wages.

A few weeks later, I had a meeting with the program director from the larger organization that umbrellaed all of the other subsidiaries. (I was employed by one of the subsidiaries.) He asked me how things were going, and I said, "Do you want me to be honest?"

"Absolutely!" he replied.

So, I told him how I was feeling. He said he would like to try to make some changes, and we dreamed up some different ideas and implementation strategies. I was again assured that the organization needed me. Although I was very unhappy, I held onto those words, thinking that maybe there would be a different opportunity there for me, that I could maybe move into a different role under him, where I would be happier.

I had a meeting with my director shortly after, and he asked how my meeting went. I didn't disclose everything, but I said it went well and that I was hopeful we could do some good work together. We continued to meet on a semi-regular basis.

My boss informed me that the ministers of addiction and mental health and some other "officials" were coming for a tour of the unit. It wasn't anything I wasn't used to, so I said I could handle it.

He wouldn't allow me to. He said he had to be there, and at least the team lead would have to be there, too. *Okay, whatever*, I thought.

I switched gears and said, "Hey, I have some interesting statistics that they may want to know." I continued, "Jail alone, without any other intervention, actually increases recidivism by about seven percent. If we offer other interventions..." And I shared some additional quantitative data.

He replied "That is good information. Do you know that to be true?"

I couldn't believe it. I am not someone who would spew data that was inaccurate or that I could not back up. This was yet another shot to the stomach. It felt so condescending. I disengaged from the conversation and contributed the bare minimum until our conversation ended.

I'd been informed of the time for our visitors' arrival, so I went down to the unit to check and found they were not there. They showed up a few hours later than expected, and nobody took the time to let me know when they did arrive. I thought that was so strange. Since I was the manager with a ton of experience and knowledge, why wouldn't they include me?

When I walked down to the unit to meet with everyone, I joined in late. They were standing in a closed circle with me outside of it. I felt so awkward, but I stayed. After bragging about themselves and offering the least-intelligent answers I'd heard (e.g., to "So, tell me, does this program actually work?" the director responded, "Yes, it does"). *I couldn't believe it.* That would have been a prime opportunity for me to share my statistics and information, but they kept me silenced and at bay.

One lady who was part of the group said to her counterpart, "Who is that girl?" referring to me.

My director didn't say anything, but the director of the jail replied, "This is Chelsey, and she is really well known in this community for the work she has done."

I thought, *Thank you for saying that and highlighting my efforts.* This comment meant so much to me, because I'd been made to feel so small by my own "leaders."

The next day, when I was in a meeting with my director and the director of operations, they said to me, "Chelsey, you just need to learn how to talk to government officials."

*What?! You didn't even give me the opportunity.* Plus, during my time in Drug Treatment Court, I'd had no problems arranging a meeting with our mayor to talk about our program and the impact it was having on our community. He had come to a Drug Treatment Court day and observed court with one of his staff. We had many conversations following that. I had no problem talking to officials; this was not my first rodeo. But I needed the space and trust to be able to do so.

Another difficult conversation occurred with the director of operations, when I was asked if I had ever tried acceptance therapy. While that is not always a bad thing, it was like they were constantly projecting their own shit on me. I would describe these as microaggressions.

For example, when I mentioned how I was trying to show up authentically and share my struggles, they said, "Feelings aren't facts." While this may be true, it felt very dismissive and lacking in humanity. Very transactional. I watched them behave that way toward others, too. I even wondered why they stayed working in our program. But nowhere else was paying that kind of money for people with lived experience and very little, if any, post-secondary education.

I had been experiencing what I now recognize as heart palpitations, prior to beginning my employment there, but they grew worse during my time here, until they appeared almost daily. That was when I decided I needed to make a doctor's appointment, to figure out what was going on. The last thing I needed was a heart attack.

I was referred to the cardiologist, who hooked me up to a monitor to record all of my irregular heartbeats, any palpitations, and any activity I engaged in over twenty-four hours. A week or so after wearing the monitor, my doctor asked to see me, so we could review the results. They had noticed one irregular heartbeat but were not concerned.

My doctor asked, "Are you exposed to any stress or anything like that?"

"Work is stressful right now," I said.

She asked me to continue monitoring my heart, and if anything changed or if I had shortness of breath, I was to go straight to the emergency room.

A while later, when I met with the program director from the larger organization for a follow-up, he asked if things were any better. I told him they were not. He made arrangements to fly to meet with me in my community, a week or so later.

We met in person at a local coffee shop. He said, "I am so confused as to why they won't let you bring your skillset in and add the assessment tool you want to use."

We had a good conversation, until he gave me some very bizarre advice (though it also turned out to be some of the best). He said, "Whatever you do, Chelsey, do not quit. Let them fire you, so you get severance."

My first thought was, *What the hell? Who says something like this?*

Then, he asked, "Have you ever been fired before?"

I'm sure my face said it all. I thought, *Why is he asking like this is something to be proud of? Who the hell has been fired before and wears it like a badge of honor?*

He continued, "I've been fired three times by [the doctor who spearheaded the entire organization]."

That made me really wonder about the organization on a deeper level. *Who fires someone three times and hires them back? Don't people only get fired for being shitty?*

I left that meeting still feeling hopeful that something would change and maybe I would find my way out of the current subsidiary where I worked and into somewhere happier. The last thing that program director said was, "Being fired is the most liberating feeling. You should try it sometime."

A week after our meeting, on a Wednesday at 8:15 a.m., as I was getting ready to go to work, my phone rang. An Edmonton phone number. I immediately knew.

"Hello?" I said when I picked up.

"Hi, Chelsey. I am calling to inform you that you are being fired without cause." We exchanged some other words around benefits, severance, and all of that stuff, and the conversation ended shortly after.

I felt a sense of, "What the fuck do I do now?" along with much relief. After a little cry, I called my mom to tell her the news and then said to myself, "I know what I'll do now. I'll start my own consulting company."

I got to work. I looked into what I needed to do to start my own company, and I put work out on all of my social media platforms that I was looking for work. Two days later, I got a call from someone I knew asking if I was actually looking for work. We had a chat about a potential project, and he asked me to submit a proposal.

I had no idea what I was doing, but I was determined to figure it out. A few weeks later, I got my first contract. I was also accepted into a business course that I had applied to. In that same time period, I found out I had been accepted by this very publishing company, to publish my first book.

*Damn. That guy was right. Being fired truly is the most liberating feeling!*

# Chapter 43

## The Assessment

In mid-August, 2025, I received an email from my lawyer. My heart started to race. I wondered, *Do I owe more money? What's changed? What fresh hell awaits me now?* It's hard not to let our minds wander to the darkest places.

The email read, "The assessor has agreed to the $10,000 for the assessment to be completed, which means you will need to pay $2,500 up front to retain her, and then another $2,500 once the assessment is completed." Then, the email described who would be included in the interview process, along with a general idea of how they would be conducted. I saw that Rosie was going to be interviewed. I did not understand why, since she was not a parent of Grace. I also couldn't help but to feel that it would be those two adults' word against mine. To be honest, I felt this was like the situation was stacked against me.

I sent an email back to inquire why Rosie would be interviewed, while I did not have the opportunity for anyone else on my side to be interviewed. I didn't have a partner, but I felt like there were enough adults who'd been involved in much of what had happened, they should be able to share their experience in this madness, as well. The answer I received was that partners are often disproportionately involved in child abuse, which he did not think was the case with Rosie, but the assessor would do her due diligence.

*What the heck does that even mean?* I was so sick of being dragged through the mud, coughing up thousands upon thousands of dollars, just to try to justify that this was domestic violence and show why we were victims of it. The amount of money we'd have to spend to retell our story was was insane, and the assessment was the least trauma-informed of any system I had ever worked within. Nobody seemed to listen or care.

The thought crossed my mind: *Maybe, if we end up dead, people will listen.* But it shouldn't take the death of women and children to make a difference. We had enough evidence that showed this is preventable.

We began the waiting game until the assessment could be scheduled. I was told I would have to drive up to Calgary for both my assessment as well as Grace's. This was kind of annoying and meant a lot of commuting for us, but I did have some hope this assessment would be what we needed to make this all come to an end.

I hated the month of August. It was one of my worst months since 2020. It should have been full of excitement: it was summer time, with my birthday, my brother's birthday, and my parents' anniversary all falling within the same week. But it's hard to be excited when something drastic always happens. I proceeded with extreme caution. I dreamed of the days, months, and years when I wouldn't have to deal with this shit anymore. No more traumatic experiences, no more retelling our story.

I feel things on such a deep level, I really wished I had a soft place to land. I felt tired of fighting all of these fights on my own.

August 26, 2025 was my birthday. I turned thirty-eight years old. I reflected on what the past year had held for me and what I wanted this next year to look like.

This last year had been filled with court battles, starting a new job, losing a job, and starting my own business. Grace became a preteen, with all of the emotions that come with that. While I found some peace, I longed for more. I felt really proud of what I had been able to do with my life, despite the circumstances and ongoing battles. It was a sign that resilience is within all of us. We have to choose to embrace it and allow for it to get us through the tough times. We also need to give ourselves the space to decompress.

A few days later, I was an emotional wreck. Remember how I just said we can't be in fight mode all the time? I think I finally hit a breaking point (and not my first one, either). I shall call this chapter of my life my "soft-girl era." I've always said, when the walls come down, and I feel safe enough, I will be a mess. I think I am slowly getting there.

Life is funny. As you do the inner work and navigate life and all of its experiences (good and bad), you uncover so much more about yourself. The work truly never ends. It's a beautiful process in and of itself, but I would be lying if I said it was easy. *Nothing worth doing is easy.* It can be exhausting at times, too. As you do this work, it makes finding "your people" a lot harder, at least in my experience anyway. Not many people can get to the depths of self-awareness. Or maybe it's just that they don't want to. But I find it harder to connect with others in a meaningful way, when they are not in the same place mentally or spiritually. With that being said, I'm embracing this opportunity and will see what comes my way in this soft-girl era.

By winter 2025, the meetings for our assessment had finally been scheduled.

I drove up to Calgary to meet with the assessor, whose role is to be the voice of the child. I become super-frustrated and retriggered by all of my thoughts and emotions around this assessment. I'd never understood why we had to pay an arm and a leg to have this assessment done, when Grace also had a court-appointed lawyer to represent her, as the child, and to be her voice in the custody process. And that also came at a cost.

When I arrived in Calgary and parked at the appointment address, I realized I was a few blocks off of 17th Avenue, which is a pretty popular area and busy street. I wondered if I was in the right space. I walked down the street and right past the building, which looked somewhat abandoned and had a large for sale sign on the front yard. It could definitely use a facelift.

At the door, I was greeted by the assessor, who was warm and welcoming and created a safe space for me to share my story. I didn't think I would be as triggered as I was, when I started to retell my story, but the way she asked questions brought things up for me that I'd thought I had processed. Johnny's words and statements had haunted me for years, while lying within my subconscious. Every so often, in these vulnerable moments, when there was so much at stake, they came to the surface. No matter the amount of work we do to heal from trauma, the impact of words like his never truly goes away. What matters, however, is our ability not to believe them anymore and not to allow them to hijack us.

While I was thinking, *I am so tired of sharing my story over and over again, while feeling like nobody is listening,* the other side of my brain told me, *This is exactly the person I need to share my story with.* I understood how her report would be the document we needed to make this come to an end.

When I left her building, closing the door behind me, I held my head high and said to myself, "This is it, Chelsey. This is exactly where you needed to be. This may have been the best $5,000 you've spent."

I met with the assessor a second time, to complete the entire history of what had happened, though this time it was virtual. Again, it was quite an emotional process. It felt good to release and share my story. It felt like I was shedding layers I'd been unaware of, deep within my subconscious. I don't think we are ever done healing. The deeper we heal, the more comes to the surface.

The assessor asked me a somewhat rhetorical question, "What are we doing here?" And confirmed, "The police have never done anything for you?"

We spoke briefly about domestic violence and how the Divorce Act now mandates that domestic violence be taken into consideration. However, this does not appear to apply to common law, or at least when I was leaving Johnny it was never mentioned to me. That means many of us are left without the privilege of having DV considered if we were never married. I am not sure how much of a privilege it is in such a flawed system, but it sounds nice in theory.

A few weeks later, I drive Grace up to Calgary for her interview. The assessor's role is to assess parents, stepparents, and the child, plus any others they deem necessary. I had asked if my parents were able to participate, since they had been a part of most things that happened. I felt it was not fair that I be the only adult presenting our perspective in the story, apart from Grace, of course. Johnny had also threatened to beat my dad up last summer in front of Grace, which I thought would warrant a conversation. Sometimes, I am still so skeptical of processes because I have been failed time and time again.

As Grace and I arrived at the office, another couple was leaving. The woman was in tears, and the man had a very stoic visage, as he walked ahead of her. It seemed like a heightened and uneasy situation. I felt sadness for the woman. Even though I had no idea what her story was or what had just taken place, I could relate to what it feels like to feel so defeated. She continued walking down the street as the man got into a vehicle and drove away.

This was another representation of broken systems. I wondered, *What has her experience been? Is she another woman who is being dragged through the mud, having to beg and plead for someone to believe her? Does she fear for her life? What messages has she been given?"* I hope she's okay and finds her way through.

As we stood on the porch, waiting to be let into the office, Grace said, "That lady was really upset."

I said, "Sometimes, sharing the most difficult parts of our lives can be hard."

Grace agreed. "But I won't cry."

"It's okay if you do," I told her.

I sat inside with the assessor and Grace briefly, while the assessor explained her role, what she would and would not say, and all of the other typical things psychologists have to do when obtaining ascent (which is like consent, but a bit different when minors are involved; as the parent, I had provided consent for her to participant in this process). After a few minutes, I left to wait outside.

When I returned to pick Grace up, she and the assessor met me at the front door. The assessor told me we would have to schedule a second meeting, because they did not get through everything today. I agreed and waited for her assistant to send me some dates.

Grace and I made the most out of our trip to Calgary, including a trip to IKEA, to decompress and take our minds off of the situation.

A week or so later, we again commuted to Calgary, so Grace could finish her interview with the assessor, this time with my mom to keep me company. Virtual was not an option in this case, because parents can claim coercion or influence by the other parent. I agreed, because I knew that Johnny would 100% pull that card, as he had in the past. His constant argument was parental alienation and saying I have been trying to ruin his character and career.

While Grace had her meeting, my mom and I walked around the neighborhood then nestled into a cozy coffee shop off of 17$^{th}$ Avenue. The appointment was scheduled for two hours, but just over an hour later, I received a text from the assessor saying they were done. My mom and I quickly finished our coffee and walked back to the office. The assessor said they now had everything they needed.

As we walked to the car, Grace said, "I cried again."

I told her that was okay. "Do you feel good about what you said and how the meeting went?"

She nodded yes and then settled into the backseat. We were going to head to the mall to get something to eat and pick up some new socks, but I could see Grace's face looked visibly upset. I asked if she was okay, and she again nodded yes, but her tears started flowing.

I asked her if she wanted a hug. When she nodded, I stopped the vehicle and went out to give her a hug. She let the tears flow, saying, "I'm so glad this is all going to be over."

A few days later, there was a new email from my lawyer. *Now what?* I never knew what to expect. He informed me that Johnny had retained a new lawyer. I received another email from the assessor's administration asking me to pay an additional amount. I felt scammed by this point, because it wasn't like just a few dollars; it was hundreds. I asked for clarification around this new expense, but all I was told was I had no option but to pay it, as it was for courier fees and report writing. *Make it stop.*

A month or so later, my lawyer received the assessment via email. My heart sank when I saw it. I'd waited so long for this assessment, but now, I was scared to read it, even though the anticipation was killing me.

As soon as I began to read, I felt triggered. During his interview, Johnny disclosed that I threatened to kill myself when he'd tried to leave me. In another part, he went on to say that I'd left him one time before and only came back because I could not afford anything on my own. He claimed everything was always about money for me.

I couldn't believe some of his outright lies in that interview. Then, I read Rosie's interview, also full of lies. She purported that every time we saw them in public, I called security on them. She also said they had to pay me X dollars in child support, yet they weren't even allowed to watch any of Grace's sports. She said they had put all of Grace's money in trust, as they had done for all of their other children, as it was distributed. I didn't believe that for a second.

Their interviews were not as long as mine, which I found interesting. Reading through the assessment did get my back up: it felt like it made excuses for Johnny's poor, abusive behavior because of his being a first responder and having been diagnosed with ADHD. I felt like the assessor minimized everything that had happened to me and Grace.

I recognize that I am not trained to write these assessment reports and maybe they must be written in a certain way, but I felt like its recommendations were very focused on "family therapy" and individual therapy. The assessor asserted I needed to go to counseling for my PTSD, which I felt was a bit silly when I made clear that, when I was diagnosed with PTSD from a work-related incident, I had taken off work for ten months and attended intense trauma therapy to work through what had happened. *That wasn't the issue. Being continuously exposed to my abuser was.* I'd been cleared to return to work.

I felt like I was being blamed. I also recognize that, because I am emotionally tied and invested in the assessor's report, it was hard for me to read it objectively. I called my friend immediately after and talked with her. I didn't want to share the assessment due to confidentiality, but I needed a voice of reason.

In reading the section where Grace was interviewed, I thought she did a good job, and it seemed to be quite thorough. But then, I panicked, worrying, if I had a copy of this assessment, wouldn't Johnny *also* get a copy? I felt like we were at risk, given what Grace had disclosed.

I emailed my lawyer's assistant and told her that I was fearful for mine and Grace's safety, given the sensitive information this assessment included and the possibility of the final determination not going the way Johnny wanted it to. My lawyer called me back the next day.

We talked it through, and he reassured me that this assessment was exactly what we'd thought it would be. It said all the things we thought it would say. Grace and I had always spoken our truth. I knew that, too. Still, I told him I was scared for our safety.

As much as I respect my lawyer, I felt like he minimized my fears, saying, "Johnny won't do anything. He may just throw a fit, as he always does, but I don't think he's going to do anything."

*Why are people so quick to dismiss others' fears?* I wondered. *We are the ones who have to deal with the outcomes daily.*

Together, he and I reviewed what my lawyer would ask for in court. Hopefully, we could soon wrap this all up.

He said, "You will have to see each other for child support reviews, but otherwise, this entire battle is nearly over. I think we are through the worst of it, Chelsey. I think we can put this bed."

As I drove to the gym, I got emotional. This had been the longest, toughest battle of my life, and one I had fought hard for. Not only for me, but for Grace, her safety, and her wellbeing.

One of the things that pissed me off the most was the assessor's indicating this was "high conflict." I am so sick of professionals calling this "high conflict" and not recognizing it for what it is: *domestic violence.*

It's like the system expects me to be this battered, sobbing, broken woman, sitting in a corner, which would give them permission to call me a victim of domestic violence. Or maybe I'm supposed to show up with a bunch of bruises. I really don't know what it takes for the system to call it what it is. Maybe it isn't until women are in a body bag for it to be identified as domestic violence. It's a little too late by that point.

# Chapter 44

## Breaking Free from the Chains

The next few months, anticipating my court battles coming to an end, were a wild ride. It felt like I was truly breaking free from the chains that had held me back for so long.

I read a meditation about a boy who asked many deep, probing questions that had opened his heart. Many people came into his life, but they always left. A girl entered his life but never answered the questions; she just fluttered around and eventually left. He wanted so badly to be held that he uprooted himself and left the shade of his own heart and began to live. I was a bit confused by the ending of this meditation. What I ended up taking away from it was that sometimes we limit ourselves and get stuck in feelings and a piece of the picture, instead of seeing the whole picture. So, in order to see the whole picture, we need to break free from the chains that bind and hold us back from truly living and experiencing all that life has to offer.

We need this freedom to truly live the most authentic and aligned version of ourselves.

Sometimes, people link their happiness to love, and while love is important, it's not the only thing we need in life. Love doesn't have to come from an intimate partner, either; it can come from within and all around you. How I wish I'd learned this long ago, but perhaps I wasn't ready to receive that lesson then, and so, my life unfolded the way it was meant to.

*"There are many paths to take in life. Sometimes, you don't know where they will lead, but that's not the purpose. It's about the journey and lessons along the way. For the path chosen may lead you to even greater destinations."*

–Mark Nepo.

On September 23, 2025, I wrote a journal entry based on my daily meditation practice. It was about getting back up, no matter how many times we fall, and taking the lessons that come with it. Nepo writes, "Repetition is not failure. Ask the waves, ask the leaves and the wind."

No matter how many times we fall or have to start over or learn the same lessons, we suffer pain as often as necessary for us to learn to break and to heal. We learn what we need to, until we learn the humility of acceptance.

Many major life events that could happen to someone have happened to me, and I am not even forty yet. I plan to include many of these experiences and life lessons in my next book, because there's so much more there. After heartbreaks and leaving everything behind to flee abuse, to being fired, almost taking my own life on more than one occasion, depression, anxiety, PTSD, and sexual assault, I'm still here.

While waiting for our lawyers to meet and discuss next steps, Johnny struck again. I received a call from the orthodontist's office after they spoke to Johnny and he'd told them many time we could not use his dad's benefits to get Grace's braces, that the court order instead said that Johnny and I had to pay for her orthodonture 50/50. He'd repeated, "You cannot use my dad's benefits. Chelsey can pay out of pocket for her portion."

The lady in finance at the dental office said, "I tried to explain to him that it was best for Grace, and by using his dad's benefits, there would be no cost to either of us. But he did not want to hear me and was adamant we couldn't use his dad's assistance for the benefits."

I explained to her that I also told Johnny how I did not currently have benefits, being out of work, and that we would both have to pay out of pocket, if benefits weren't figured out.

She replied, "I don't want to get into trouble, but if you can get clarification from his dad to use his benefits, we will proceed." I informed her that I had already spoken to him just days prior and received his consent.

Once my lawyer and I connected again, his message was music to my ears. His saying we could likely wrap this up was such great news, and it made me quite emotional. During our conversation, I said, "I am done pumping money into this system. It's broken, and it causes more harm than good. Grace will be fourteen this year. Enough is enough."

We talked about child support allotments; there was still a lot of money under discussion regarding that, along with back pay. My lawyer told me, if Grace chose to attend post-secondary, Johnny would be expected to participate financially in that, as well. I could handle those conversations, when necessary, but I needed to be done with the back-and-forth about parental alienation, denial of abuse, and what felt like forced contact between him and Grace. I finally put my foot down.

Family reunification works when it involves healthy parents. Reunification does not work when one parent takes no responsibility for their actions and chooses to laugh about them, instead, while continuing to blame true victims.

I was provided with an opportunity to break free from the chains in more ways than one.

# Chapter 45

# The Letter

Amidst the chaos and silence of my court battles and living life, I had another interesting experience. Several months before, my friend and I had been texting about dating, guys, and how awful the dating world was.

She mentioned how she'd been chatting recently with a guy she'd met online. "He's a cop—you might know him." When I asked his name, she told me his name.

I knew I'd seen this individual on dating apps before, and I'd always swiped *no*. I told my friend, "I know who he is."

To be honest, I never thought it would go anywhere, so I left it alone. I just shared my own experience with her and explained why I didn't like him. You may be wondering who this cop is, so I won't keep you guessing. He's the cop that had threatened to arrest me.

As time went on, they slowly developed a relationship. In the back of my mind, I thought maybe he wasn't going anywhere. I wondered what does this mean for our friendship? The thing I value most about our friendship is the ability to have difficult conversations.

One night, the two of us went out with two of her friends. The topic of their relationship came up. One of her friends was putting pressure on her, asking why they weren't exclusive yet. I didn't want my friend to get hurt, but I was hoping she would go on to find someone better. For some reason, I just didn't trust him and what was going on. My friend told the group how I didn't like him, so then they wanted to know why not, which I openly shared.

My friend heard me raise some additional concerns about him, but then the conversation returned to the others' pressure for her to become something official with this man, though their relationship was still in the early stages. She described something nice that he'd done for her, something she'd told others about before. I began to think, *I hope my hate for him doesn't impact her ability to tell me the good things that go on in whatever this relationship or friendship is.*

The next time we hung out, it was just the two of us. I told her how I was feeling and that I didn't ever want her to feel like she couldn't share the good things about their relationship with me, despite my feelings. We had a good conversation about that.

We discussed my experience and thoughts again as she and I got ready to go to a "women in business" event. I had been writing about this cop in my book at this time, so I was definitely heightened, emotionally, after just reliving some of that trauma through writing.

She said to me, "Maybe he was going through a rough time that day or something happened. She added, "He's a really good guy."

"Maybe so," I said. "But I've also seen and heard some pretty horrific things in my career, and I have never behaved that way. It's not an excuse. They should be able to turn it off and be present for the next call."

During that discussion, I felt it was better to agree to disagree, since we were each seeing different versions of him. I said, "If he treats you well, that's great, but I did not have a great experience with him."

She replied, "I know."

A few months later, this friend arranged a girl's night out dinner for about ten of us. I didn't know many other girls, but it was fun nonetheless. I got a new hairdresser out of the night, so that's always a win.

At the end of the night, I told my friend I had her stuff in my car and to come grab it. She said she would and that she was waiting for that guy to come pick her up, because she did not drive.

My heart started to race. *Shit. Really?* We keep chatting until she received a message that he was there. She said to me, "He's here," and we both walk up to the front to leave.

Not only was he there, he was physically in the building, coming inside to get her. I didn't acknowledge him, just walked past him.

My friend followed me outside. "Chelsey, wait up."

I was more triggered than I'd realized. It was cold outside, so I went to get to my vehicle, but also, I didn't want to be near him. At my vehicle, we chatted briefly, then she asked, "Would you ever have a conversation with him? He cares about you. He asks me how you're doing. He even asked the other day."

I did wonder whether he actually did care or was just trying to get with my friend. I replied, "I'm not sure, but not right now. I am far too triggered by him, and now, he's a bit too close for comfort."

I'd hoped he would remain "over there": as a cop, someone I didn't have to deal with in my personal life. But there he was, with my friend, and their relationship seemed to be getting stronger.

A week or later, I found I had been thinking about this conversation with her quite a bit. Then, I thought, *What a cool opportunity for me to tell him how he impacted me that day when he showed up. The impact he had on Grace. And to encourage him to do differently next time.*

How you show up matters. It's not often that cops get to hear our side of things. No matter how he responded, this was an opportunity for me to heal further on my own journey and to let go of my hate for him.

A few days later, I texted my friend. "Hey, I've been giving it some thought as to whether I wanted to talk to [him] or not, and I decided I would like to write him a letter. What are your thoughts?"

She agreed, saying he would like that. So, I wrote him a seven-page letter.

*Dear Officer,*

*I never thought I would get the opportunity to directly share how our last interaction impacted me. Not only me, but my daughter, too. When I was asked if I would ever have a conversation with you, my first response was, "No," because I wasn't ready. Moments later, I realized that, in time, I would. As I sat and reflected, I thought the best way for me to do this was to write, as I am much better with written expression, especially when there is so much emotion attached to this whole experience.*

*I want to be clear in that I am aware you are not responsible for the broken systems we work in, and I don't place the blame solely on you. You had an opportunity to show up differently on December 23, 2020, though, and you didn't.*

*I have been dealing with police and the justice system for almost a decade, because of domestic violence. When you arrived at my house shortly after 9:00 p.m. that night, initially I felt a sense of relief. Knowing it was you and having worked with you in the downtown core during my time at CMHA. I also felt safe and that, finally, maybe someone would hear my concerns. These thoughts and feelings of safety immediately disappeared once you stood in my door way and said, "This is the fifth time we have responded. You know I could arrest you for this." For not forcing my daughter to go to her dad's. I told you what was going on, why she didn't want to go. Not only did you make that comment to me, you said it in front of my daughter, who has forever worried since then that I may go to jail and that you had the power to put me there, for protecting my daughter.*

*I explained to you the abuse that had occurred and why Grace didn't feel safe, that I understood I was technically breaching my parenting order, but it was for good reason and in the best interest of my child. I pointed to her as she stood at the top of the stairs, listening and observing, to go and talk to her, and ask her why she didn't want to go to her dad's. You looked up at her momentarily but didn't seem eager or interested in what either of us had to say.*

*You continued to stand in my doorway with an authoritative stance as I asked you how many more women and children need to die by DV before you actually took it seriously. Those words came out because I was frustrated and scared, but deep down, I was terrified that anything I said that you didn't like would have me hauled away in the back of the cop car. You carried an attitude like this was the last place you wanted to be that night. It's an image and a conversation that I will never forget, as it's a permanent memory and shaped a strong opinion of you and our police service.*

*I went on to tell you the history and involvement with the school counselor, and how Johnny tried to take Grace from school, which prompted more police contact. I also told you that I was tired of telling my story over and over again only for nothing to be done, as was my daughter. It really hurt when it was you treating me the same way, given that we had a working relationship and I respected you.*

*You asked me what I hoped for in the future, which seemed to completely derail the trajectory of the conversation, and to this day, I don't understand the intent behind that question. I didn't think you actually cared to know, but fearful of what may happen if I didn't answer, I answered. I told you that I wanted Johnny to get the help that he needed, so he could engage in a healthy way. I wanted them to have a relationship, but not at the expense of her (Grace's) safety and mental health.*

*Timmy* [name changed of this officer] *had responded to a call previously, and I was thankful for that because he cared. When I showed him my court order and explained how Grace said she didn't feel safe, he said that was enough, and he would not make her go. I was present when he asked Grace why she did not want to go, and she told him that her dad abused her. When I told you this, you told me that Timmy put in his notes that Grace did not disclose why she didn't want to go.*

*This felt like another hit to me—another effort for you to cover up or not want to do the work required with DV cases. And it reassured me that even when you think you know someone and trust the police to do their jobs and document accordingly, with honesty and integrity—you can't. We are supposed to call the police when we feel in danger, and trust we will be protected. I don't feel that way. I do not trust that I can call or that anything will be done. Some have proven me wrong, but I still hold a lot of mistrust for police as a whole (recognizing a few good ones exist).*

*You then asked me if I wanted this to be investigated. Which should have been your call. Not mine. Why would I get a choice? You followed that question with, "If you do, you'll have to go down to the station."*

*I felt like you were trying to pass the buck, so you could get the fuck out of dodge. Little did you know, I'd had a terrible experience with an officer at the front, when I'd made attempts to file a complaint at the "complaint" desk with a uniformed officer. I asked you if the station was open at this time, to which you responded, "It should be." Again, making me feel like you didn't care. You didn't want to do your job. It was solidified when our conversation continued.*

*You asked me if Johnny could be charged with anything under the criminal code. That's your job to determine that. I asked you why all of the officers who had responded, not one of you had asked to hear the recording I have of Johnny physically dragging Grace out of my vehicle, as she was screaming for her life, grasping at anything to prevent her from being taken, screaming she can't breathe.*

*You asked if I still had the video, I told you I did. I told you neighbors had come out that night, asking if we were okay. You asked me to send you the video, which I did. You told me that you would be in touch with me the following day after 6:00 p.m., as you were on nights. As you left, you said, "Great, I'll have to write a book about this."*

*I want you to consider that statement and how it made me feel. You may not know what it feels like to be a victim and fight a system this way, but imagine for a moment being in my shoes, feeling as though you aren't believed. That at every turn your situation is minimized, and in the scariest moments of your life and your child's, nobody, especially those who are supposed to protect you, don't. You are left to fight on your own.*

*I later looked up the police standards in Alberta and learned that neither you nor any other responding officer followed any of that protocol.*

*Let's go back to our situation. You said I would hear from you the following day/night and that you would send my information and the video to the family violence unit. I never heard from you again. Meanwhile, I was left to fear for my safety. It was disheartening to say the least, to feel like it really didn't matter to you.*

*You may have thought things got better from that point on, but that couldn't be further from the truth. It continued to get worse, which is a story for another time.*

*The RCMP had to get after LPS. And over two years after the incident, Johnny finally got charged with assault with a weapon on Grace. This is truly unacceptable, and it came after fierce advocacy on my end and the RCMP. I was finally connected with the family violence unit, which made these things possible, and I am forever grateful for Wes Yasinski and his compassion. He was finally someone I felt heard me and understood the severity. It shouldn't have taken this much fighting to get here though. There was an NCO (No Contact Order) put into place (November 2022-November 2023). There is so much more to this story, too.*

*EPOs followed. Johnny has held Grace hostage and become aggressive, among other things. All of this comes with more in-depth stories for another time.*

*I have been failed by systems for many years. But I continue to show up and fight, because I have to. I have done a lot of work on myself, but I will admit, you triggered me. You came too close for comfort, being with my friend. I didn't think this would happen or you would ever end up in my inner circle for me to have to deal with or recognize, but here we are.*

*So, as we enter this next chapter, I've come to this conclusion. I don't want my friend to have to hide or feel like she cannot share the good things between you, because of my thoughts and feelings toward you. I want her to be happy and treated well. I think it would be a tremendous healing opportunity for us to engage in a dialogue, after you have read this and digested where I am coming from. I want you to know that I am not coming from a place of hate but rather mistrust and hesitancy, as there is still a lot of emotion tied to this and, in the bigger picture, because my fight isn't over yet.*

*With that being said, I welcome a conversation for us to come to a common understanding and see what we can build from there.*

*I will close with this final thought.*

*I don't know what you were going through the night you responded, but I want you to know that how you show up for people, on and off duty, matters and leaves lasting impressions (good or bad). You have to be able to put your biases and belief systems aside and be present for that person and their circumstances.*

*Thank you for taking the time to read this. I look forward to future conversations.*

*Chelsey*

It took a couple of weeks for my friend to give him the letter, but eventually, it made its way to him. She said he was interested in a conversation, however I have yet to hear anything. I have come to the conclusion that writing this letter and knowing he received it are all the healing I need.

If I were that officer and I received a letter from someone who felt they were treated poorly by me, I would have taken every opportunity to find a way to have a conversation with that person. This was a clear indication he didn't care about me. He only cared about getting with my friend.

This was a courageous step on my part, and a huge step in letting go.

# Chapter 46

# The Waiting Game

After the PN7 assessment was completed and the lawyers had an opportunity to review it, it was my understanding we would be back in court to get a final court order, including updated child support and back pay.

My lawyer and I wanted to avoid trial because that process is very expensive, but I knew the option was on the table given how Johnny does not agree to anything and is so resistant. I believed we might just need a judge (not the one who'd seized on our file) to make a final order based on the information presented to them, with potential witnesses.

Over many years, we had completed multiple JDRs yet still had no conclusion or final orders. In order to get a trial in Canada, you must attend at least one JDR; going straight to trial with no attempts to mediate is not an option. Throughout this fight, I had been more than fair and made multiple attempts to mediate with Johnny. However, we had not reached a successful conclusion.

Johnny and his lawyer continued to claim parental alienation and draw out the process, refusing to agree to any of our proposed orders, which only delayed the process further.

On March 16, 2026, my lawyer had a meeting scheduled with Johnny and Grace's lawyer. Following that meeting, plans were to be made to set a trial date.

I heard from my lawyer in June that Johnny's lawyer was now trying to stall the process yet again and ask for another JDR. My lawyer is not interested in that approach, and neither am I. I made it clear I was done spending money on this and wanted to wrap it up.

My lawyer and I drafted an edited agreement, with a proposal of conditions much better than what Johnny would get in court after going through a trial. My lawyer sent it off to Johnny's lawyer that afternoon, so she would have an opportunity to read it prior to their court date on June 11, 2026.

Court was adjourned to July 2, 2026. It was my understanding that my lawyer and Grace's lawyers were going in to set trial dates; that was the entire purpose of this appearance. At the end of June, I received a call from my lawyer to say Johnny's lawyer had countered our offer. In return, my lawyer thought we should offer them something he believed was even better. We discussed what this could look like and then would put it into an order.

Our goal was to obtain a final order, so we no longer have to revisit the issue of child support every year. This would become a standing order until Grace turns eighteen years old. I wasn't in court on July 2, 2026, since my lawyer was scheduled to be present.

A few days later, my lawyer emailed me with a quick update. Johnny's lawyer had adjourned court yet again. Now, court was scheduled for the following week.

During that appearance, Johnny's lawyer fired him and took herself off of the record. This was the third lawyer Johnny had during our legal proceedings, and the latest firing meant only one thing: court would be adjourned yet again.

However, the judge made it very clear to Johnny, whether he retained a new lawyer or not, court would be adjourned only until July 30, 2026. At that time, they would set trial dates; this court process has been going on for two years, and resolution was a must. He could bring one witness, as could I.

My lawyer put our offer on the table again, so all parties were aware, including the judge. The judge agreed, reiterating the same message to Johnny. He had a timeline to either retain another lawyer or decide to self-represent.

My lawyer informed me that Johnny did not take to this lightly. He argued in court for negotiation and was quite upset as he spoke, like there has been no prior attempts. His requests were denied, and the next court date was scheduled for July 30, 2026, in order to set a trial date.

When I spoke to my lawyer over the phone, he assured me it would be quite difficult for Johnny to find yet another lawyer on such short notice, someone who could review the file and get up to date on everything. If a lawyer did agree, Johnny would be paying a large retainer fee.

My lawyer added he also planned to request that Johnny cover the costs of the trial, since we had provided Johnny with a new offer, one that was much better than our initial offer and similar to what he could expect to get in court. However, he and his previous lawyer did not respond to this offer.

July 30, 2026 came and went. A few days later, I received a call from my lawyer indicating Johnny had retained another lawyer. Court was adjourned yet again, so the new lawyer could review the matter.

This felt like another gut punch. *How many lawyers is he going to blow through, and much longer are we going to drag this out for?*

I am still waiting on a trial date.

# Conclusion

## How Do You Do It?

As I continue to wait, I don't stop advocating or sharing my story. If anything, this has given me so much more motivation to inspire hope and create systems change.

I had dinner with an RCMP officer recently, someone I worked together with in one of my previous roles and remained connected to, even after my career took a different path. I shared a part of my story and experience with the RCMP.

He said, "Our practice has gotten much better than before."

I replied, "As of 2024, I can confirm the process had not improved much, based on my experience."

As we continued to talk, he listened intently and then apologized for his RCMP service. It's not his fault, but I appreciated his apology and willingness to listen and understand.

During the conversation, he said, "Wow, you're amazing. How have you become so resilient, despite all of this?"

I wished I had a better answer, but here is what I know for sure.

What inspires me is resilience: what the toughest lessons can teach us and who we become through the process, even when it feels like there is no way out and systems are stacked against us.

I believe we have to dig deep and heal ourselves. We are not responsible for the things that have happened to us, but we are responsible for our own healing and how we show up in the world. It's important to learn to love ourselves again, and find value in who we are and in our stories. Through this process, we can create meaningful systems change and inspire others.

We can define our experience or let them define us. I chose to define mine. Perspective is everything.

If you are interested in learning more about Chelsey or her services, please visit her website at https://www.roots-and-rise.org. Or follow her on these social media platforms:

Instagram: @roots__and__rise
Facebook: Roots & Rise Coaching and Consulting
Substack: Chelsey De Groot
TikTok: roots__and__rise
YouTube: Chelsey De Groot @rootsandrisecc

# Acknowledgments

I want to start off by thanking those who have sat with me in the darkest moments of my life, for you became the guiding light to help me navigate through. To all of my friends and family, you know who you are.

I want to give a special shout out to a few people who, despite the broken system, stayed the course with me and connected me to the right people. Corporal Leanne Beattie, who was a steady voice of reason and support while dealing with the RCMP and holding other police services accountable. Wes Yasinksi from our local police service, who was the first officer who made me feel heard, valued and seen. And Justice Sylvia Oishi, who was the first judge to observe our relationship power dynamics in the court room and took actions that allowed me to feel a bit safer, even for a moment in time. Thank you for allowing me to be seen and heard.

I also want to thank Adonus Wiseman and her victim support service dog, Marlee. The unwavering support and advocacy Adonus showed me, does not go unnoticed. Marlee walked alongside Grace during appointments and provided foundational support and safety to Grace every step of the way. I am forever grateful. Victim support animals do not get enough credit for the work they do.

To my daughter, who has been on this entire journey with me. You may not always have had the best version of me or the best experiences, due to our circumstances, but you are the reason I have fought so hard, strived for all that I have, and continue to use my voice for change. You are my reason for everything, each and every day. I hope I have now provided you with the safety and comfort you deserved all along.

To all readers out there, I hope you find hope and resilience through your own story and know that your experiences do not have to define you. You get to define them, as you have the power to choose. If you are in the middle of leaving or are currently experiencing domestic violence, I hope you find the help you need. It's out there. This doesn't have to be the end. It may be the beginning of a life that is even better than imagined. Even in the darkest moments, there is beauty on the other side.

To my publisher, Landon Hail Press, SJ, and the entire team, thank you for believing in me and allowing me to share my story in such an authentic, raw, and vulnerable way. To my beta readers, Dawn and Adina, thank you for taking the time to read my story and provide me with honest feedback. To my photographer, Bailey Parkinson, thank you for allowing space and storytelling through your photos, to capture exactly what I wanted this book cover to look like. You made it so easy, fun, and authentic.

To all of those women and children who are no longer here to tell your story, this is for you.

# About the Author

Chelsey De Groot is the founder of Roots & Rise Coaching and Consulting and the co-founder and Vice President of the National Survivors Coalition. Chelsey brings more than twenty years of professional expertise together with real-world initiatives across justice, corrections, child welfare, Housing First initiatives, problem-solving courts, Indigenous partnerships, and organizational development.

Through Roots & Rise, Chelsey works with leaders and institutions ready to evolve practice, advance methodology, and improve outcomes across the communities they serve. Grounded in Risk-Need-Responsivity (RNR) principles and values-based leadership, her work bridges organizational capacity, professional education, cross-sector collaboration, and public events to build more effective, human-centered approaches to safety.

www.ingramcontent.com/pod-product-compliance
Lightning Source LLC
LaVergne TN
LVHW100135061126
851857LV00010B/93
* 9 7 8 1 9 5 9 9 5 5 9 2 4 *